Programming
for
Non-professionals

Buxing   Jiang

Asian Culture Press

Cover Design: Tao Liu
Cover Image Source: Storyset
Used under Freepik Company's open license

Interior Formatting: Buxing Jiang
Translator: Zhen Guo, Buxing Jiang
Editor: Judy Liu

ISBN: 978-1-957144-96-2

Library of Congress Control Number: 2024911015

Published and distributed in the United States by Asian Culture Press LLC, June 2024

Asian Culture Press LLC
1942 Broadway St., Suite 314c
Boulder, CO 80302
United States

For information regarding reprints, adaptations, or other licensing inquiries, please contact the author at jiangbuxing@scudata.com

Preface

Programming, like driving, has increasingly become a basic skill of modern people. There is no need to say the benefits of mastering programming skills and being able to use programming to deal with problems in daily work and life.

However, at present, almost all the programming languages in the IT field are designed for professionals, and they set a threshold too high for employees in other job positions to learn and master in daily work. This also indirectly leads to the difficulty of finding a book about programming for this kind of people and putting what they have learned into practice.

In fact, it is not difficult to understand the basic concepts and logic of programming. With an appropriate programming language and book tutorials, programming can become a skill that most people can master like driving.

This book hopes to help this process.

The content of this book can be divided into two parts.

The first part is the foundation, which introduces the basic concepts of almost all programming languages. After understanding these knowledges, you can quickly grasp the key content and master a new language. However, only learning these contents, you can only handle some arithmetic problems that you almost never encounter in your work, and you can't apply what you have learned. Nevertheless, these contents are still necessary as a basis.

The latter part is about the most common structured data and its processing methods in daily work. After obtaining these knowledges, you can handle the tasks of tables and data analysis and so on efficiently. The content of structured data computing described in this book is far beyond the current traditional system based on relational algebra. Many operation types are incorporated into the book for the first time all over the world, and mastering these operations is very important for structured data processing.

This book is not for professional programmers who have an in-depth understanding of programming. It does not involve professional contents such as object orientation, event driven, framework and so on. Most of the knowledge here can be understood and mastered by beginners, but a small amount of content is relatively difficult. The part marked with * in the section name can be used as optional reading content to deepen the understanding of programming. It doesn't matter if you skip it and it won't affect the learning of other parts and daily work application.

The programming language used for examples in this book is called SPL, and the development environment is called esProc. It is an open source and free software. The download address of the ready-made installation package can be found in the resource information section in the appendix of the book. The specific installation process is very simple and will not be described in detail here.

SPL is the simplest programming language in the industry that has all the basic features of programming and can easily process structured data computing. Other languages are either too difficult or too cumbersome (including Python, which is very popular at present), and are not suitable for beginners. For a more detailed explanation, please refer to the two small articles in the appendix.

Table of Contents

1 DOING ARITHMETIC 1

   1.1 DATA 1

   1.2 VARIABLES AND STATEMENTS 4

   1.3 FUNCTIONS 8

2 DOING JUDGEMENT 11

   2.1 LOGIC OPERATION 11

   2.2 BRANCHING STRUCTURE 13

   2.3 COMMENTS AND JUMPS 16

3 DOING LOOP 19

   3.1 SINGLE LAYER LOOP 19

   3.2 MULTILAYER LOOP 21

   3.3 CONDITIONAL LOOP 23

   3.4 ENDLESS LOOP 26

4 SEQUENCE 29

   4.1 SEQUENCE 29

   4.2 LOOP OF SEQUENCE 32

   4.3 MULTI-LAYER SEQUENCE 34

   4.4 UNDERSTANDING OBJECTS 36

5 SEQUENCE AS A WHOLE 39

   5.1 SET OPERATIONS 39

   5.2 LOOP FUNCTIONS 41

   5.3 LOOP FUNCTIONS: ADVANCED 43

   5.4 ITERATIVE FUNCTION[*] 47

   5.5 POSITIONING AND SELECTION 48

   5.6 SORTING RELATED 52

   5.7 LAMBDA SYNTAX[*] 55

6 REUSE 58

   6.1 USER-DEFINED FUNCTIONS 58

   6.2 RECURSION[*] 60

   6.3 REUSABLE SCRIPT 63

7 STRING AND TIME 67

   7.1 STRING 67

   7.2 SPLIT AND CONCATENATE 71

   7.3 DATE AND TIME 77

8   DATA TABLE 81

   8.1   STRUCTURED DATA 81

   8.2   TABLE SEQUENCE AND RECORD SEQUENCE 85

   8.3   GENERATION OF TABLE SEQUENCE 91

   8.4   LOOP FUNCTIONS 94

   8.5   CALCULATIONS ON THE FIELDS 98

9   GROUPING 104

   9.1   GROUPING AND AGGREGATION 104

   9.2   ENUMERATION AND ALIGNMENT 109

   9.3   ORDER-RELATED GROUPING 113

   9.4   EXPANSION AND TRANSPOSE 116

10   ASSOCIATION 121

   10.1   PRIMARY KEY 121

   10.2   FOREIGN KEY 124

   10.3   MERGE 130

   10.4   JOIN 132

11   BIG DATA 140

   11.1   BIG DATA AND CURSOR 140

   11.2   FUCTIONS ON CURSOR 143

   11.3   ORDERED CURSOR 147

   11.4   BIG CURSOR 150

12   DRAWING GRAPHICS 155

   12.1   CANVAS AND ELEMENTS 155

   12.2   COORDINATE SYSTEM 159

   12.3   MORE COORDINATE SYSTEMS 164

   12.4   LEGEND 168

APPENDIX 172

   MORE RESOURCES 172

   WHAT PROGRAMMING LANGUAGE SHOULD NON PROFESSIONALS LEARN? 173

   ACTUALLY, YOU WILL NEVEL BE ABLE TO MASTER PYTHON 176

1 DOING ARITHMETIC

1.1 Data

Start esProc, click File > New from the menu bar to get a grid interface below:

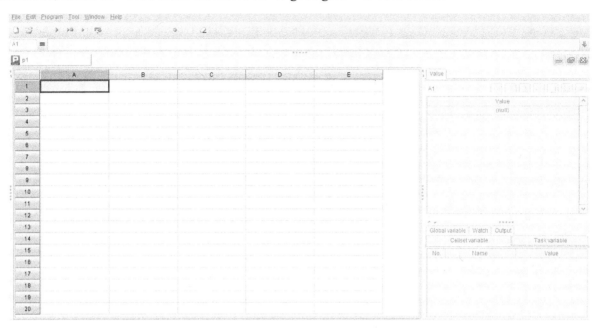

We write SPL code in this Excel-like grid, but of course this is not Excel.

Most programming languages only support text style code. Generally, the code is executed from front to back if no special code is to change the order. SPL is slightly different. SPL code is written in a grid which will be called a cellset later, where all cells are filled with codes and executed from front to back. Specifically, it is executed cell by cell. Each cell is executed from left to right in each row, and then the cell of the next row is executed. Though they are not essentially different, the grid style coding is more nonprofessional-friendly, which you will appreciate more as you know SPL better.

Programming books have been accustomed to starting with a simple "Hello,World" example program, a legacy of early command-line era and a third wheel for Contemporary GUI operating systems. And we just omit it.

A computer program should be able to do what a calculator can do. Let's see how SPL does the arithmetic by coding in the cell:

	A	B
1	=3+5	=1-2+3-4
2	=3+5*7	=6/2
3	=1*(2+3)	=1*(2-3*(4+5))
4	=1.5*1.5	=2*1.5
5	=1/2	=1.0/2
6	=65536*65536*65536*65536	

| 7 | =1.000000001*1.000000001 | |
| 8 | =65536.0*65536*65536*65536 | |

(Instead of taking a screenshot each time, sometimes we just code in the cell)

The equal sign preceding the code in each cell is compulsory (just hold your why for a while). The parentheses must be in English format; error will be reported if they are in the Chinese format (try finding what kind of error it will report).

Now press Ctrl-F9 to execute the program and the background of the code area turns pale yellow. Click a cell and you can view its value in the right-hand section:

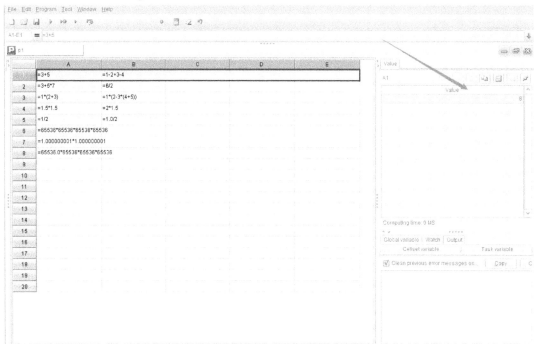

Before the execution, the background of the code area is white and a click of a cell containing code will not display a value on the right-hand section. Unlike Excel, SPL does not compute automatically. Generally, computer programs do not automatically execute an action until a special **Execute** operation tells them to do that.

Look at those computed results:

Like an Excel formula, a SPL formula has multiplication represented by *, division by /, and performs computation in the order of multiplication and division first and then addition and subtraction.

Like an Excel formula, each layer in a SPL formula is represented by parentheses rather than brackets or braces, and error will be reported if the wrong symbol is used.

Also like an Excel formula, a SPL formula computes both positive numbers and negative numbers.

Results of A1, B1 and A2 are integers written without decimal points. Results of B2 and B4 are integers written with decimal points, as shown by 3.0. Why are there decimal points in the latter but there are not in the former?

Because computers identify numbers with decimal points and integers as different types of numbers. The former is **floating point numbers** and the latter **integers**.

We do not care the type of numbers when doing arithmetic. But in computer program, however, to identify the **data type** is a foremost and basic task, and critical for getting result correct because integers and floating-point numbers are stored and processed in different ways.

Is it necessary to distinguish integers from floating-point numbers since we can treat integers as floating-point numbers where the fractional part is 0? Why don't we just use floating-point numbers?

It is mathematically OK. But there are technical problems for computers to perform the related operations. Since it is much simpler to store and compute integers than process floating-point numbers, processing integers of floating-point format is as inefficient as processing real floating-point numbers. So that is not a wise choice to make particularly when the computation mainly involves integers. As computers cannot know the difference, it is the programmers' job to make the right decision.

Most programming languages differentiate integer from floating-point number but allow them to appear in the same expression. To compute the expression, we will convert the integer to the floating-point number (an integer can be always converted to a floating-point number, and not vice versa). The result of a division operation could be a floating-point number, so SPL specifies that the quotient should always be of the floating-point format to ensure that data type of the result is explicit and definite. SPL also defines a type of division operations that return integers. This type of division is represented by the backslash (\). See what =6\3 and what =5\3 will get respectively if you are interested.

Let's move on to view A6's computed result. It is 0. What happened?

A large number requires a larger space to be stored. The computer's memory, however, is limited. The machine cannot represent an infinitely large number. We thus put a restriction on the size of data. Most contemporary programming languages have two representations for integers: 32-bit binary integers and 64-bit binary integers. This means the largest number computers can represent are 2^{32} or 2^{64} (The actual size is half smaller because the other bit is used to represent the negative number). Error will happen once the computed result exceeds the limit.

The largest integer SPL can handle is 64 bits. 65536^4 exceeds the limit and error happens. Unfortunately, almost all programming languages, including SPL, do not report the error but let it be. Programmers can only rely on themselves to avoid the mistake.

Why do the 32-bit integers and 64-bit integers are selected? Two foremost reasons are usability and efficiency. 32-bit integers are sufficient for most operations, 64-bit integers occupy too much space and are less computationally efficient, which makes them necessary only in certain few occasions, the 16-bit integers are often inadequate, and to invent another type of integers makes the list a little crowded (Actually 16-bit integers and even 8-bit integers were once used on early computers. Interestingly all these types of integers are 2^n-bit. There have never been such bits as 18 or 25)

Like the other contemporary programming languages (early programming languages may have different conventions), SPL calls 32-bit number integers and 64-bit numbers **long integers.**

The fact is that both 2^{31} and 2^{63} are extraordinarily large numbers. Since it is rare that such a large number is used, it is not that important to dig deeper.

A7's computed result is also not what we expect. And why?

Same as integers, storage space is limited for floating-point numbers. On the other hand, floating-point numbers are finite (approximately $\pm 10^{308}$) and can only be represented by a limited precision of about 18 significant figures (Extra figures should be discarded). Thus A7's error happens.

In addition , this is important, contemporary computers uses binary numbers to perform calculations. The binary counterpart of a decimal integer can retain the original precision. But a decimal finite decimal, such as 0.1, probably becomes a recurring decimal - you can think about the principle behind it yourself - which cannot be precisely represented by computers after it is converted to a binary number. Deviation can be accumulated to lead to unexpected error when the imprecise number undergoes a series of operations.

Yet, integers are always precise after a series of operations, and thus the first choice on all possible occasions.

Let's look at A8. Unlike A6, it records 65536 as 65536.0, which tells the computer that this is a floating-point number instead of an integer. SPL will convert a number to floating-point format, which has a far greater range than integer, for computations to get the correct result instead of an over-limit number.

But what does 1.8446744073709552E19 mean?

This is the scientific notation conventionally used by all programming languages. Here it represents the number $1.8446744073709552*10^{19}$. In a cell code, number $1.23*10^{-20}$ can also be represented by 1.23E-20.

Apart from integers, long integers and floating-point numbers, other data types in SPL include huge numbers (which represent numbers of any length and precision but process slower), strings and date, time and datetime. All will appear in the following sections.

Understanding the basic data types is the foremost thing to learn a programming language.

1.2 Variables and statements

The area of a circle is $S = \pi r^2$. Now we write a piece of code to caclualte the area of a circle with the specified radius. Here we take 3.14 as the value of π.

	A
1	5
2	=3.14*A1*A1

Execute the code and view A2's value, which is the area of a circle whose radius is 5.

To calculate the area of another circle whose radius is 7.8, we just need to change A1 to the specific value and then execute the code. Now A2's value is the current circle's area.

It looks like that Excel is more convenient. The spreadsheet tool can automatically calculate after you enter a new value. But this is not the key point. We just let it be.

Let's examine the expression in A2. It contains a cell name. It references A1's value at computation and uses the new value whenever there is a change to A1. That is, this expression references a value through the name of cell containing it.

It is easy to understand for one who is familiar with Excel.

Programming languages call named data the **variable**, like A1 and A2 (We can write =A2*4 in A3 to calculate the area of a ball with A1 being the radius). A3 is also a variable. All cells in the cellset are variables.

Then we can reference a variable in a computing expression. A recomputation of the expression with a new variable value will get a new result. So coding only once for computing multiple expressions of same pattern. It is convenient and error immune. Computers are indeed good at doing the repetitive work.

Excel also has this merit.

Is the variable thus named because it is variable?

That's it. A variable can get a new value in a program, as the following piece of code shows:

	A
1	5
2	=3.14*A1*A1
3	>A1=7.8
4	=3.14*A1*A1

A2 and A4 have same expressions, but they get different results after execution. A3 modifies A1's value to 7.8 when executed. A4 then takes the new value for A1 to do the computation.

This is different from Excel. The spreadsheet tool cannot modify a cell value by writing a formula in another cell.

Instead of the equals sign =, A3's code is headed by the sign greater than sign >. In SPL, a cell whose content begins with = is called a **calculation cell** and one whose content starts with > is called an **executable cell**. A calculation cell calculates the expression after the equals sign and puts result into the current cell. An executable cell executes the action after the greater than sign but will not put any value into the current cell. In the above code, A3's value is still null after it is executed.

Cell A1 in the above piece of code, with neither the equals sign nor the greater than sign, is called a **constant cell** in SPL. It is used to define a **constant**.

Many programming languages have the concept of **constant variable**, which can be understood as the named constant. The constant variable value cannot be changed at running time of the program once it is set. The constant variable can also be regarded as a variable that can only got assigned once. The introduction of constant variable aims to avoid changing the variable value that should be kept unchanged when code is wrongly written.

SPL does not have the strict concept of constant variable. The value of constant cell A1 in the above code can be modified by the execution of an executable cell.

Generally, a program written with a programming language is in text format, sentence by sentence. The sentence-wise format is more apparent in programs written in earlier programming languages. Each sentence describes an action to be carried out. Such a sentence is called **program statement**. A piece of program is made up of a set of program statements.

SPL does not feature this sentence-wise coding format. In a SPL program, code in a cell can be treated as a statement. Both a calculation cell and an executable cell are statements.

In most programming languages, programmers need to name variables. SPL supports user-defined names, too, as shown in the following program:

	A
1	>r=5
2	=3.14*r*r
3	>r=7.8
4	=3.14*r*r

Here letter r, rather than A1, is used to name the variable. Results are the same.

In the following interface, variable r is displayed in the right bottom section.

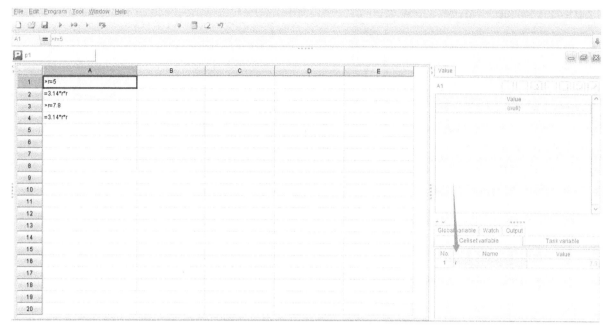

The advantage of a meaningful user-defined variable name is unforgettable and not easy to confuse, such as the r used in the above program. It is the same r as the one in the formula for area of a circle.

Sometimes when the variable is used for storing an intermediate result, you can give it a not so meaningful name. But there is a probability that it is a namesake. In SPL, you can name a variable after the cell name. This is one of the small conveniences that the grid-style coding format has but that the text coding format does not have.

There are two variables, a and b, and we need to exchange their values, for instance. The general program is as below:

	A
1	>a=5
2	>b=3
3	>c=a
4	>a=b
5	>b=c

The newly defined variable c can be renamed after the cell name:

	A
1	>a=5
2	>b=3
3	=a
4	>a=b
5	>b=A3

Like in Excel, when the cell name is used as the variable name in SPL and when a row or column is inserted or deleted, the cell name referenced in an expression will be automatically adjusted to get the right result. SPL's another Excel-like feature is to use the dollar sign $ to fix a cell to the specific row and column when a row or a column is inserted or deleted.

esProc also offers some commands and their shortcuts on the Edit menu. When you are familiar with the SPL features, you will find that its grid-style coding format is far more convenient than the text coding format.

By the way, SPL is a case-sensitive programming language. The lowercase r and the uppercase R generate different effects. The cell name used as a variable name should be the uppercase. Al represents a cell variable while al is only an ordinary variable. Some programming languages are case-insensitive, where the lowercase r and the uppercase R produce same effects.

A sign that can be used as a variable name is usually made up of letters and numbers and must not begin with a number. It can contain the underline (The sign _ is generally treated as a letter and can be placed at the beginning). SPL also allows using the Chinese character in a variable name. **Identifiers** are the jargon for the signs that can be included in the variable name.

Another question: Does a variable have a data type?

There are two types of programming languages. One is the strong typed languages, such as Java and C/C++. They require that a variable's data type be declared before it is used. If variable x is declared as the integer type, it cannot be used to store a floating-point number. If it is assigned a floating-point number, it will be automatically converted into an integer (and lost information during the process). The other is the weak typed languages, such as SPL. In SPL, users do not need to declare the data type for a variable; the appropriate type will be naturally generated during the computation.

Does it show that the weak typed languages are more convenient to use?

It does in terms of usage convenience. But as a strong typed language declares the data type of a variable in advance, the computer knows how to store the variable before execution and thus gets a better performance. A weak typed language decides the storage method after the result is obtained, which makes computing performance poorer. Besides, it cannot detect the error if the data type is mistakenly changed.

There is no perfect thing of the kind.

Take the formula for the area of a circle as an example. $S = \pi r^2$ is in essence an equation. It tells that the area of a circle S is equivalent to πr^2. In fact, the equation will still hold if they switch positions.

Now we write the formula in SPL statement to calculate the area of a circle:

>S=3.14*r*r

Is it an equation too?

No!

In a programming language, a statement that sets the value of a variable is called the **assignment statement**. It represents an action, rather than being a mathematic equation. It should not be written as follows:

>3.14*r*r=S

It makes no sense. The computer will report an error for it.

An assignment statement calculates the expression on the right of the sign = and assign the result to the variable on the left the sign =. The calculation of the expression is irrelevant with the variable. The assignment will only begin after the calculation is finished.

This way an equation that is mathematically impossible will become a common assignment statement, as shown below:

>X=X+1

It denotes that the current X value plus 1 and the result will be assigned to X. Suppose the X's value is 3, then its value will become 4 after execution.

You will basically understand the concept of variable if you can figure out what X=X+1 means. This can be counted as the first small barrier in the course of learning program design and a concept that Excel does not have.

Look at this piece of code:

	A
1	>a=5
2	>b=3
3	>a=a+b
4	>b=a-b
5	>a=a-b

Try to change the initial values of both a and b multiple times and execute the program to see the final values of both variables. You can first make a guess and then try to prove your conclusion using the variable assignment principle.

Early computers have small memories. One fewer variable means less memory usage, and programmers invented the crazy code to achieve this goal.

1.3 Functions

As we have said, data has types. A division operation may get a result of floating-point number. If we need to get an integer, by rounding about the result, for instance, what should we do?

It seems that we haven't introduced a method for doing this. Even if the result is an integer (like 6/3), it will be represented by a floating-point number (3.0). How will it be converted into an integer that can be identified by the computer?

We need int() function to get this done.

	A
1	=int(6/3)
2	=int(100/3+0.5)

int(x) calculates the integer part of x:

$$int(3.0)=3, \quad int(3.1)=3$$

$$int(-3.0)=-3, \quad int(-3.1)=-3$$

(Here = represents a mathematical equation rather than an assignment statement)

The concept of function is introduced as early as in a high school mathematics textbook. For the time being, we can consider that the function concept in the programming language is the same as that in the mathematics. Both have the independent variable (which is called **parameter** in programming languages) and dependent variable (which is called **return value** in programming language). In the equation y=f(x), x is the parameter and y is the return value, or we can say f(x) **returns** y.

int(x) takes number x as the parameter and returns the integer part of x. It is called **integer function**.

By the way, int(x) returns a 32-bit integer. long(x) is used to convert a number (an integer, a floating-point number, or a long integer) to a long integer. There is also the float(x) function for converting a number to a floating-point number,

8

Usually, a practical program written in a specific language uses many ready-made functions that the language predefines. These ready-made functions are also called **library functions** like they are stored in and retrieved from a library of functions. Generally, a skilled programmer needs to be familiar with hundreds of frequently used library functions. It is important and necessary to learn to use the library functions if you want to master a programming language.

The significance of library functions lies in the reusability. The ready-made code for a specific operation that is packaged into a library function is convenient to use anywhere, anytime, while a rewriting is troublesome and error prone.

Moreover, most of the time programmers who develop high-level application cannot write code for implementing the low-level operations. They can only be achieved through library functions. It is almost impossible to implement int(x) function in SPL (It's almost because hardcoding can make it if efficiency is completely not a concern. You can try to do this when you finish the relative section in this book).

You might be curious about how library functions come into being since they cannot be written in your currently used language?

Generally, a programming language is developed in another more foundamental programming language. Its library functions can be written with this more foundamental language. SPL, for instance, is developed in Java, so the library functions it cannot write are written in Java; Java is developed in C language, so the library functions it cannot write are written in C language; and an assembly language can write any library functions (though functions in this level are already beyond recognition).

This is another issue.

Actually, the concept of function in the programming language is wider than that in the high-school mathematics.

A function does not necessarily have parameters. SPL pi() function, for instance, returns π only . To calculate the area of a circle, we use the following code:

```
>S=pi()*r*r
```

A function may not have a return value, like output(x) function.

	A
1	>output("Hello,World")

Execute the code and we can view Hello, World in the right bottom section on the following interface.

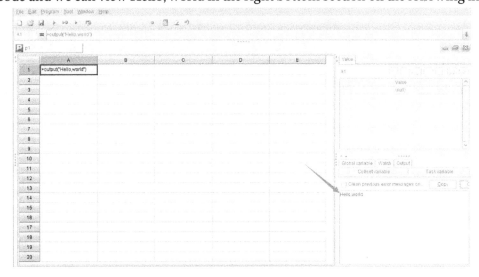

output(x) function outputs the value of x to the output window on the right bottom section, so it will not return a value.

A function that does not return a value execute an action instead. It is more like a statement.

The word **function** also has the meaning of purpose or activity. This shows that the value return is the purpose or the target activity we want to achieve. For programmers, value returning is not the only significance of functions, they use them to do anything that can be done.

In this sense, we, sometimes, call the use of a function **calling** it, like it is called up to perform a specific task.

Like functions in mathematics, functions in programming languages may have more than one parameter. max(x,y), for instance, returns the larger one of x and y.

Some functions have a fixed number of parameters. The power function power(a,x) that returns a^x always have two parameters. max() function, however, can have more parameters. Both max(1,2) and max(3,4,5) are allowed.

The parameters of a SPL function can have default values. Parameter n in pi() function takes 1 as its default. pi(n) means $n\pi$, but in most cases the function returns 1π. So pi() means pi(1). It is important to know the parameter default values, otherwise you may not understand the code written by others.

Not all programming languages support parameter default value.

All features introduced as yet are not beyond Excel.

2 DOING JUDGEMENT

2.1 Logic operation

If we want to calculate the absolute value of a number (in fact, SPL has an abs() function, but here we use other methods to try), we need to judge whether the number is greater than 0 or less than 0. We introduce the if() function to achieve this:

=if(x>0,x,-x)

if(a,b,c) function has three parameters, where a is a condition. If the condition holds, b is returned, otherwise c is returned.

Using if function, max(x,y) can also be realized:

=if(x>y,x,y)

Most modern programming languages have a data type called **boolean**. It has only two values: true and false.

Conditional judgment, such as the above x>0 or x>y, is also understood as a kind of calculation expression in programming language, just like our conventional arithmetic expression, except that its calculation result is a boolean value. When this condition holds, its calculation result is true, otherwise the calculation result is false.

The stricter description of if(a,b,c) function is as follows: if a is true, b is returned; otherwise, c is returned.

To convert a data of other types into boolean, you can use the bool(x) function. If x is not null, it will return true, otherwise it will return false. In fact, there is no distinction between null and false in SPL.

Since Boolean value is also a kind of data, it should be able to participate in operation. Let's take a more complicated example: given a year, calculate how many days there are in that year.

We know that there are 365 days in a normal year and 366 days in a leap year, so we just need to judge whether the year is a leap year or not. The complete rule is this: if a year is divisible by 4 and cannot be divisible by 100, or it is divisible by 400, it is a leap year. For example, 2004 is a leap year (divisible by 4 but not by 100), 2000 is a leap year (divisible by 400), 1900 is not a leap year (divisible by 4 but also by 100). The SPL expression is as follows (y is the year to be judged):

=if(y%4==0 && y%100!=0 || y%400==0,366,365)

The last two parameters are easy to understand. Let's explain the first parameter, that is, y%4==0 && y%100!=0 || y%400==0 .

% is used to calculate the remainder of the division operation, == is used to determine whether the operands are equal, y%4==0 indicates whether the remainder of y divided by 4 is equal to 0, that is, whether y can be divisible by 4. If y can be divisible by 4, then the result of y%4==0 is true, otherwise it is false. For example, 2004%4==0 is true, while 1998%4==0 is false.

SPL retained the habit of C language, using != to indicate "not equal to" , while many programming languages use <> to indicate "not equal to". Other comparison operators in SPL, such as >=, <= and so on, are the same as most programs.

So, y%100!=0 can determine whether y can not be divisible by 100. Similarly, 1900%100!=0 is false, while 1998%100!=0 is true. Similarly, y%400==0 will be used to determine whether y can be divisible by 400.

What are the remaining && and || ?

These are the boolean operators, && stands for "and", which is usually called **AND** in programming; || stands for "or", which is called **OR** in programming. Both && and || are binary operators, that is, like addition, they have two operands. The operation rules of && and || are as follows:

true && true = true
true && false = false
false && true = false
false && false = false
true || true = true
true || false = true
false || true = true
false || false = false

In fact, they are the normal meanings of "and" and "or". The priority of && is higher than ||, that is to say, if there are no parentheses, && will be calculated first and then ||, just like multiplication and division before addition and subtraction. If this expression is written as y%400==0 || y%4==0 && y%100!=0, it will get the same result.

There is also a very common operator ! with single operand, meaning "not", and the operation rules are as follows:

!true = false
!false = true

! is a little bit like the minus sign "-" in arithmetic, and its priority is higher than &&.

SPL retained the C language operators, while some programming languages directly use the words AND and OR and NOT to express &&, || and !.

Now, we can understand y%4==0 && y%100!=0 || y%400==0, it really correctly expresses the rule of leap year judgment.

Here's another question. Why do we use two equal signs ==, instead of using one equal sign as in arithmetic expressions?

This is because SPL retained the habit of C language, and considers the assignment statement such as a=x as an operation expression, which also has a calculation result, that is, x. For example, if we write =a=5 in cell A1, SPL will not report an error but will execute normally, and we can see that not only variable a has a value of 5, but also cell A1 itself has a value of 5. Because a=5 is also understood as a calculation formula, its calculation result is 5, which can be assigned to cell A1.

But after such an agreement, if we also use = to judge equality, we can't distinguish it. Therefore, the C language stipulates that two equal signs == should be used to judge equality, so it will not be confused with assignment operation. SPL also applies this rule.

After getting used to it, we will see the advantages of this convention, which can make the code much simpler. But there is also a risk. It's easy to write = when it's time to write ==. Originally, we want to judge the equality, but we made an assignment instead. We should pay special attention to it when writing codes.

It should be noted that not all programming languages are regulated in this way. For example, BASIC language does not regard assignment as an operator. a=5 only completes assignment without a calculation result. It also uses one equal sign to judge equality. The advantage is that it's not easy to make mistakes, but the code can be cumbersome sometimes.

Still, there is no perfect thing of the kind.

2.2   Branching structure

We can make some judgments with the if() function, but in some cases, we need the if statement.

Let's review the quadratic equation $ax^2 + bx + c = 0$ we learned in middle school. We can use the formula $x = \frac{-b \pm \sqrt{b^2 - 4ac}}{2a}$ to find the solutions,but we need to pay attention to $b^2 - 4ac$. If it is greater than 0, there are two solutions. If it is equal to 0, there is only one solution. If it is less than 0, there is no real solution.

We will program to find solutions of the equation. The coefficients a, b, c will be filled in cells A1,B1,C1, and the resulting solutions are required to be written in cells A2 and B2. If there are two solutions, fill in both A2 and B2; If there is only one solution, only A2 is filled in; If there is no solution, it will not be filled in.

	A	B	C
1	3	8	4
2			
3	=B1*B1-4*A1*C1		
4	if A3>0	>A2=(-B1+sqrt(A3))/2/A1	>B2=(-B1-sqrt(A3))/2/A1
5	if A3==0	>A2=-B1/2/A1	

sqrt() in B4 and C4 is a square root function, which need not be explained in detail. The point is that if statements appear in A4 and A5.

if is followed by a logical expression. If the result of this expression is true, the program will continue to execute the cells to the right of the if cell; If the result of the expression is false, the program will skip those cells to the right of the if cell and go directly to the next line for execution.

Note that this if is not the if() function mentioned in the previous section. It may not be followed by parentheses(if parentheses do exist, parentheses will be regarded as a part of the logical expression, and a layer of parentheses outside the expression will not change the calculation result of the expression), and it must be written at the beginning of the code in the cell.

This is the simplest form of the if statement: if the condition is true, it will be executed to the right, otherwise it will be executed directly down.

There is no error in this code, but there is a small problem. Judge whether A3 is greater than 0 in cell A4, and if it is true, B4 and C4 will continue. And then what? The program will still be executed to A5, and it will be judged whether A3 is equal to 0 again, but this is an unnecessary action and a waste of time. Only if "A3 is greater than 0" is not true, it is necessary to judge whether A3 equals 0.

How to avoid this redundant action? The code can be written like this:

	A	B	C
1	3	8	4
2			
3	=B1*B1-4*A1*C1		
4	if A3>0	>A2=(-B1+sqrt(A3))/2/A1	>B2=(-B1-sqrt(A3))/2/A1
5	else	if A3==0	>A2=-B1/2/A1

The if in cell A4 and the else in cell A5 form a pair. If the judgment in A4 is true, the cells to the right of A4 will be executed. If it is not true, the program will see if there is an else under A4. If there is, it will execute the cell to the right of this else.

else means "otherwise", that is, the action to be executed when the previous if is not true.

This program uses the formula of quadratic equation, but the premise is that the equation is really quadratic, that is to say, it assumes that A1 is not 0. If A1 is 0, the B4, C4 and C5 of the above program will be divided by 0. Let's continue to improve this code, so that it can deal with the case that A1 is 0, that is, the equation degenerates into a linear equation.

	A	B	C	D
1	3	8	4	
2				
3	if A1==0	>A2=-C1/B1		
4	else	=B1*B1-4*A1*C1		
5		if B4>0	>A2=(-B1+sqrt(B4))/2/A1	>B2=(-B1-sqrt(B4))/2/A1
6		else	if B4==0	>A2=-B1/2/A1

Looking at this section of code, it is obvious that B4:D6 is moved from A3:C5 of the previous section, that is, the else processing to be performed after the judgment in A3 is not true. However, B4:D6 takes up three rows, not just the cells to the right of A4.

At this time, we will introduce the concept of SPL **code block.**

For any cell, if the lower and the lower left of it are all empty, then the block area formed by the right and the right lower cells of it is called its code block. Take A4 for an example, A5 and A6 below it are all empty, so the block area from B4 to D6 is called A4's code block. For A3, the A4 below it is not empty, so its code block is only B3:D3, and cannot be extended to line 4 (A4 is not empty). That is to say, all the cells to the right of a cell must belong to its code block, but whether the lower line to the right of the cell belongs to its code block depends on whether the cells below and to the left of it are empty.

It's rather tongue twister to describe with words, but actually it's very intuitive from the grid layout. Look at the grid below:

	A	B	C	D
1	X	X		X
2		X	X	X
3			X	
4		X		X
5	X		X	X
6			X	X

The code block of A1 is B1:D4, because A2:A4 is empty and A5 is not;

The code block of B1 is C1:D1, because B2 is not empty;

The code block of B2 is C2:D3, because A3:B3 is empty and B4 is not;

The code block of C3 is D3:D3, because B4 is not empty;

The code block of A5 is B5:D6, because A6 is empty.

Code blocks are designed to limit the scope of a statement. If the condition of if is true, the code block of the cell where the if is located will be executed; If not, the code block of the corresponding else cell will be executed.

Some programming languages use curly brackets or BEGIN...END to enclose the statements to be executed. The programming language using this scheme has no requirements for writing format. However, for the sake of readability, people still use text indentation to write the code into this ladder shape to see the scope of each statement. SPL does not use bracket scheme, but directly uses ladder like code blocks to limit the scope of statements, which will force the code to have a certain format.

The above code can also reverse the condition of A3, and the square root calculation can be done only once:

	A	B	C	D
1	3	8	4	
2				
3	if A1!=0	=B1*B1-4*A1*C1		
4		if B3>0	=sqrt(B3)	
5			>A2=(-B1+C4)/2/A1	>B2=(-B1-C4)/2/A1
6		else	if B3==0	>A2=-B1/2/A1
7	else	>A2=-C1/B1		

The code block of A3 is B3:D6, which will be executed when the judgment condition of A3 is established, otherwise, the code block B7: D7 of A7 where else is located will be executed.

We have to further consider the case of equation degeneration, that is, A1 and B1 are both 0. At this time, if C1 is also 0, then any number is the solution of the equation. If C1 is not 0, then the equation has no solution.

	A	B	C	D
1	3	8	4	
2				
3	if A1!=0	=B1*B1-4*A1*C1		
4		if B3>0	=sqrt(B3)	
5			>A2=(-B1+C4)/2/A1	>B2=(-B1-C4)/2/A1
6		else	if B3==0	>A2=-B1/2/A1
7	else	if B1!=0	>A2=-C1/B1	
8		else	if C1==0	>output("Any")

When the equation degenerates to 0=0, the code does not fill in any solution and outputs an any at the bottom right.

Like the above code, else has if in the code block. This situation is not uncommon in reality, which will lead to the wide code, because every additional layer of if needs to be indented to the right, the code is not very beautiful and easy to read.

Many programming languages, including SPL, provide syntax to bind else to if after it, and the above code can also be written as follows:

	A	B	C	D
1	3	8	4	
2				
3	if A1!=0	=B1*B1-4*A1*C1		
4		if B3>0	=sqrt(B3)	
5			>A2=(-B1+C4)/2/A1	>B2=(-B1-C4)/2/A1
6		else if B3==0	>A2=-B1/2/A1	
7	else if B1!=0	>A2=-C1/B1		
8	else if C1==0	>output("Any")		

Write the else and the if immediately following the else together. These else if and the first if form a complete if statement. It is equivalent to judging a batch of mutually exclusive conditions respectively, executing the corresponding code block when a condition is established, and then ending the entire if statement.

2.3   Comments and jumps

The program code may not always be written correctly. When there is no expected result, we often can't figure out the reason. At this time, we need to debug the program to locate the error.

In the early days, the primitive debugging method was to output the intermediate results of the program to see which step was wrong. The development environment of modern programming language basically provides perfect debugging function, which can execute code step by step to see whether the direction of the program is consistent with the expectation, and whether the intermediate results are consistent with the expectation.

esProc also provides these functions, all on the program menu. It's difficult to describe the use of debugging functions in words. You can find it out quickly after trying several times. We won't elaborate here. SPL codes are written in the cells, and each execution unit is a cell. It's easy to check the value of cells and variables midway, and it's naturally very convenient for debugging.

Now that we have learned the branching structure, the program is no longer always going from top to bottom. It may go through different paths under different data. You can use the program debugging function to observe the direction of the above programs.

In the process of debugging, sometimes we want to see the running effect when a piece of code is skipped and not executed. However, if we delete this code, we may need to add it back later, which is troublesome.

In this case, comments can be used. Almost all programming languages provide comment statements or functions. In SPL, if a cell starts with /, it is considered as a **comment cell**. This cell will be automatically ignored and skipped during execution. If a cell starts with //, the cell and its code block will be ignored and skipped.

You can try to add / or // to some cells to see what changes will occur in the code display.

In the following code, A7:D7 and D5 will be ignored and skipped, that is, the second solution will not be calculated, and the case that B1 is not 0 will not be handled.

	A	B	C	D
1	3	8	4	
2				
3	if A1!=0	=B1*B1-4*A1*C1		
4		if B3>0	=sqrt(B3)	
5			>A2=(-B1+C4)/2/A1	/>B2=(-B1-C4)/2/A1
6		else if B3==0	>A2=-B1/2/A1	
7	//else if B1!=0	>A2=-C1/B1		
8	else if C1==0	>output("Any")		

It's very convenient to use comments to control debugging. You can change this code into comments when you don't need to execute it, and change it back when you need to execute it again. The main body of the code doesn't need to be deleted.

The original intention of the invention of comments is to enable programmers to write some code related notes in case they can't understand the code after a long time. Of course, this role still exists, good program codes always have detailed and clear comments. In SPL, the text written directly will be regarded as a constant cell, which does not affect the execution of the program. It can play the role of comments, and the role of a comment cell is more used to facilitate debugging.

if statement can change the direction of the program, many programming languages also provide a more simple and crude way to change the program flow, that is, goto statement. Let's rewrite the code of solving quadratic equation to feel it (only consider the case that A1 is not 0):

	A	B	C
1	3	8	4
2			
3	=B1*B1-4*A1*C1	if A3<0	goto A6
4	if A3==0	>A2=-B1/2/A1	goto A6
5	=sqrt(A3)	>A2=(-B1+A5)/2/A1	>B2=(-B1-A5)/2/A1
6			

There is an extra empty line in the code, but the logic seems very clear, avoiding the long if… else block.

A more complete case can also be rewritten with goto:

	A	B	C	D
1	3	8	4	
2				
3	if A1==0	if B1==0	if C1==0	goto A9
4			>output("Any")	goto A9
5		>A2=-C1/B1	goto A9	
6	=B1*B1-4*A1*C1	if B6<0	goto A9	
7	if B6==0	>A2=-B1/2/A1	goto A9	
8	=sqrt(B6)	>A2=(-B1+A8)/2/A1	>B2=(-B1-A8)/2/A1	
9				

The goto statement has been controversial since it came into being. Many computer scientists complain that it can mess up the flow of programs. When a program is running normally, we don't know what will happen when a goto statement appears, and it is very difficult to debug when the program goes wrong. Therefore, some programming languages simply do not provide goto statement, and do not allow casual jumping.

However, sometimes when the program level is deep, when the conditions are appropriate, jumping out with a goto statement will make the code clearer. If goto is not used, it is likely to make repeated judgments to avoid executing statements that should not be executed. Our attitude towards goto should be: don't ban it, but use it carefully. Generally speaking, we can keep this principle: always jump out from the depth of multi-layer code (for example, SPL code blocks have obvious levels), not jump in; Jump forward, not backward (though not forbidden).

goto is always userd with if, that is, jump when a condition holds (or does not hold). goto, when it has nothing to do with if, is meaningless. Jumping forward will make the code in the middle useless (instead, it can be used for debugging, playing the role of comments mentioned earlier); Jump backward and the program will never end.

However, in SPL, if you accidentally write a program that will not end, don't worry. When the code is running, the development environment is not dead. You can use the debugging function to terminate the program.

3 DOING LOOP

3.1 Single layer loop

So far, all the code we have written is executed once from top to bottom and then ends. if statements may cause some code to be skipped and not executed. The overall flow of the program is still from top to bottom, and no code will be executed multiple times.

In fact, what computers are best at is repetitive work, that is, to execute the same code over and over. Obviously, we should not copy the code repeatedly, which requires the ability of the program language to loop.

Let's calculate 1+2+... +100:

	A	B
1	=0	
2	for 100	>A1=A1+A2

Only two lines are OK. After the program is executed, the A1 value becomes the answer we want: 5050.

Almost all programming languages use the keyword for for loop statements, and SPL is no exception.

for 100 in A2 means that the code block of A2 will be executed 100 times. Here, the code block of A2 has only B2, that is, B2 will be executed 100 times. During execution, the cell value of A2 will start from 1, add 1 after each execution, and finally become 100.

A2 cell with for is called **loop cell**. The code block of A2, that is, the code to be repeatedly executed, is called the **loop body** of A2. A2 itself is also called the **loop variable** of the loop, and it will change from 1 to the number of cycles.

Let's look at this code. We have understood the statement x=x+1 before. A1=A1+A2 in the loop body is similar, that is, each time we add A2 to the current A1, A2 will increase from 1 to 100, so A1 will add 1, 2,...,, until 100, and the operation of 1+2+...+100 is completed.

We can also use this structure to calculate 1+3+5+...+199, that is, the first 100 odd numbers.

	A	B
1	=0	
2	for 100	>A1=A1+(2*A2-1)

This time, it's still to add 100 numbers, so we need to loop 100 times, the loop variable A2 will still change from 1 to 100, but the number to be added is no longer a direct loop variable, and it needs to be calculated through the loop variable (2*A2-1).

Now we do a slightly more complex operation. According to Taylor formula: $= 1 + \frac{1}{1!} + \frac{1}{2!} + \frac{1}{3!} + \cdots$, add the first 20 terms to calculate the approximate value of the natural logarithm base e.

	A	B
1	=1	=1
2	for 20	>B1=B1*A2
3		>A1=A1+1/B2
4	=exp(1)-A1	

Here, we need to introduce an auxiliary variable B1 to store the factorial value n!, It is also calculated step by step in the loop. Finally, the result is accumulated in A1. Use the expression of A4 to see the difference between the calculated result and the actual value. The function exp(1) will calculate the value of e, i.e. the power of e^1.

This code can not loop too many times, because n! is going to get very big, and it's going to get out of the range of floating-point numbers very quickly.

Fibonacci sequence is such a sequence: the first and second terms are all 1, from the third term, each term is equal to the sum of the previous two terms, written out as 1,1,2,3,5,8,... This is a famous rabbit sequence. If you are interested, you can search its origin. I won't repeat it here.

Now let's calculate the nth term of the Fibonacci sequence, n>2.

	A	B
1	=1	=1
2	20	
3	for A2-2	=A1+B1
4		>A1=B1
5		>B1=B3

B1 is the result we need. A2 is the number of terms we want to compute, which is n.

The number of loops in a for statement is not always a constant, but can also be a calculation expression A2-2. Because the first two terms already exist, we only need to calculate n-2 times. There is no loop variable used in this loop body. A3 only controls the number of loops.

Calculate the next item in B3, and then fill in A1 and B1 respectively to replace the original items. In this way, for each loop, A1 and B1 are equivalent to moving forward once in the Fibonacci sequence, from the first and second items to the second and third items, and then to the third and fourth items,... At the end of the loop, they will become the n-1 and n items, and B1 is the result we need.

This code can also be written one line less without the intermediate variable:

	A	B
1	=1	=1
2	20	
3	for A2-2	>B1=A1+B1
4		>A1=B1-A1

Debug it and try to find its logic by yourself.

We learned the goto statement in the previous section. In fact, we can use goto and if to create the effect of the for statement. For example, in the first example of 1+2 +...+100:

	A	B
1	=0	=1
2	if B1<=100	>A1+=B1
3		>B1+=1
4		goto A2

Here A1+=B1 is equivalent to A1=A1+B1. Similarly, B1+=1 is equivalent to B1=B1+1. This is a simplified way of writing in C language, and this style is retained in SPL. x+=y is equivalent to x=x+y. Similarly, subtraction, multiplication, division can be written like this, but addition is the most commonly used.

Using if and goto to create loops, a loop variable (B1 here) needs to be defined artificially. First, an initial value of 1 is assigned to the loop variable. Then the if statement is used to judge whether the loop ends or not. If not, the loop body will be executed. After execution, the loop variable will be added by 1, and then goto will be used to jump back. If the loop end condition is true, the if statement will no longer execute the loop body.

Obviously, the loop written by the for statement is simpler than the if...goto structure, and it is not easy to make mistakes (if the action of adding a loop variable by 1 is omitted accidentally, the loop created by if...goto will never end). Moreover, such goto violates the principle of not jumping backward. So we don't usually use if...goto to create loops.

3.2 Multilayer loop

Just as if... else may be found in the code block of if and else, there can be for again in the loop body of for, which we call **multi-layer loop**.

Narcissus number refers to such a three-digit number, the sum of the cube of each digit is equal to the number itself. Now we want to calculate all Narcissus numbers between 100 and 999.

	A	B	C	D	E
1	for 9	=100*A1	=A1*A1*A1		
2		for 0,9	=B1+10*B2	=C1+B2*B2*B2	
3			for 0,9	=C2+C3	=D2+C3*C3*C3
4				if D3==E3	>output(D3)

We haven't learned the concept of set yet, and can't save all the Narcissus numbers found in one set. So in cell E5, we use the output() function to output the Narcissus numbers, which can be seen in the lower right corner.

A new grammatical form for 0,9 appears in B2 and C3. Usually, the statement for n means that the loop variable will change from 1 to n, but sometimes we want to change the start and end values. We can also write the loop statement as for a,b, which means that the loop variable will change from a to b, where a and b are integers. If b>a, the value of loop variable will be a,a+1,...,b, b-a+1 times in total; if b<a, the value of loop variable will be a,a-1,...,b, a-b+1 times in total.

Cell A1,B2,C3 respectively loops through each digit of the three-digit number. This is code for three-tier loop. The outermost layer A1 loops through the hundreds digit, the middle layer B2 loops through the tens digit, and the innermost layer C3 loops through units digit. Because there are 10 possibilities for tens digit and unis digit from 0 to 9, if it is written as for 10, it needs to subtract 1 in the later operation, which is troublesome, so it is easy to write it as for 0,9 directly.

In multi-layer loop, the complete inner loop will be executed every time the outer loop body is executed. In this way, A1 will loop 9 times and B1 will be executed 9 times; B2 itself will loop 10 times, and C2, as a statement in the loop body of B2, will be executed 9*10=90 times; D3 and E3, as statements in the body of C3, will be executed 9*10*10=900 times.

The three-digit number and the sum of cubes of each digit are calculated by D3 and E3 respectively. The calculation of B1,C1 and C2,D2 is to try to make the calculation amount smaller. When the number of units digit changes in a cycle, the number of hundreds and tens is temporarily unchanged, so it is unnecessary to repeat the calculation for the hundreds and tens every time. This is also a matter of attention when coding. The execution times of inner loop body statements may be very many, and a little less computation will reduce the total calculation amount, thus greatly improving the performance of the program.

Now you can execute the program by yourself, and check the output at the bottom right to see which Narcissus numbers are calculated.

By the way, we use multiplication when we calculate cubic here, and we also used multiplication to calculate square when we talked about quadratic equation before, why not use power() function directly?

Actually, power() can be used when calculating square before, but it can't be used here. Because power() is calculated by exponent and logarithm, it will return a floating-point number. But it needs to be compared accurately here, and it is not reliable to use floating-point numbers. So we'd rather multiply it three times. Also because of this, we should write for 0,9 instead of for 10, otherwise it is a bit troublesome to write multiplying B2-1 three times.

We did not use power() to calculate square before, on the one hand, it is not difficult to write self multiplication twice, on the other hand, it will be much slower to calculate with exponent and logarithm, so it is also written as self multiplication.

These are also details that you need pay attention to when programming.

This code can also be optimized. If the sum of cubes of each digit is larger than the three-digit number, it is unnecessary to loop the units digit any more. Because when the hundreds and tens are unchanged, when the number of units digit is looped to the next, i.e. added by 1, this cube sum will increase by at least 1 (increase by 1 only when the units digit changes to 1 from 0, and other changes are greater than 1), and the three-digit number itself will only increase by 1. Then, the gap between the three-digit number and the cube sum cannot be smaller (generally the bigger it will be) and they cannot be equal.

That is, once we find D3<E3, C3's loop is unnecessary to continue. It is impossible to find a Narcissus number under the condition that A1 and B2 are unchanged. It is only a waste of time and calculation.

Most programming languages, including SPL, provide break statement to abort the current loop, and the code is rewritten as follows:

	A	B	C	D	E
1	for 9	=100*A1	=A1*A1*A1		
2		for 0,9	=B1+10*B2	=C1+B2*B2*B2	
3			for 0,9	=C2+C3	=D2+C3*C3*C3
4				if D3==E3	>output(D3)
5				else if D3<E3	break

This code has one more line, but the computing performance is much better than before.

In fact, the analysis of single digit just now holds true for tens digit, because the cube of numbers 0-9 must not be less than itself. If C2<D2, then there must be D3<E3. At this time, there is no need to do the third level loop.

The code can be further optimized:

	A	B	C	D	E	F
1	for 9	=100*A1	=A1*A1*A1			
2		for 0,9	=B1+10*B2	=C1+B2*B2*B2	if C2<D2	break
3			for 0,9	=C2+C3	=D2+C3*C3*C3	
4				if D3==E3	>output(D3)	
5				else if D3<E3	break	

The above analysis can be extended to the hundreds digit, but it doesn't make any sense. Please think about the reason here. The optimization of this code is basically over now.

3.3   Conditional loop

for n and for a,b are both loop with definite number of cycles, but sometimes we don't know how many times to loop. To end the loop only when a condition is true (or not), and repeating the loop body before that, this kind of loop is called **conditional loop.**

In fact, for n and for a,b can also be understood as such a loop, that is, ending the loop when the loop variable exceeds n and b (exceeding does not necessarily mean greater than). Conditional loop is a more general form of loop.

There is a classical method to calculate the greatest common divisor of two numbers, which is called successive division method. Two positive integers a and b, assuming a>b, replace a with the remainder of a divided by b, now a<b, and then replace b with the remainder of b divided by a, and then a>b,..., and so on, until one of a or b is 0, then the other one that is not 0 is the greatest common divisor of the original a and b. Because a and b exchange positions repeatedly to calculate the remainder, it is called successive division method.

This is the way Euclid, a Greek geometrician, invented more than 2000 years ago. Interested readers can prove it by themselves. We use program code to implement it here.

Set the original two numbers in the cells A1 and B1.

	A	B
1	7215	2345
2	for B1>0	=A1%B1
3		>A1=B1
4		>B1=B2

The calculation result will be shown in A1.

The code of cell A2 is for B1>0, for is followed by a boolean expression. When it calculates true, the loop body will be executed once, and then return to A2 to calculate the boolean expression again. If it is still true, the loop body will be executed again . . .; Until the boolean expression is evaluated as false, the loop ends.

This logic can realize Euclidean division. We don't know how many times to loop, only know that when B1 is 0, the loop can be terminated.

Most programming languages have conditional loops, but they usually use while.

Words like if, else, for will be used in the program code to represent certain special statements, called **reserved words** or **keywords** of the program language. These reserved words are of special significance and cannot be used as identifiers such as variable names. All programming languages have a number of their own reserved words.

SPL does not want to have too many reserved words, and it is not ambiguous to use for to represent conditional loop, so it does not retain the more common reserved word while.

Let's do another exercise related to divisor, prime factorization, which is the content of mathematics lesson in primary school.

The method is very simple. Given a positive integer n, we divide it by 2, if it is divisible, then we get a factor 2. We divide n by 2 to get a new n, continue to divide it by 2, . . . ; until it is not divisible by 2, if n becomes 1 at this time, it's over. If n is not 1, continue to divide it by 3 and repeat the process; Continue to divide n by 4,5, . . .; in the end, n is always changed to 1, and it's over.

As we said before, because we haven't learned set yet, we can output the prime factors we find out.

Let n fill in cell A1 first.

	A	B	C
1	7215	=2	
2	for A1>1	for A1%B1==0	>output(B1)
3			>A1=A1\B1
4		>B1+=1	

Pay attention to that \,which means integer division,is used in cell C3, otherwise floating-point number will be calculated, and the next A1% B1 can not continue.

This is a two-layer loop code. It can also be written as a single-layer loop:

	A	B	C	D
1	7215	=2		
2	for A1>1	if A1%B1==0	>output(B1)	
3			>A1=A1\B1	next
4		>B1+=1		

Replace the for of cell B2 with if, and then add a next in cell D3.

We already know the function of if. What's the function of next here?

next means to proceed to the next round of loop header and no longer execute the code that has not been executed after it in the loop body. Here, if the code is executed to the next of D3, it means that B4 will be skipped and will not be executed, and the program will directly go to the next loop, that is, it will go back to A2 to judge A1>1 and decide whether to continue to execute the loop body.

Think about this logic process carefully. B1 starts with 2. If A1 can be divisible by 2, output the 2 in C2, divide A1 by 2, and then go back to A2 again to enter the next loop. At this time, B1 is still 2, because next will skip B4, and the statement B1+=1 is not executed. After all the factors of 2 are calculated, the if of cell B2 will not hold, and then it will enter cell B4 to execute B1+=1, change B1 into 3, and then enter the next loop. This single-layer loop can achieve the same effect as the above two-layer loop.

It should be noted that if next is used in the loop of for n or for a,b, the loop variable will still change in the next loop. For example, the previous example of finding odd sum can also be written with next:

	A	B	C
1	=0		
2	for 200	if A2%2==0	next
3		>A1+=A2	

When an even number is encountered, the condition of B2 is established, it will be executed to the next of C2 to enter the next loop, and the loop variable will still be added by 1; When the number is odd, it will be executed to B3 to execute accumulation, and the loop body will be executed 200 times.

In multi-layer loop, next followed by the name of loop cell can make the outer loop directly enter the next round. For example, the Narcissus number mentioned above can also be written as follows:

	A	B	C	D	E	F
1	for 9	=100*A1	=A1*A1*A1			
2		for 0,9	=B1+10*B2	=C1+B2*B2*B2	if C2<D2	next A1
3			for 0,9	=C2+C3	=D2+C3*C3*C3	
4				if D3==E3	>output(D3)	
5				else if D3<E3	next B2	

It seems that using next achieves the same effect as break, but the mechanism is different. next B2 of cell E5 will directly enter the next round of B2 loop, and if it is break, it will jump out of C3 loop. In this example, the effect of the two is the same, because there is no code of the B2 loop after the C3 loop ends, and the B2 loop ends too.

If the code changes to this:

	A	B	C	D	E	F
1	for 9	=100*A1	=A1*A1*A1			
2		for 0,9	=B1+10*B2	=C1+B2*B2*B2	if C2<D2	next A1
3			for 0,9	=C2+C3	=D2+C3*C3*C3	
4				if D3==E3	>output(D3)	
5				else if D3<E3	next B2	
6			>output("B2")			

When E5 code is next B2, C6 will not be executed; If it is break, C6 will still be executed. You can try it and understand the difference by themselves.

3.4 Endless loop

What happens if you don't write anything after for, neither the number of loops nor the loop condition?

This kind of loop is called **unconditional loop**, commonly known as **endless loop.** In theory, this loop will be executed endlessly and never stop, just like goto which is not used with if.

This obviously doesn't makc sense. We shouldn't write a program that can't be terminated.

However, it's not uncommon to see endless loop code in reality. What's the matter?

Because we also have break and if.

An endless loop is not really an endless loop, only that when we write a loop statement, we are not sure how to write the end condition of the loop. It needs to be determined during the running process of the loop body. In this case, we will write an endless loop at the beginning of the loop, and use if to judge the end condition of the loop in the loop body. If it is true, we will use break to jump out of the loop.

A real endless loop really doesn't make sense. However, if the if used to trigger a break is wrongly written, the pseudo endless loop may become a real endless loop, which should be paid special attention to when coding.

Set a four digit x, split the four digits respectively, use these four digits to form the largest four digit a, and then form the smallest four digit b. Here, we also consider the first few digits that are 0 (actually three digits, two digits or even one digit) as reasonable four-digit numbers. Then calculate a-b to get a new four-digit number, regard it as x and repeat the process, so that the calculation can be repeated infinitely.

If the new x is the same as the previous x in a certain round of calculation, it is obvious that if the calculation continues, only the same x will appear, and it is meaningless to continue. We call x at this time "digital black hole", once the number of black hole appears, the operation can be stopped.

Write a piece of code with endless loop, randomly choose a four digit x as the starting value, take finding the number of black hole as the ending condition, and output all the x in the process.

	A	B	C	D	E
1	1234				
2	for	=A1\1000	=A1\100%10	=A1\10%10	=A1%10
3		=max(B2,C2,D2,E2)		=B2+C2+D2+E2-B3	=min(B2,C2,D2,E2)
4		if B3==B2	>C3=max(C2,D2,E2)		>D3-=(C3+E3)
5		else if B3==C2	>C3=max(B2,D2,E2)		>D3-=(C3+E3)
6		else if B3==D2	>C3=max(B2,C2,E2)		>D3-=(C3+E3)
7		else	>C3=max(B2,C2,D2)		>D3-=(C3+E3)
8		=B3*1000+C3*100+D3*10+E3		=B3+C3*10+D3*100+E3*1000	
9		>output(A1)	=B8-D8	if C9==A1	break
10		>A1=C9			

The initial value is placed in A1.

Because we haven't learned the knowledge of set, we can't use the function of set sorting. The most troublesome part of this code is B3:E7, which is used to sort the four digits from large to small. B2:E2 solve the four digits respectively. The max/min function is used to calculate the maximum digit in B3 and the minimum digit in E3. D3 is the sum of three digits except the maximum digit. Then, B4:B7 respectively judge which of B2:E2 is the largest digit, the remaining largest is the second largest digit, and then subtract it and the smallest from D3 to get the third largest digit. The final B3:E3 are the four digits from large to small. If we have the knowledge of set, the sorting can be completed in one cell.

However, it's good to review the if... else structure again in this troublesome way.

The following code is simple. Calculate the maximum and minimum four-digit that can be formed respectively, and subtract to get a new x. if it is the same as the previous one, the loop will be ended. Otherwise, the new x will replace the old x to continue the loop.

Try it on your own to see if this code can stop and which number can it stop at?

Again, if the program does not end due to wrong code, you can use the debugging function to force it to stop.

Up to now, we have known several structures to control the flow of program:
1) Sequential structure: execute from top to bottom
2) Branching structure: according to the conditions to determine the different direction, will skip some code, the overall direction is still forward
3) Loop structure: repeatedly executing a piece of code, including loops formed by goto

If we do not consider the function call, we can say that all programming languages have only such a few process structures. We have learned them all.

If we review the examples we have done, we will find that the programming language does not help us find a way to solve the problem. When we encounter a problem, we still need to come up with a solution ourselves, that is, to solve the problem through a series of steps (using the combination of the above three basic structures), which are usually called **algorithms**.

The function of programming language is to provide a way to describe the algorithms that human beings think of, so that the computer can understand and execute. A good programming language can more succinctly describe people's ideas, and programming will be fast; A bad programming language may be very troublesome, and it will be more difficult to think of a solution description than a problem solution.

In any case, don't expect programming languages to help us come up with algorithms. If you can't think of an algorithm, there is no solution to the problem.

4 SEQUENCE

4.1 Sequence

In the previous programs we wrote, there are only a few original input data. The data processed by loop code is also calculated by code according to some rules, not the original data. In practice, the original data we need to process is often a large number of data, and we need to use the concept of set.

However, most programming languages do not retain the term set, but use **array** to represent batch data. SPL uses the term **sequence** to emphasize the order between batch data. Sequence and array can be understood as the same thing, only that the idiom is different, and sequence is mainly used in this book.

A batch of data in order can form a sequence, which can be stored and named by a variable name. The data forming the sequence is called the **members** of the sequence, and the number of members forming the sequence is called the **length** of the sequence.

In SPL, write the data in turn in square brackets and separate them with commas to get the sequence constants, such as:

	A
1	[1,2,3,4,5]
2	=[3,9,0,2,2.3,9.8]
3	=[]

A1 and A2 are sequences, where A1 is a constant cell and A2 is a calculation cell. A3 is also a calculation cell, and its result is an empty sequence, that is, a sequence without members. The length of an empty sequence is 0. However, an empty sequence is not a null value.

In many programming languages, the members of an array must be of the same data type. However, there is no such requirement in SPL. Members of a sequence can have different data types, but in most cases, the sequence is composed of members of the same data type.

Sequence members can use other variables or expressions:

	A	B	C	D
1	3	=4+8	=pi()	=3*C1
2	=[3,A1,D1,3*B1]	=[B1,C1+A1,0]		

A2 and B2 can also define a sequence, but the sequence that needs to be calculated must be defined by the calculation cell, and it needs to be executed before it has a value.

SPL can also use a cell range to define a sequence like Excel:

	A	B	C	D
1	4	8	3	2
2	5	2	0	-5
3	=[A1:D2]			

A sequence of length 8 is calculated in A3. The members are arranged from left to right and from top to bottom in the order of cells. This sequence is equivalent to [4,8,3,2,5,2,0, - 5].

You can access the member corresponding to a **sequence number** by adding the number in parentheses after the sequence variable. You can either get the value or assign the value:

	A	B	C	D
1	4	8	3	2
2	5	9	0	-5
3	=[A1:D2]	=A3(2)	=A3(5)	>A3(4)=3
4	=A3(1)+A3(3)	=A3(A3(4))	=A3(A4)	

After execution, the cell values of B3 and C3 is 8 and 5 respectively. After D3 is executed, the fourth member of A3 will be changed to 3(was 2 before), but the value of D1 will not be changed. When A3 is assigned, the value of D1 has been copied to the member of A3. When A3 is changed, it has nothing to do with D1.

Sequence members can participate in operations, and can also refer to other members of the sequence as sequence numbers. A4 will be calculated as 7, B4 will be calculated as 8, C4 will be calculated as 0.

The sequence number of a sequence member, sometimes is referred to as its **position** in the sequence.

If you click the cell where the sequence is located, the development environment can also display the value of the sequence, which will be listed as a table, such as A3 of the above code:

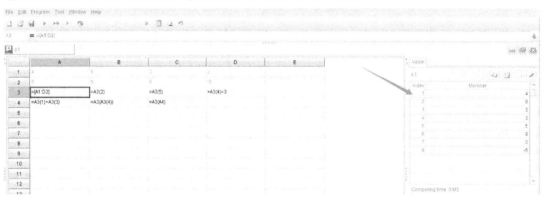

In SPL, the sequence number of sequence members starts from 1, and the reference of a member uses parentheses. In some programming languages, the serial number of array members starts from 0, and the reference of a member uses brackets. This should also be noted when learning programming language.

In fact, a sequence variable can be simply understood as a group of variables with the same name, which should be distinguished by sequence numbers. Each member can be regarded as an independent variable. If the sequence number exceeds the limit, it is equivalent to referring to a non-existent variable, and the program will report an error.

The above-mentioned method of generating a sequence needs to write out the members one by one (in fact, it is the same when generating sequence with cell range). If we want to generate a sequence with hundreds or thousands of members, this method is obviously out of the question.

In SPL, the syntax of the expression [x]*n can be used to generate a sequence of length n and each member is x. For example, [0]*100 will return a sequence with 100 zeros as members, so we can create a sequence of any length.

The sequence created by this method will have an initial value for all members. So, can there be a sequence with no initial value, just with vacant positions?

In fact, this is meaningless. Any variable in a computer program will always occupy some memory space, and there will always be some data in the space. The only difference is how to interpret the data according to the variable type. There is no "vacuum" value that does not occupy the space. We usually say the null value, that is, null, is also a data type, it also takes up some storage space. You can also use [null]*n to generate a sequence, but it is not much different from [0]*n in space occupation.

In SPL, null and 0 are different, that is, null!=0 will be evaluated as true, similar to SQL; But in some programming languages, null and 0 are the same thing (such as C).

We'll talk about how to generate and process a sequence with uncertain length later.

Having learned sequence, we can change the previous example of calculating the Narcissus numbers and write all the Narcissus numbers into a sequence:

	A	B	C	D	E	F
1	=0	=[0]*100				
2	for 9	=100*A2	=A2*A2*A2			
3		for 0,9	=B2+10*B3	=C2+B3*B3*B3	if C3<D3	break
4			for 0,9	=C3+C4	=D3+C4*C4*C4	
5				if D4==E4	>A1+=1	>B1(A1)=D4
6				else if D4<E4	break	

Assuming that there are at most 100 Narcissus numbers (actually far less than 100), generate a sequence of length 100 in B1. A1 is the number of Narcissus numbers currently found. For each one found, let A1 increase by 1, and then fill in the corresponding member in B1. Finally, those members in the front of B1 that are not 0 are all the Narcissus numbers.

We will reform the problem of prime factorization later.

Let's use sequence to implement a classic algorithm: bubble sorting.

Giving a group of numbers, or a sequence, we need to rearrange the members of the sequence from small to large.

The algorithm process of bubble sorting is as follows: scan the sequence from head to end, if the size of adjacent members is not appropriate, such as the previos number is larger than the next one, then exchange the two numbers. After a scan, if an exchange action has occurred, it is necessary to scan again until no exchange has occurred in a scan, and the sorting is completed.

	A	B	C	D
1	=[3,4,12,4,6,9,3,5]		=A1.len()-1	=true
2	for D1	>D1=false		
3		for C1	if A1(B3)>A1(B3+1)	=A1(B3)
4				>A1(B3)=A1(B3+1)
5				>A1(B3+1)=D3
6				>D1=true

The data to be sorted is in A1. After the outer loop starts, D1 is set to false to assume that this is the last loop, and then the sequence is scanned. If the size of adjacent members is not appropriate, the exchange is implemented, and D1 is set to true, so that the next outer loop can be carried out. If there is no exchange, D1 remains false and the outer loop ends.

There is another common variant of bubble sorting:

	A	B	C	D
1	=[3,4,12,4,6,9,3,5]		=A1.len()	=C1-1
2	for D1	for A2+1,C1	if A1(A2)>A1(B2)	=A1(A2)
3				>A1(A2)=A1(B2)
4				>A1(B2)=D2

Please try to understand the principle of it by yourself.

With sequence and its sorting ability, we can simplify the previous problem of black hole number, and use the variant of bubble sorting to sort (from large to small here):

	A	B	C	D	E
1	1234				
2	for	=[A1\1000,A1\100%10,A1\10%10,A1%10]			>C6=D6=0
3		for 3	for B3+1,4	if B2(B3)<B2(C3)	=B2(B3)
4					>B2(B3)=B2(C3)
5					>B2(C3)=E3
6		for 4	=C6*10+B2(B6)	=D6*10+B2(5-B6)	
7		>output(A1)	=C6-D6	if C7==A1	break
8		>A1=C7			

With sequence, we can use loop (B6:D6) to calculate the four-digit number. Before that, we need to fill C6 and D6 with 0(cell E2), and then we can correctly calculate the maximum and minimum four-digit numbers through the loop of B6:D6. In cell E2, as mentioned before, a=x is also regarded as a calculation expression, and will have a value. D6=0 will be calculates as 0 at the same time of assigning 0 to D6, and then it is assigned to C6. As a result, both C6 and D6 become 0.

4.2   Loop of sequence

With loop, we can implement some aggregation operations for a sequence, such as the previous max/min.

	A	B	C
1	=[3,4,12,4,6,9,3,5]	=-999999	=999999
2	for A1.len()	if B1<A1(A2)	>B1=A1(A2)
3		if C1>A1(A2)	>C1=A1(A2)

A1.len() in cell A2 will return the length of sequence A1. This function in the form of x.f() will be discussed later, and we just let it be here.

This is a standard algorithm for calculating the maximum amd minimum value. For the maximum value, set the target value to a very small number, and then compare it with the sequence member in turn. If the current member is found to be larger, replace the target value with the current member, and then get the maximum value at the end of the loop. The minimum is the opposite process.

The sum is also simple:

	A	B
1	=[3,4,12,4,6,9,3,5]	=0
2	for A1.len()	>B1+=A1(A2)

However, we always need to write an A1.len(), and then use the sequence number A1(A2) when referring to members, which is a bit troublesome. In fact, the sequence itself can also be looped. max/min can be written as follows:

	A	B	C
1	=[3,4,12,4,6,9,3,5]	=-999999	=999999
2	for A1	if B1<A2	>B1=A2
3		if C1>A2	>C1=A2

for can be directly followed by a sequence, the number of cycles is the length of the sequence, and the loop variable is each member of the sequence in turn. There is no need to write the length of the sequence, and there is no need to use the sequence number to access members.

It's also easy to write sum:

	A	B
1	=[3,4,12,4,6,9,3,5]	=0
2	for A1	>B1+=A2

In recent years, programming languages have begun to support this kind of set type loop writing method. The early programming languages did not have a strong set concept, so they could only use the previous sequence number writing method.

However, there is a problem. We don't know the loop number of the current loop. For example, when we calculate the maximum value, we want to know not only what the maximum value is, but also which member is the largest. It is relatively simple if we use the above-mentioned sequence number writing method:

	A	B	C
1	=[3,4,12,4,6,9,3,5]	=-999999	=0
2	for A1.len()	if B1<A1(A2)	>B1=A1(A2)
3			>C1=A2

When we find a larger member, just write down its sequence number. Finally, C1 will be the sequence number of the maximum value.

SPL has taken this into consideration and provided a method to obtain the current loop number even when the sequence loops:

	A	B	C
1	=[3,4,12,4,6,9,3,5]	=-999999	=0
2	for A1	if B1<A2	>B1=A2
3			>C1=#A2

When a sequence loops, there are two loop variables. The loop cell itself is a member of the sequence. After adding #, it means the loop number. Here, it is exactly the expected sequence number. This variable with # is usually called the **loop number**.

Let's take another example to judge whether two sequences of the same length are identical, that is, each member of the same sequence number is the same. It can be written using a conventional loop like this:

	A	B	C
1	=[1,2,3,4,5]	=[1,2,3,4,6]	
2	for A1.len()	if A1(A2)!=B1(A2)	>output("No")
3			break

If an unequal member is found, output no, and then jump out of the loop.

It can also be realized by a sequence loop:

	A	B	C
1	=[1,2,3,4,5]	=[1,2,3,4,6]	
2	for A1	if A2!=B1(#A2)	>output("No")
3			break

The code for this comparison can also be written as follows:

	A	B	C
1	=[1,2,3,4,5]	=[1,2,3,4,6]	
2	for A1.len()	if A1(A2)!=B1(A2)	break
3	if A2<=A1.len()	>output("No")	

After finding an unequal member, jump out of the loop and judge outside the loop. A3 code means that the loop variable still has a value after the end of the loop, and if the loop ends normally, its loop variable will be filled with the number of cycles plus one, which is equivalent to the value of the loop variable if there is another round of loop.

When using a sequence loop, at the end of the loop, the loop variable will be filled with a null value, and the loop number is not defined any more.

4.3 Multi-layer sequence

The members of a sequence can also be sequences, and a multi-layer sequence can be formed in this way. For example, [[1,2,3],[2,3,1],[3,1,2]] is a legal sequence, and each member is also a sequence.

Let's look at how members of a multi-layer sequence can be referenced:

	A
1	=[[1,2,3],[4,5,6],[7,8,9,10]]
2	=A1(2)
3	=A1(3)(2)
4	>A1(1)(3)=0
5	=A1.len()
6	=A1(3).len()
7	>A1(2)=0

Try to execute the above code and observe the running results to understand the actions of member reference and assignment of multi-layer sequence.

The result of A2 is sequence [4,5,6]; A3 gets the second member of the third member sequence, namely 8; After A4 is executed, the third member of the first member sequence becomes 0, which used to be 3; A5 is the length of the sequence, which is 3, and A6 is the length of the third member sequence, which is 4; After A7 is executed, the second member sequence will be changed to 0, and this member will no longer be a sequence.

Multi layer sequence can also be displayed on the interface. After the above code is executed, click A1 to see its value on the right.

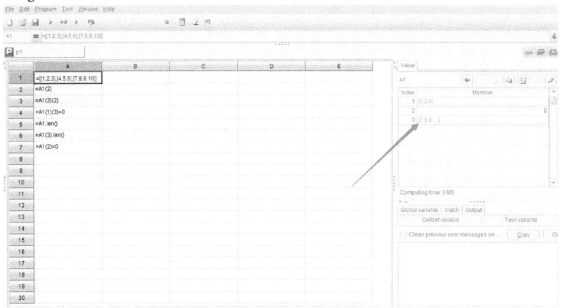

The sequence members will also be displayed as a sequence. At this time, double-click a sequence member (such as the third member pointed by the arrow), the members of this member sequence will be displayed:

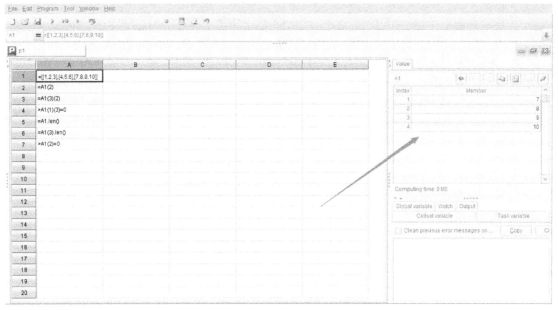

The sequence composed of n sequences of length m can be understood as a two-dimensional structure, and each member sequence can be written as a row, and it can be regarded as a table of n rows and m columns. Therefore, some programming languages also call a two-layer sequence as a two-dimensional array, and even have done some special processing, and can support the writing method of x(i,j) to access the member of the i-th row and j-th column. There is no special understanding in SPL, it is simply understood as the j-th member of the i-th member sequence, that is, written as x(i)(j).

Obviously, there can be more of these levels, in terms of array, there can be more dimensions.

We use the two-layer sequence to calculate the Pascal triangle:

```
1
1   1
1   2   1
1   3   3   1
1   4   6   4   1
......
```

Pascal triangle is composed of N rows of numbers. The n-th row has n numbers. The m-th number of the n-th row is the sum of the (m-1)-th and m-th numbers of the (n-1)-th row. The n-th row number of Pascal triangle is exactly the coefficient of term x^i in $(1+x)^n$, that is:

$$(1+x)^1 = 1 + 1x$$
$$(1+x)^2 = 1 + 2x + 1x^2$$
$$(1+x)^3 = 1 + 3x + 3x^2 + 1x^3$$
$$(1+x)^4 = 1 + 4x + 6x^2 + 4x^3 + 1x^4$$

......

The code is simple:

	A	B	C	D
1	5	=[0]*(A1+1)	>B1(1)=[1]	>B1(2)=[1,1]
2	for 3,A1+1	>B1(A2)=[1]*A2		
3		for 2,A2-1	>B1(A2)(B3)=B1(A2-1)(B3-1)+B1(A2-1)(B3)	

Calculate to the (A1+1)-th row, the result is a 2-layer sequence, which is saved in B1.

B1 generates a sequence of length A1+1, which is ready to be filled in. C1 and D1 are filled in the first two rows. The A2 loop is calculated from the third row. B2 generates a sequence of length A2, with members all be 1, for the current row, and then calculates from the second column to the A2-1 column, because the first and A2 columns of this row are all 1, and it is unnecessary to calculate them.

4.4   Understanding objects

Let's take a look at an example code:

	A	B
1	=4	=A1
2	=[3,4,12,4,6,9,3,5]	=A2
3	>B1=3	=A1
4	>B2(2)=0	=A2(2)

The value of A1 is assigned to B1, and then B1 is changed in A3. If you look at A1, you will find that it has not changed and still is the starting value. That is, the =A1 in cell B1 copies A1, and is irrelevant to the original A1.

Similarly, the value of A2 is assigned to B2, and then one member of B2 is changed in A4. Now we can see that the member of A2 has been changed! This shows that the assignment of sequence is different from that of integer, and the assignment in B2 does not copy A2. A2 and B2 are actually the same thing.

Unlike the single values of integer and floating-point, the sequence is a complex data type composed of a batch of values. This kind of data will occupy a large space in the computer to store, and is not suitable to be directly stored in the memory space occupied by the variable itself, and needs special space and needs to be managed uniformly.

The computer will give a number to every memory space, so that it can find the space with this number later on. This number is also called the **address** of the memory space, which is very similar to the address we use in daily life. For the complex data type of sequence, the variable stores not the data itself, but its address.

The address of the memory space is also called **pointer** in many computer materials.

Back to the above code, the assignment statement of B2 only copies the address of sequence A2, not the value. After execution, A2 and B2 store the address of the same sequence. At this time, if you change the member of B2, that is, if you change the member of that sequence, you will also see the change from A2. Similarly, if you change the member of A2, you can also see the change from B2.

The simple values of integer are completely copied when they are assigned values. If you change one of them, it has nothing to do with the other.

The computer community is also used to call the complex data types such as sequence as **objects.** We'll come across more types of objects later.

An object usually has many functions related to it. For the function f with object x as the main parameter, it can still be written in the traditional form of f(x,...), but in order to show that f is strongly related to x, we often write it in the form of x.f(...), and also call f the **function** or **method** of object x. For example, the function x.len() that returns the length of sequence x.

A large number of functions in SPL are written in the form of such objects.

In the previous code, we need to know the maximum length of a sequence when we want to use a sequence. We first create a sequence with a certain length and then fill in the members in the execution process of the program. It is not convenient. We can not always know the length of the sequence to be used in the program(for example, the number of Narcissus numbers in the previous example, maybe 100 are not enough). If it is long, it will waste space, and if it is short, it will lead to overflow error.

In fact, for the sequence object, SPL provides ways to change its length, which is, to be exact, to insert and delete members.

	A
1	=[1,2,3,4,5,6,7,8,9]
2	>A1.insert(1,0)
3	>A1.delete(5)
4	>A1.insert(0,10)
5	>A1.insert(8,78)

Execute the program and observe the changes in A1.

A.insert(i,x) will insert a member x before the i-th position of sequence A, and the original i-th, (i+1)-th,... members will move backward in turn; If i is 0, x is inserted to the end, that is, appending a member. A.insert(...) will increase the length of the sequence. A.delete(i) will delete the i-th member, and the sequence length will be reduced.

We rewrite the Narcissus number program using insert() function:

	A	B	C	D	E	F
1	=0	=[]				
2	for 9	=100*A2	=A2*A2*A2			
3		for 0,9	=B2+10*B3	=C2+B3*B3*B3	if C3<D3	break
4			for 0,9	=C3+C4	=D3+C4*C4*C4	
5				if D4==E4	>B1.insert(0,D4)	
6				else if D4<E4	break	

Create an empty sequence in B1, and then append a member in E5 for each narcissus number found. Finally, B1 is the sequence composed of all Narcissus numbers. The length of the sequence is exactly the number of Narcissus numbers, and there is no waste of empty positions.

Pascal triangle can also be implemented in a similar way:

	A	B	C
1	5	=[[1],[1,1]]	
2	for 3,A1+1	=[1,1]	>B1.insert(0,[B2])
3		for 2,A2-1	>B2.insert(B3,B1(A2-1)(B3-1)+B1(A2-1)(B3))

B1 initializes the first two rows. In the loop of each following row, a sequence with only head and tail is generated in B2, added to the end of B1, and then the calculation of B2 is completed by inserting the intermediate value in B2 by the loop.

Pay attention to the action of appending B2 to B1 in cell C2. When adding a sequence member to a two-layer sequence, add a layer of [] to the parameter, that is, the [B2] here. This is because the insert() function actually allows a sequence to be inserted into the original sequence at a time. When x is also a sequence, A.insert(i,x) inserts the members of x before the i-th member of A in turn (if i is 0, append to the end). To insert sequence x as a whole (the case of this example), you need to add a layer of [], as a sequence with a length of 1, otherwise, insert() function will take x apart and insert the members one by one.

We'd like to say a light digression here.

In fact, once the memory space in the computer program is created, its size is fixed and can not be changed. The insert() function can change the length of the sequence, and the action behind it is to recreate a larger memory space, copy the original members of the sequence, and discard the original space (return to the operating system).

It is conceivable that insert function will be a very slow action. Frequent use of insert() function will lead to continuous creation and moving of storage space(of course, the memory space will not be recreated every time, it will be created a little larger at once, and be recreated again if not enough), resulting in low performance of operation. We should get used to avoiding it in code.

This principle is applicable to any programming language.

5 SEQUENCE AS A WHOLE

5.1 Set operations

Now, we have learned to use a sequence, but this sequence looks like what we said before, it is a batch of variables with the same name. When we operate on these sequence members, we still refer to and assign values one by one. In this chapter, we learn how to operate a sequence as a whole.

Sequence is essentially a set, so it is easy to think that it can support set related operations, that is, intersection, union, etc.

SPL provides four set operators:

	A	B
1	=[1,2,3,4,5,1]	=[4,6,4,5,1]
2	=A1|B1	=B1|A1
3	=A1&B1	=B1&A1
4	=A1^B1	=B1^A1
5	=A1\B1	=B1\A1
6	=A1|1	=A1&1
7	=1|B1	=1&B1
8	=A1\1	=B1\1

A1|B1 appends the members of sequence B1 to sequence A1 to form a new sequence and return, which is called concatenation. While &,^,\ are the set union, intersection and difference operations of common significance. We used to represent the integer division operation with \, here we use it on the sequence to represent the difference set.

It is important to note that, unlike the mathematical disordered set, the sequence is ordered, which will lead to the difference between A1&B1 and B1&A1, and that the sequence intersection and union operations in SPL do not meet the exchange law. The ordered set also allows duplicate members. When performing intersection, union and difference operations, it will be more complex than the set without duplicate members. Please carefully observe the above operation results to understand the operation rules in this case.

In addition, SPL also supports the operation between a sequence and a single value, which is equivalent to the operation with a one-member sequence. The single value can be placed to the left or right of the operator.

We use the set operation to rewrite the narcissus number program:

	A	B	C	D	E	F
1	=0	=[]				
2	for 9	=100*A2	=A2*A2*A2			
3		for 0,9	=B2+10*B3	=C2+B3*B3*B3	if C3<D3	break
4			for 0,9	=C3+C4	=D3+C4*C4*C4	
5				if D4==E4	>B1|=D4	
6				else if D4<E4	break	

Concatenate the calculated narcissus number to the current sequence with | operation. You can see that the set operation also supports |= syntax.

Pascal triangle:

	A	B	C
1	5	=[[1],[1,1]]	
2	for 3,A1+1	=[]	
3		for 2,A2-1	>B2|=[B1(A2-1)(B3-1)+B1(A2-1)(B3)]
4		>B1|=[1|B2|1]	

Use inner loop to calculate the middle part of the current row, and then concatenate 1 before and after it respectively, and then concatenate it as a whole to the end of the target 2-layer sequence.

As a kind of data, sequence can also be compared:

	A
1	=[1,2,3,4]==[1,2,3,4]
2	=[1,2,3,4]!=[1,3,2,4]
3	=[1,2,3,4]<[1,2,4]
4	=[1,2,3,4]<[1,2,3,4,5]

The results of these judgments are all true. The conventional dictionary sorting method is used in sequence comparison. Each pair of members is compared in order, and the values of the first pair of unequal members is used to draw the comparison result of the sequences; If it is always equal, the longer sequence is considered larger; If all the corresponding members are equal and the length is the same, the two sequences are considered equal. In particular, because of order, the sequences composed of same members are not necessarily equal.

We used [0]*n to generate an all-0 sequence of length n. SPL also provides the to() function to generate a sequence of integers.

	A	B
1	=to(5)	[1,2,3,4,5]
2	=to(2,6)	[2,3,4,5,6]
3	=to(5,1)	[5,4,3,2,1]
4	=to(6,2)	[6,5,4,3,2]

The result of column A is equal to the sequence of constants in column B.

SPL refers to the sequence whose members are all integers as an **integer sequence**.

Regarding the loop statements we have learned, we can find that for n, for a,b are basically equivalent to for to(n) and for to(a,b). Here we say basically equivalent rather than equivalent, because the loop variable values of the former two at the end of the loop are different from those of the latter two.

The sequence numbers of the sequence members are also integers. We can get the members from a sequence to form another sequence according to the sequence numbers specified by the members of an integer sequence. For sequence A and integer sequence p, in SPL, A(p) can be used to represent [A(p(1)),...,A(p(k))], k is the length of p. A (p) is called the **generated sequence** of A.

	A	B
1	=[9,8,7,6,5,4,3,2,1]	=A1([5,2,6])
2	=A1([1,2,3,5])	=A1.to(5)
3	=A1(to(3,7))	=A1.to(3,7)
4	=A1(to(5,A1.len()))	=A1.to(5,)
5	=A1(A1)	=A1(A1|to(9))

B1 will get the 5th, 2nd and 6th members of A1 to form a sequence, i.e. [5,8,4]. For the sequence composed of some continuous members in a sequence, it can be obtained by the to() function of the sequence. A2, A3 and A4 can be simplified into B2,B3,B4. Note the writing methods of B2 and B4, and the comma in B4 cannot be omitted.

A5 and B5 are interesting calculations. Please observe the results of them by yourself.

Usually, the generated sequence is part of the original sequence(which can be called a sub sequence at this time), but an integer sequence may also have duplicate members, so the generated sequence is not always the sub sequence of the original sequence.

5.2   Loop functions

Previously, we used the loop statements to complete the sum and max/min operations for the sequence members, but the loop statements are very troublesome, and we need to set the initial value first and then calculate step by step. SPL takes this into account and provides some common functions for sequences.

	A	B
1	=[3,2,1,8].sum()	
2	=[3,4,1,0,5].max()	=[4,5,2,3,2].min()
3	=[3,null,4,5].len()	=[3,null,4,5].count()
4	=[3,null,4,5].avg()	

It's easy to see the meaning from the names of these functions, and then execute this code to observe the operation results to confirm. count() is a bit like len(), but count() does not count members whose values are null. avg() is defined as sum()/count(), not sum()/len().

We will popularly call the functions that calculate the sequence into a single value **aggregate functions**, which are equivalent to aggregate the set.

These aggregate functions all use the object syntax of x.f(). In fact, SPL also supports writing these functions in traditional form, while sequence members are used as parameters:

	A	B
1	=sum(3,2,1,8)	
2	=max(3,4,1,0,5)	=min(4,5,2,3,2)
3	=count(3,null,4,5)	
4	=avg(3,null,4,5)	

We've used the max/min function before.

It should be pointed out that len() is not regarded as an aggregate function. It actually gets an attribute of the sequence and does not actually traverse the sequence members to calculate the result. Therefore, len() does not have this way to write the sequence members as parameters.

We know that using to(n) can generate sequence [1,2,…, n], and then use sum() function to get the sum, so we can easily calculate 1+2+…+100 with to(100).sum(), which is much simpler than the previous code of loop statements.

So, what about the sum of the first 100 odd numbers? Seems to have to write loop statements?

No, SPL has thought about this and provides a way to generate a new sequence of the same length from an existing sequence. This expression to(100).(~*2-1).sum() can calculate the sum of the first 100 odd numbers.

We can understand the left to(100) and the right .sum(), but what is the .(~*2-1) in the middle?

For the sequence A, A.(x) denotes a sequence of the same length formed by calculating the expression x for each member of A in the same order. In expression x, the symbol ~ is used to represent the member of A which is participating in the calculation.

[1,2,3].(~*2-1) is [1*2-1,2*2-1,3*2-1], that is [1,3,5]. Just replace ~ with each sequence member in turn, and ~ is actually the loop variable when the sequence loops.

In this way we can understand to(100).(~*2-1).sum(). Similarly, to(11,20).(~*~).sum() can calculate the sum of squares of 10 numbers from 11 to 20.

A.(x).sum() is a common writing method. In SPL, it can be simplified to A.sum(x), which is simple and easy to understand. Furthermore, the functions on to(n) are also commonly used, and SPL allows them to be simplified as n.f(…).

1+2+…+100 can be written as 100.sum(), and the first 100 odd sum can also be written as 100.sum(~*2-1). Isn't it very simple?

The functions that calculate on each member of the sequence and get a new result after traversing all the members are generally called **loop functions**. A.(x), aggregate functions and simplified form of A.f(…) are all loop functions.

Euler found a formula related to π: $\frac{\pi^2}{6} = 1 + \frac{1}{2^2} + \frac{1}{3^2} - \frac{1}{4^2} + \cdots$ We use it to calculate π in reverse, just one expression:

    =sqrt(1000.sum(1/~/~)*6)

The accuracy of the first 1000 items is enough.

There are many formulas related to π, here is another one: $\frac{\pi}{4} = 1 - \frac{1}{3} + \frac{1}{5} - \frac{1}{7} + \cdots$ With the help of if function, it is easy to implement:

    =1000.sum(if(~%2==1,1,-1)/(2*~-1))*4

The syntax of loop function is very concise and efficient.

Let's simplify the example used in learning loop, and calculate $e = 1 + \frac{1}{1!} + \frac{1}{2!} + \frac{1}{3!} + \cdots$

When we used loop statements before, we used an intermediate variable to calculate n!, But it seems that it can't be written in ~?

Actually you can also use an intermediate variable in an expression. The code without loop statements is rewritten as follows:

	A
1	>nf=1
2	=1+20.sum((nf*=~,1/nf))

The expression in sum uses the comma operator, that is, (a,b,c,…,x) will calculate a,b,c,…,x in turn, and the final result is x. (nf*=~,1/nf) will calculate nf*=~ (recall that = can be used as an operator), then calculate 1/nf, and the final result is 1/nf. Comma operator is also invented by C language and inherited by SPL. It can be used to write a small number of multi-step operations in an expression to avoid writing multiple statements. The expression of the comma operator usually needs to be written in parentheses to ensure that it will not be misidentified. For example, if the outer parentheses are not written here, it may be considered by the sum() function to be multiple parameters to perform sum, which leads to the wrong result.

Now that we've learned the usage of the comma operator, we can also use it to combine two pieces of code into one:

	A
1	=(nf=1,1+20.sum((nf*=~,1/nf)))

For Fibonacci sequence, we can calculate the first n terms of the sequence since we have the weapon of sequence:

	A
1	>a=0,b=1
2	=20.((b=a+b,a=b-a))

A2 will calculate the first 20 terms of Fibonacci sequence. The expression here does not use ~, which acts as a loop variable. The loop function is only used to realize repeated calculation.

This code seems a little difficult to understand. Its principle is the same as the example code when we talked about loop statements before. We will not elaborate on it any more. Please think for yourself, draw the process on the paper and execute it by yourself.

5.3   Loop functions: advanced

SPL provides ~ symbol as loop variable in loop functions, which can simplify a lot of code originally written with loop statements. But we know that the loop statement for sequence also provides the symbol to obtain the loop number (add # before the loop variable), so is there something similar in the loop function?

Yes, simply use the # symbol.

	A
1	=[3,4,3,6,1,4]
2	=A1.sum(if(#%2==1,1,-1)*~)

A2 calculates the difference between the sum of odd and even members of sequence A1.

Using #, we can calculate the sequence by contraposition addition of members of two sequences with the same length.

	A	B
1	=[3,8,2,4,7]	=[9,2,6,1,0]
2	=A1.(~+B1(#))	

A2 will calculate [A1(1)+B1(1),...,A1(5)+B1(5)].

Sequence A stores the sales of a company from January to December in turn. Now we want to know the maximum monthly growth, that is, the maximum difference between a member and the previous member. This can be realized with #.

	A
1	=[123,345,321,345,546,542,874,234,543,983,434,897]
2	=A1.(if(#>1,~-A1(#-1),0)).max()

When #>1, that is, not January, we can calculate the growth of this month compared with last month. The last month value can be obtained by A1(#-1), and the growth amount can be obtained by being subtracted by the current month value ~, and then get the maximum difference.

In the calculation of loop function, it is very common to refer to an adjacent member. SPL provides a special symbol ~[-1] to represent A1(#-1). The code can be simplified as follows:

	A
1	=[123,345,321,345,546,542,874,234,543,983,434,897]
2	=A1.(if(#>1,~-~[-1],0)).max()

~[-i] denotes the i-th member before the current member, and ~[i] denotes the i-th member after the current member, that is, A1(#+i). Different from using A(i) to get a sequence member, when using [], the calculated sequence out of sequence range will not report an error, but will get a null value.

Let's try an example of refering to a member after the current member, to calculate the average sales value of each month and the months before and after it, that is, in the nth month, calculate the average sales value of the (n-1)-th month, the nth month and the (n+1)-th month, which is called moving average. We only calculate a 2-month average for January and December.

	A
1	=[123,345,321,345,546,542,874,234,543,983,434,897]
2	=A1.(avg(~[-1],~,~[1]))

Note that we can't simply add up and divide by 3, but use the avg() function, which will correctly handle the situation with null values.

We can also simplify the calculation of Pascal triangle by means of ~[]:

	A	B
1	5	=[[1],[1,1]]
2	for 3,A1+1	=B1(A2-1).(~+~[-1])
3		>B1|=[B2|1]

Here we make use of the convention that ~[-1] will get null when it is out of bounds.

In addition, ~[] can get a continuous subsequence. For example, for the previous data, we want to use the monthly sales sequence to calculate the monthly accumulated sales, the code can be written as follows:

	A
1	=[123,345,321,345,546,542,874,234,543,983,434,897]
2	=A1.(~[:0].sum())

~[:0] means from the sequence head to the current member, which is equivalent to A1.to(#). The complete writing of this grammar is ~[a:b], which gets A1.to(#+a,#+b). If a is omitted, members will be retrieved from the beginning, namely A1.to(#+b); If b is omitted, members will be retrieved till the end, namely A1.to(#+a,).

The method of getting a subsequence can also be used for the previous example of getting the moving average:

	A
1	=[123,345,321,345,546,542,874,234,543,983,434,897]
2	=A1.(~[-1:1].avg())

Similar to loop statements, loop functions may be nested in multiple layers. For example, we calculate the sum of the products of each two members in two sequences.

It's not hard to write with loop statements:

	A	B	C
1	=[4,3,2,8,7]	=[9,2,6,1,0]	=0
2	for A1	for B1	>C1+=A2*B2

But if we write with a loop function, there will be an obstacle:

	A	B
1	=[4,3,2,8,7]	=[9,2,6,1,0]
2	=A1.sum(B1.sum(~*~))	

This writing is obviously wrong. The innermost ~*~ will calculate one square. We originally wanted to multiply the ~ of outer A1 by the ~ of inner B1, but now there is only one ~ symbol, and we can't distinguish it.

This problem can be solved by introducing an intermediate temporary variable:

	A	B
1	=[4,3,2,8,7]	=[9,2,6,1,0]
2	=A1.sum((a=~,B1.sum(a*~)))	

In addition, SPL also stipulates that adding a variable name before ~ can represent specified ~, while ~ without a variable name will represent the innermost layer ~, which makes it easy to write:

	A	B
1	=[4,3,2,8,7]	=[9,2,6,1,0]
2	=A1.sum(B1.sum(A1.~*~))	

A1.~ denotes ~ of outer layer A1, and another ~ without leading variable denotes ~ of inner layer B1.

If the outer loop function is for a sequence without a variable name, it can't be referenced. In this case, we need to use a variable to assign values in advance and give it a name artificially.

	A	B
1	=to(9)	=A1.sum(to(~,9).sum(A1.~*~))
2	=9.sum(to(~,9).sum(~*~))	

To calculate the sum of all multiplication terms in the 9*9 table, we need to give to(9) a name, in order to distinguish the layers in the multi-layer loop function. While it is impossible to distinguish the inner and outer layers by writing 9.sum(...) directly, because 9.~ is not a legal formula.

Sometimes the inner and outer layers are the same sequence, even if it is copied to a different variable, they still cannot be distinguished:

	A	B
1	=[4,3,2,8,7]	=A1.sum(A1.sum(A1.~*~))
2	=A1	=A2.sum(A1.sum(A2.~*~))
3	=A1.(~)	=A3.sum(A1.sum(A3.~*~))

The writing of B1 has the same result as writing sum(~*~) directly, and it is impossible to distinguish the inner and outer layers. The writing of B2 seems to be able to distinguish, but A1 and A2 are actually the same object (review the content of the previous chapter). In the calculation of loop function, ~ is recorded in this sequence, and the inner and outer layers can still not be distinguished by only using different variable names; To write like B3, copy A1 to a new sequence, ~ of A3 and ~ of A1 will be different, and the correct result can be executed.

It's the same rule for #, and you can try to understand what the following examples are calculating:

	A	B
1	=[3,8,2,4,7]	=[9,2,6,1,0]
2	=A1.max(B1.max(A1.~-~))	
3	=A1.max(B1.max(A1(A1.#)-B1(#)))	
3	=A1.max(B1.max(A1(#)-B1(A1.#)))	

SPL also has a function A.run (x), which is similar to A.(x). This function also calculates x in turn, but still returns A, not the sequence of x.

What's the use of this?

x can be an arbitrary expression. We said that = is also a suitable operator. When using A.run(x), we can use ~=… to change itself. For example, A.(~=~*~) will change A into a sequence of the square of its members, which is different from A.(~*~). The latter will return a new sequence, while the former modifies the original sequence.

It still seems there is no much difference? The new generation of sequence is no different from the modification of the original sequence for subsequent calculations.

When only ~ is used for calculation, there is no big difference (there will be a big difference when we talk about records and table sequence later). But if we refer to adjacent members with the help of the [] symbol, the result will be different.

For example, A.run(~=~[-1]+~) will change A into a sequence of cumulative values. While A.(~[-1]+~) is different, it does not calculate the cumulative value, but only the sum of adjacent values. Because a new sequence will be generated in the latter, and ~[-1] and ~ are all of the original sequence A, which will not be changed in the calculation process; However, the former does not produce a new sequence in the calculation process, and ~[-1] will be changed by the last round of calculation, resulting in the effect of cumulative value.

The results of A.run(~=~[-1]+~) and A=A.([:0].sum()) are the same, and both of them can calculate the cumulative values, but the former needs much less calculation, because it is calculated on the basis of the previous round, while the latter needs to calculate from the beginning every time.

You can try it with code.

With this mechanism, we can simplify the calculation of e, abandon the use of a temporary variable, and use only one expression:

=1+20.run(~=~*if(#>1,~[-1],1)).sum(1/~)

The 20.run(~=~*if(#>1,~[-1],1)) will get the sequence of factorial values [1!,2!,…,20!]. Before each cycle, ~[-1] is already the factorial value of the previous round, and then *~ is the factorial value of the current round. For the first round of loop, we need to process with if, because SPL specifies that any number multiplied by null results in null, which is different from addition and requires special handling.

With the sequence of factorial values, it is easy to get the result with another step of doing sum.

The power of loop functions is huge, and you can write very simple and elegant code if you use them properly.

5.4 Iterative function[*]

We can also use more basic **iterative function** to complete the calculation of *e* without using a temporary variable.

Iterative function A.iterate@a(x,a) of sequence A has two parameters x and a. We'll neglect the @a here for the moment, simply think that @a is a part of the function name, i.e., the function name is iterate@a. We'll talk about this @ soon.

As a loop function, A.iterate@a(x,a) will calculate x for each member of A, ~ and # can be used in expression x to represent the current member and sequence number of A in the loop, which is the same as other loop functions. The difference is that the symbol ~~ is also provided in the iterative function, which is used to represent the x calculated in the previous cycle. When the loop starts, the initial value of ~~ is the parameter a. After all members loop, return the sequence of ~~, which has the same length as A.

The function A.iterate (x,a) without @a is defined as the last member of A.iterate@a(x,a), that is, the intermediate process is no longer integrated into the sequence, only retain the last ~~.

Let's go through a few examples:

1. A.iterate(~~+~,0)

The initial ~~ is 0, the current member ~ will be added to ~~ in each round of the loop, and finally we'll get the sum of all members, namely A.sum().

2. A.iterate@a(~~+~,0)

@a retains the results of each round of calculation, that is, the cumulative value from the beginning to the current member, which is equivalent to A.([:0].sum()).

3. A.iterate(if(~~<~,~,~~),-inf())

inf() is infinity, -inf() is negative infinity, which is the minimum number. In each cycle, if the current member ~ is larger than ~~, ~~ is replaced by ~, and the final result is A.max().

4. A.iterate(if(~~>~,~,~~),inf())

This is similar to the previous one, and will get A.min().

5. A.iterate(if(~,~~+1,~~),0)

After analysis, we can see that it will be calculated as A.count().

It seems that the iterative function is the "parent function" of these aggregate functions, which can be defined by the iterative function. It is easy to define an operation of successive multiplication of sequence members with iterative function: A.iterate(~~*~,1). Factorial operation is a special case: n.iterate(~~*~,1).

In fact, A.(x) can also be interpreted as A.iterate(~~|[x],[]) or A.iterate@a(x,null). Iterative function is indeed the "parent function" of other loop functions.

Now we can calculate *e* in one line:

=1+20.iterate@a(~~*~,1).sum(1/~)

The iterative function in the middle will also be calculated as a sequence of factorial values.

5.5   Positioning and selection

It is a common operation to extract a subsequence from a sequence (that is, to extract a subset from a set). We have learned to use the to() function and sequence of numbers to extract a subsequence according to the position of members.

Sometimes we want to get members from the end of a sequence in the reverse order. Of course, we can use the length of the sequence to calculate the sequence number, but it's a bit troublesome. SPL provides functions that can use the reverse order.

The function A.m(i) will get the i-th member of A. if i<0, it will get the -i member counting from the end, that is

A.m(i)=A(if(i>0,i,i+A.len()+1))

Similarly, when p is a sequence of length k with negative members, there is a function

A.m(p)=[A.m(p(1)),...,A.m(p(k))]

A.m(-1) is often used to get the last member of A. Pascal triangle can be simplified a little bit:

	A	B
1	5	=[[1],[1,1]]
2	for A1-1	=B1.m(-1).(~+~[-1])
3		>B1|=[B2|1]

We can also select members by a certain step size:

A.step(k,i)=[A(i),A(i+k),A(i+2*k),...]

Starting from the i-th member, select one every k.

A.step(2,1) will select the odd numbered members, and A.step(2,2) will select the even numbered members.

Of course, it is more common to select members that meet a certain condition:

A.select(x) returns a sequence of members in A that make x true, where x can use the symbols allowed in loop functions such as ~ and #. The select() function is called a **selection function**, and is also a loop function.

The select() function is very common. Let's give some examples:

	A	B
1	[13,30,45,23,42,98,61]	
2	=A1.select(~%2==0)	[30,42,98]
3	=A1.select(~>30)	[45,42,98,61]
4	=A1.select(~>~[-1])	[13,30,45,42,98]
5	=A3.select((~-~[-1])%2==0)	[98]

The constant sequence of column B is the result of the select() function in column A, and A5 is further selected on the basis of A3.

In fact, A.step() can also be represented by select() function, that is

A.step(k,i)==A.select(#-i>0 && (#-i)%k==0)

The sequence number is used as a condition to achieve the result of selection.

48

Using these functions, we calculate the prime numbers below 1000:

	A	B	C
1	=to(1000)	>A1(1)=0	
2	for 2,31	if A1(A2)==0	next
3		>A1.step(A2,2*A2).select(~>0).run(A1(~)=0)	
4	=A1.select(~>0)	=A4.select(~[1]-~==2).([~,~+2])	

A composite number below 1000 always has a prime factor of no more than $\sqrt{1000}$ (<32). We only need to use the integers below 32 to filter the sequence to(1000), and exclude all the multiples of these numbers (fill in the corresponding members as 0). The remaining members that are not 0 must be prime numbers.

A1 generates the target sequence, B1 excludes 1(1 is not prime), that is, fill the member of the position with 0. Then A2 loops from 2 to 31, if the member at this position is already 0, it means that it is a composite number, leave it alone, skip to the next cycle. If it's a prime number, pick out the positions of all its multiples, that is, A1.step(A2,A2*2). Pay attention to start from A2*2 and skip A2 itself, because A2 is a prime number and needs to be kept. Then, the members in these positions may have 0, which indicates that they have been screened out in the previous round. To exclude them, use select(~>0) to keep those that are not 0. The members in these positions are multiples of A2, that is, composite numbers. Set the members in these positions to 0, and then enter the next round.

At the end of the loop, select the remaining non-zero members, which are all prime numbers. By the way, B4 calculates all twin prime pairs (prime numbers with difference of 2) on this basis, using the select() function and A.() that we've learned, and the result is a two-layer sequence.

The selection function will get members out of the sequence. In the other way round, we will also care about whether a data is in the sequence and its position in the sequence.

The function A.pos(x) will return the position of x in A. More strictly, it is to find an i such that A(i)==x. If multiple A(i) are the same as x, it will return the first one. If not, it will return null. The latter case is more commonly used, that is, whether the return value of pos function is null is used to determine whether a data is in the sequence.

Similarly, there is an A.pseg(x) function. For a sequence A with increasing member value, that is, A(i)<A(i+1), the function will return the segment where x belongs, that is, if A(i)<=x<A(i+1), pseg() will return i; If x<A(1), it will return 0; If A.m(-1)<x, A.len() is returned. We take the increasing sequence as an example to explain the principle, actually it also works for decreasing sequence, but these less than signs should be changed to greater than signs.

In our daily work, we often need segmented statistics, such as age, sales amount, etc. We can use the pseg() function in these cases, but we will give these examples after we have learned structured data.

In theory, there may be duplicated values in the previous example of digital black hole, that is, a becomes b, b becomes c, and c becomes a again. In this case, it will lead to endless loop, but our current program can't discover this situation. Only because we have done our homework in advance, we know for sure that there is only one single black hole in the four digits, so the code is written like that, but it may not be the case for other digits.

The pos() function can be used to find this kind of loop, and the pseg() function and insert() function can also be used to improve the sorting.

	A	B	C	D
1	5	12345	=A1.run(~=if(#>1,~[-1]*10,1))	
2	for	=[]	=C1.(B1\~%10)	
3		for C2	=B2.pseg(B3)	>B2.insert(if(C3==B2.len(),0,C3+1),B3)
4		=C1.sum(B2(#)*~)		=C1.sum(B2.m(-#)*~)
5		=@|B1	>output(B1)	>B1=B4-D4
6		if B5.pos(B1)	break	

This program can find the digital black hole of any number of digits. A1 is the number of digits and B1 is the starting value.

Here we use the various techniques we have learned before, C1 uses run() to calculate a sequence [1,10,100,...], C2 uses it to get the number of each digit. Sorting needs only one line now, and the current result is saved in B2. B3 loops for each digit. In C3, pseg() is used to find out where the new digit should be inserted. In D3, insert() function is used to insert it. At the end of the loop, B2 is the sequence sorted from small to large. B4 and D4 use C1 again to calculate the large number and small number. The @ in B5 stands for itself. When the program starts to run, it will automatically clear all the cell values. The expression will continuously accumulate the calculated numbers and record them in a sequence. In B6, if it is found that the newly calculated number is already in the sequence, it means that the duplicated value appears and the program should be stopped.

It should be noted that pos() and pseg() are not loop functions, and the symbols such as ~, # can not and need not be used in the x of their parameters. If they are used, they are considered to belong to the loop function of the upper layer (these functions may be nested in a loop function).

These principles will be further explained at the end of this chapter.

We care about the members that meet the conditions, but sometimes we also care about the positions of those members. For example, we want to find out in which months the sales amount has increased from a sequence of 12-month sales amount. Using the select() function can only find the growing members, but not the positions of the growing members.

The A.pselect(x) function can help us by returning the sequence numbers of members that make x true. In terms of the symbols of a loop function, select() will return a sequence of ~ and pselect() will return the corresponding #. pselect() is called the **positioning function.**

Let's try:

	A	B
1	[13,30,45,23,42,98,61]	
2	=A1.pselect(~%2==0)	[2,5,6]
3	=A1.pselect(~>30)	[3,5,6,7]
4	=A1.pselect(~>~[-1])	[1,2,3,5,6]

We expect the result of column A to be the value of column B, but it is not? A2, A3 and A4 return 2, 3 and 1 respectively, which is only the first value in the sequence of column B.

What's going on?

It turns out that the pselect() function is defined as such, it only returns the first # that satisfies the condition.

So, what should we do if we want to return all the qualified #, like select?

	A	B
1	[13,30,45,23,42,98,61]	
2	=A1.pselect@a(~%2==0)	[2,5,6]
3	=A1.pselect@a(~>30)	[3,5,6,7]
4	=A1.pselect@a(~>~[-1])	[1,2,3,5,6]

Just add @a after the function name.

What is this?

The writing method of @a is invented by SPL, which is called **function option.** In theory, pselect and pselect@a are two unrelated different functions, but these two functions are very similar. They are both for sequences, and the parameters are the same. Although the functions are not exactly the same, they are very similar. In this case, we are more willing to regard one of them as a variant of the other, and use similar names when naming, which will be more convenient for understanding and memorizing.

But these two functions are still different and need to be distinguished. In SPL, we use the same name to name these two functions, and use the character after @ to distinguish them. It seems that a function has different modes: when there is no @a, pselect only returns the first one, and when there is @a, pselect will return all values.

There are many functions with options in SPL, and there are often more than one options. For example, pselect() also has a @z option, which means to search from the end and in reverse direction. In the above example, A1.pselect@z(~%2==0) will return 6. Moreover, these options may be used in combination, A1.pselect@az(~%2==0) means to find all the # that meet the condition from the end and in reverse direction, and the result will return [6,5,2].

There is no order in the writing of options, pselect@az and pselect@za are the same.

Correspondingly, the select() function has a @1 option, which means that the first member satisfying the condition will be returned. The reason for this design is that it is more common for select() to return all values, while it is more common for pselect() to return the first.

SPL function options can greatly simplify the code. At present, there is no such syntax in other programming languages, and the function of some languages also has the concept of option, but it generally exists as an independent parameter. We will see later that in structured data processing, parameters are very complicated, and it is not convenient to pass option information as parameters.

We use the max() function to find the maximum value of the sequence members. Similarly, we may also care about the position of the maximum value. SPL also provides A.pmax() function to return the position of the maximum value in sequence A.

The maximum value of a sequence is unique, but there may be more than one member with the maximum value. Therefore, pmax() is similar to pselect(), by default it returns the position of the first maximum value. If the option @a is added, it will return all positions, and @z will search from the back to the front.

The pmax() function is not difficult to understand, so we don't give examples here. And, of course, there is also pmin() function.

We mention pmax() here to deepen the understanding of positioning function. pmax() is also a positioning function. Positioning is a common operation, but there is no corresponding library function in many programming languages. SPL pays special attention to this kind of operation.

Forget to mention that the pos() function also has @a and @z options.

It's easy to ignore that there is another selection function maxp() that is related to max().

A.maxp() is defined as A(A.pmax()), which is the member that returns the maximum value.

If you think about it, isn't it A.max()? Why create a new function?

It's still different. In a simple way, A.pmax() has the @a option, which may return multiple values, so that A.maxp@a() may also return a sequence, but A.max() will not.

However, even if A.maxp@a() is a sequence, the members are all the same. It doesn't seem very interesting.

The bigger difference is in the case of with parameters. A.max(x) returns the maximum x, while A.maxp(x) returns the member that maximizes x. For example:

	A	B
1	[13,30,45,23,42,98,61]	
2	=A1.max(~%10)	8
3	=A1.maxp(~%10)	98

See the difference?

We know that A.max(x) is A.(x).max(), A.pmax(x) is also equal to A.(x).pmax(), but A.maxp(x) is not A.(x).maxp(), it is still defined as A(A.pmax(x)).

max() returns the maximum value itself, while maxp() returns the member that makes the maximum value appear. For just a sequence, they are the same, but with an expression, you can find their difference. In the structured data processing that will be covered later, this kind of calculation is very common. For example, we often care more about the product that leads to the highest sales amount than the highest sales amount itself.

max() is not a selection function, it returns a value. maxp() returns a member(or sequence of members), and is a selection function. Like positioning function, selection function is also a big kind of operation.

Of course, there is also minp() function.

5.6   Sorting related

In order to solve the problem of digital black hole, we have written several sort codes. Sorting is really a very common action, so SPL provides sorting function directly.

A.sort() will return a sequence that arranges the members of A from small to large. Of course, we often use sorting from large to small, just use the @z option.

The sorting function returns a sequence composed of the original members of the sequence, which can be understood as a type of selection function. It also has a corresponding positioning function, A.psort() will return a number sequence p, so that A(p) is arranged from small to large. In other words,

A.sort()==A(A.psort())

Please try to understand the meaning of this equation.

Try it. As a rule, the result of column A is the constant of column B.

	A	B
1	[13,30,45,23,42,98,61]	
2	=A1.sort()	[13,23,30,42,45,61,98]
3	=A1.sort@z()	[98,61,45,42,30,23,13]
4	=A1.psort()	[1,4,2,5,3,7,6]
5	=A1(A4)	[13,23,30,42,45,61,98]

With the sorting function, the digital black hole can be simpler, without using pseg() and insert():

	A	B	C	D
1	5	12345	=A1.run(~=if(#>1,~[-1]*10,1))	
2	for	=C1.(B1\~%10).sort()		
3		=C1.sum(B2(#)*~)		=C1.sum(B2.m(-#)*~)
4		=@|B1	>output(B1)	>B1=B3-D3
5		if B4.pos(B1)	break	

Sorting function also supports the case of expression A.sort(x), but it is not equal to A.(x).sort(). It is defined by psort(), that is, A.sort(x)==A(A.psort(x)), and A.psort(x) can be defined by A.(x).psort().

This is the same as the case of maxp(), which is the common feature of selection function and positioning function. The same is true for select() function, that is, A.select(x)==A(A.pselect@a(x)), not A.(x).select().

However, SPL does not provide a function that is consistent with A.max(x) style and can directly return A.(x).sort(), so this requirement can only be calculated with this expression. This is caused by historical habits. In the early programming languages, sort() function was designed in this way.

Sorting is generally used to get a neat order, but it can also be used to disrupt the order of a sequence.

	A	B
1	=to(1000)	=A1.sort(rand())

The rand() function in B1 will return a random floating-point number between 0 and 1 in each calculation. The random number is disordered, and the order of sorting is disordered. As a result, A1, which was originally very neat, is arranged in a disordered way. If we develop a poker game, this principle can be used to shuffle cards.

The method of disrupting the order can also be used for sampling. For example, 100 numbers should be randomly selected from the range of 1 to 1000, which cannot be repeated. It's not easy to generate them randomly, and it's troublesome to regenerate them if there is repetition. It is very simple using the above sorting method, just getting the top 100 after disrupting the order.

	A	B
1	=to(1000)	=A1.sort(rand()).to(100)

We'll explain a little more about the rand() function. It is very convenient to use random numbers to generate test data. However, when we find an error in the test, we hope to run the same set of test data again to find out where the error is. But, random numbers are random, and another batch is generated after the second calculation.

In fact, there are no real random numbers in the computer, but a series of calculations are carried out to get new numbers from the numbers generated last time. When the calculation rules meet some mathematical principles, it is difficult to see the pattern, and it can also ensure that the calculated numbers can be evenly distributed within the specified range. These random numbers are called pseudo-random numbers. As long as the first number is determined, the sequence of the numbers calculated is determined.

Using this principle, we can create the same "random numbers".

	A	B
1	=rand@s(1)	=100.(rand())
2		=100.(rand())
3	=rand@s(1)	=100.(rand())

rand@s(s) function sets the parameter s to the first random number, called the seed. Running this code shows that B1 and B3 are the same.

So, if the seeds used at the beginning of each program execution are same, then the generated random number sequences will all be the same?

No, when the program starts, it will automatically execute a statement like rand@s(long(now())), now() returns the current time, that is, the start time of program execution is used as the seed. This is operated by human and has enough randomness, which can ensure that different random number sequences will be obtained before each program execution.

Looking back, psort() is not only used to define sort(), but also useful. Look at this code:

	A	B
1	=50.(1000+~)	=A1.(rand(100))
2	=B1.psort@z()	=A1(A2)

The rand(n) in B1 means to return a random integer below n.

Regarding A1 as the student numbers of a group of students (Actually we should use names, but wait until we learn about strings. We just use integers as student numbers for now). B1 can be understood as the scores of these students, which correspond to the members of A1 one by one. Now we want to get the result sequence of these student numbers sorted by their corresponding scores.

It's obviously useless to sort A1, while sorting B1 can sort out the score itself, but it can't get the sorting of student numbers. Using psort() can solve this problem. Now B2 is the student number sequence that we want to sort by score.

When the number of members is large, the sorting of the whole sequence is slow and often meaningless. For example, with the sales of tens of thousands of stores, we usually only care about the top few and the corresponding sales amounts, and we are not interested in the situation after hundreds or thousands. And to get the top few, there is no need to sort the whole sequence.

SPL provides the top() function to get only the first few. Similarly, there is the ptop() function, but the syntax rules are a little different from the sort() function. Because the top() function has three cases similar to the max() function: max() that returns the value, positioning function pmax() and selection function maxp().

	A	B
1	[13,30,45,24,42,98,61]	
2	=A1.ptop(3)	[1,4,2]
3	=A1.top(3)	[13,24,30]
4	=A1.ptop(3,~%10)	[2,7,5]
5	=A1.top(3,~%10)	[0,1,2]
6	=A1.top(3;~%10)	[30,61,42]

The positioning function A.ptop(n) returns the positions of the smallest n members. When there is a parameter, A.ptop(n,x) is defined as A.(x).ptop(n). It is similar to pmax(), which is not difficult to understand. A.top(n) can be defined as A(A.ptop(n)). When there is no x parameter, it is both a value and a member. It can be analogized to max or maxp() without ambiguity. However, with the x parameter, A.top(n,x) is defined as A.(x).top(n), which is equivalent to max(), is for the value. The selection function is represented by A.top(n;x), and it corresponds to maxp(). Note that a semicolon is used to separate parameters instead of a comma.

Maybe because the word topp really does not look good, it is not used. Here n can't be omitted. In SPL, there are a lot of cases where semicolons are used to distinguish parameters (we will talk about it later), so that we can distinguish them.

Generally speaking, the function style designed in SPL is relatively consistent, and it is easy to make an analogy between different operations.

5.7   Lambda syntax[*]

Looking back at the two functions A.pos(x) and A.select(x), we say that the former is not a loop function, and the symbols ~, # can't be used in the parameter x, while the latter is a loop function, and the symbols ~, # can be used in the parameter. In fact, in the calculation process of these two functions, both of them will traverse A, that is, they will process the members of A one by one. What is the difference between the parameters of these two functions?

Before the introduction of loop function, all functions f(x) has one characteristic. If its parameter x is a calculation expression, it will be calculated before calculating this function f(). For example, max(3+5,2+1), when the computer calculates max() function, the parameters obtained are already 8 and 3. It's the same case even if there may be variables in the parameters. The calculation expression of max(x+5,y+3) cannot be calculated when x and y are not assigned, and after x and y are assigned, x+5 and y+3 will be calculated first and then transferred to max function for calculation.

That's OK. That's what we learned about functions in math class. So is the parameter of A.pos(x).

However, A.select(x) is different. This x may not be calculated before calculating the select() function. It can be calculated only in the process of calculating the select() function. For example, A.select(~%2==0), we can't calculate ~%2==0 before calculating the select() function. There is an unknown ~, which can only be determined in the process of looping A, and then we can calculate this expression.

For the function of sequence, its parameter is an expression to be calculated, which can only be calculated in the process of looping the sequence. The function with this characteristic is called loop function. Therefore, A.pos(x) and A.pseg(x) are not loop functions, while A.(x), A.run (x), A.select(x) and A.max(x) are loop functions.

For non-loop functions, even if the parameters are written as expressions, they will be calculated as specific values when they are passed in.

For a loop function, the parameter to be passed into the function is an expression, which contains some unknown variables such as ~, #. In fact, this expression can be regarded as a function with these unknown variables as parameters. In other words, the parameter of a loop function is essentially another function, not a simple value.

This is the essential difference between a loop function and non-loop function, it takes function as parameter.

The earliest programming languages did not support functions as parameters, and people were still inexperienced at that time. They simply used the experience of functions in mathematics (in fact, mathematicians have been engaged in functional analysis and studying functions of functions for a long time, but they are relatively abstruse after all). Later, in order to make code reuse more convenient, people introduced the concept of function pointer, and passed the function as a parameter to another function, so that the former can be called by the latter. However, it is still necessary to clearly define the called function with a piece of code. The code is complex and difficult to understand.

For example, A.select(~%2==0) in our example, the traditional syntax is divided into two steps: first, define a function f(x) as x%2==0, and then use A.select(f) to calculate. In the loop calculation of the select() function, the current member of A is passed into the function f() as a parameter. After calculation, the return value is obtained, and it is decided whether to add this member to the return value of select().

In fact, the calculation logic of many functions that need to be used as parameters is not complex. It can be described clearly by a simple expression, for example, this x%2==0 is very simple. It's too troublesome to define an f function for such a matter.

Therefore, people further invented the programming syntax to define a function directly with an expression. Instead of defining the f function in advance, it can be directly written into the parameter of the select() function:

> A.select(f(x):{x%2==0})

This method of temporarily defining functions in parameters is called **lambda syntax** in the industry.

With lambda syntax, code writing is much easier. Now many programming languages have begun to support this syntax.

There are still problems.

The function to be passed in must be a function with parameters, which are used to refer to some variables (the members of A here) generated in the calculation process of the host function (the select() in this example). Otherwise, if there are no parameters, it should have been calculated before calling the host function.

Therefore, in the above f(x):{x%2==0} syntax, there must be a way to specify the parameter. Use x in f(x) to tell the computer that x in x%2==0 is the parameter of the function as the parameter(a bit roundabout), and is waitting for the host function to pass the value in. If we only write x%2==0, the computer doesn't know what x is, or is it a variable somewhere else?

It's still a bit cumbersome and confusing to understand, but this is the status quo of most programming languages that support lambda syntax.

It's not over yet.

The sequence number (that is #) of A's members may also be used in the host function of select(). It is not enough for the function f() to have only one parameter, because the select() function needs to accept all kinds of functions as parameters, and the parameters of these functions must be unified, otherwise the select() function cannot call them.

Therefore, this function must have at least two parameters, and the syntax must be written as follows:

A.select(f(x,y):{x%2==0})

In this example, we don't use the y parameter prepared for the sequence number (that is #), but we have to write it in the definition.

However, we know that select() may also use ~[-1] and so on. How much more will be passed in? These parameters need to be defined as parameters of f() in advance. It's too troublesome. Just pass in the whole A and then the current sequence number. Anyway, it can be calculated. Finally, it may be as follows:

A.select(f(x,y):{x(y)%2==0})

The parameter x represents the sequence to be calculated by the host function, and the parameter y represents the sequence number of the member being calculated by the host function. The rest is written in this definition.

But that's inconvenient again.

In fact, most of the programming languages that support lambda syntax do not come to this stage, and they only support to the level of f(x):{x%2==0}. In other words, there is no way to refer to sequence numbers and make adjacent references in expressions.

So, how can we make the code simple and descriptive?

That's what SPL does now.

SPL simplifies this matter by using the symbols of ~ and # and [] to represent the parameters of the function as a parameter. Therefore, it is OK to write ~%2==0 instead of writing f(x) to specify the parameter name.

In this way, writing and understanding are simple, and because of these rich symbols, the description ability is also strengthened.

6 REUSE

6.1 User-Defined Functions

Still suppose there is no factorial function, now we want to calculate the number of combinations $\binom{n}{k} = \frac{n!}{k!(n-k)!}$.

	A	B	C
1	10	4	
2	=1	for A1	>A2=A2*B2
3	=1	for B1	>A3=A3*B3
4	=1	for A1-B1	>A4=A4*B4
5	=A2\A3\A4		

n and k are filled in A1 and B1 respectively, and the second, third and fourth lines calculate $n!$, $k!$ and $(n-k)!$ respectively.

This calculation is OK, but the almost same code has been written three times.

If the problem is more troublesome, for example, we need to calculate the coefficient sequence of the binomial theorem $(1+x)^n = \sum_{k=0}^{n} \binom{n}{k} x^k$ (that is, a line of Pascal triangle). The loop function can calculate multiple values in one statement, but it must be easy to write in the expression. If it needs several lines of code to realize the calculation, it has to use the loop statements:

	A	B	C	D
1	10	=1	for A1	>B1=B1*C1
2	for A1-1	=1	for A2	>B2=B2*C2
3		=1	for A1-A2	>B3=B3*C3
4		=@|(B1\B2\B3)		
5	=1|B4|1			

In fact, most programming languages, including SPL, allow us to write the code to be repeated as our own functions, and then call them over and over again.

	A	B	C	D
1	func	=1	for A1	>B1=B1*C1
2		return B1		
3	=func(A1,10)	=func(A1,4)	=func(A1,6)	=A3\B3\C3

The func statement of cell A1 defines a function, which is identified by A1. Its code is the code block of A1. When SPL encounters the func cell, it will skip this code block and execute the subsequent code.

There is func() function in cell A3. The first parameter is the position of the user-defined function to be called. Here is A1, which means to call the function defined at A1. The next parameter 10 is the parameter to be passed into the user-defined function A1. SPL will fill this parameter in A1, and then let the program jump to A1's code block to execute, that is, start to execute B1:D2.

We can understand the code of B1:D1, which can calculate the factorial of A1 and fill in B1. When A1 fills in 10, this code calculates 10!, and fill it in B1. Then the return statement of cell B2 returns the value of B1. At this time, the program will jump back to the place where the function was called, that is, A3, and has already got the return value of func() 10!, the cell value of A3 is 10!.

That is to say, the custom function A1 will calculate the factorial value of its parameter and return it.

Similarly, B3 will calculate 4!, C3 will calculate 6!, and finally, the number of combinations $\binom{10}{4}$ is calculated in D3.

The whole process seems a bit complicated, but in any case, the three factorial values are calculated using the same code, and there is no need to write the code three times.

To sum up: func statement is used to define a function, in which return statement is required to return the calculation result. Then use the func() function to pass in the parameter to call this function.

func() is a function. It can be used in the same way as other functions. It can be put in the expression to participate in the calculation.

	A	B	C	D
1	func	=1	for A1	>B1=B1*C1
2		return B1		
3	=func(A1,10)\func(A1,4)\func(A1,6)			

The result can be calculated correctly in this way.

Moreover, after the custom function is defined, it can be used in the loop function.

	A	B	C	D
1	func	=1	for A1	>B1=B1*C1
2		return B1		
3	10	=func(A1,A3)		
4	=1|(A3-1).(B3\func(A1,~)\func(A1,A3-~))|1			

The calculation of binomial coefficients also looks clearer.

Let's take another practical example: finding outliers in a batch of points on a plane. The method is as follows: calculate the sum of the distances from each point to other points, and then sort them from large to small. The top 10% of the points are considered as outliers because they are relatively far away from other points.

	A	B	C	D
1	100	>X=A1.(rand())	>Y=A1.(rand())	
2	=to(A1)	=A2.(A1.sum(func(A5,X(A2.~),X(~),Y(A2.~),Y(~))))		
3	=B2.psort@z().to(int(A1*0.1))			
4				
5	func			
6		return sqrt((A5-B5)*(A5-B5)+(C5-D5)*(C5-D5))		

In A5, a function is defined to calculate the distance between two points. It has four parameters, which are the abscissa and ordinate of two points respectively. Using Pythagorean theorem, the distance between two points can be calculated. When a user-defined function has more than one parameter, it will be filled from the definition cell to the right. This function is defined in A5, and its four parameters will be filled in A5, B5, C5 and D5 respectively. Thus, we will write the function body to the next line, i.e., cell B6.

Function definition can be anywhere, in front of or behind the main program will not affect the code execution.

In the main program, the abscissa and ordinate of 100 points are generated randomly. Then in cell B2, the user-defined function A5 can be called to calculate the sum of distances. This is a two-layer loop function. The inner layer calculates 100 distances and the sum (the distance between one point and itself is 0, adding one more will not make mistakes, and we don't have to exclude the point itself), and the outer layer loops the 100 points. Note the difference between A2.~ and ~ in the inner loop.

Then use psort to sort and get the sequence numbers of the top 10% points.

6.2 Recursion[*]

With the custom function, we can write recursive programs. Let's look at the factorial operation, it is a good example.

We know, n!=(n-1)!*n. That is, if we already know (n-1)!, we can use multiplication to calculate n!; However, special treatment is required when n=0, because (n-1)! is meaningless at this time, and we can not calculate 0! by (0-1)!.

Let's write a custom function to calculate factorial with this idea.

	A	B	C
1	func	if A1==0	return 1
2		return func(A1,A1-1)*A1	
3	=func(A1,0)	=func(A1,1)	=func(A1,10)

In custom function A1, it calls itself. This method of writing function code is called **recursion**.

Let's analyze the execution process of this function. If the parameter is 0, then the condition of B1 holds, continue to execute C1, return 1, the function ends, no problem. By the way, when a custom function is executed to the return statement, it will be executed and returned, regardless of whether there are statements after it.

If the parameter is 1 and the condition does not hold when it is executed to A1, the cell B2 will be executed. At this time, A1-1, that is, 1-1=0, will be used as the parameter to call the function first. After entering the function again, A1 will become parameter 0, and the A1 equal to 1 will be temporarily stored. Now that the condition of B1 is established again, it returns 1, and then returns to cell B2 before the call. The A1 stored just now is restored to 1, so it calculates 1*1=1, and returns. There is no problem.

If the parameter is 2, it will also be executed to cell B2. At this time, A1-1=2-1=1 will be passed into this function as the parameter, and A1 equal to 2 will be temporarily stored. From the above analysis, we know that it will return 1, and then restore the value of A1 to 2. When the parameter is 2, the function will return 1*2=2, which is correct.

. . . . . .

As long as the factorial of A1-1 can be calculated correctly, A1 of the current parameter can be calculated correctly.

Recursion is a bit like the mathematical induction we learned in high school. If we want to prove the proposition related to n, we need only prove these two steps:

1) The proposition is true when n = 0;

2) If n-1 is true, then n is also true.

Recursion is also similar. If we want to do a calculation related to n, the direct calculation may be troublesome. So long as we do these two steps:

1) We can do the calculation when n = 0;

2) If the (n-1)-related calculation has been worked out, we can do the n-related calculation.

We've just used the above method to calculate the factorial.

Let's try the n-th term of the Fibonacci sequence that we have done before. Its rule is as follows:

1) $F(1)=F(2)=1$

2) $F(n)=F(n-1)+F(n-2)$

The code written recursively is also very simple:

	A	B	C
1	func	if A1<=2	return 1
2		return func(A1,A1-1)+func(A1,A1-2)	
3	=func(A1,1)	=func(A1,3)	=func(A1,10)

When this code recurses to n, it depends on the two results of n-1 and n-2, and there are two initial cases(n=1 and n=2) to deal with specially.

When writing recursive code, we must pay attention to judging the initial situation. If we forget this judgment, recursion will become an endless loop and never return, and this endless loop will easily lead to memory overflow. This is because every time the recursion enters the function body again, the current variable value will be temporarily stored for recovery when it returns. If the recursion does not return, the space occupied by these variables will soon exceed the memory of the computer.

Careful readers can also analyze that it is not cost-effective to use recursive method to calculate factorial and Fibonacci sequence. The computation amount and memory of these two recursive codes are much larger than the previous loop method. Recursion is used here only as a teaching example, because the logic is relatively simple and it is easy to understand the principle of recursion.

Let's do another example that is difficult to do without recursion, calculating the full permutation of n.

The full permutation of n means that the n numbers 1, 2,..., n are lined up and all the different arrangements are listed. If n=3, there are 6 types: [1,2,3], [1,3,2], [2,1,3], [2,3,1], [3,1,2], [3,2,1]. If n=4 , there are 24 types, and the number of full permutation is n!.

It's not easy to list the n! types of permutations directly. It's easier to use recursion.

1) When n = 1, there is only one type, i.e. [1]

2) If we already have the full permutation of n-1, suppose it is a sequence p (it should be a two-layer sequence, and each member is a permutation). Now we just need to arrange n before its first, second,..., and (n-1)-th positions and append it to the last for each member of p to get n new permutations, then collect all the new permutations (n new permutations for each member of p).

Write the code in this way:

	A	B	C
1	func	if A1==1	return [[1]]
2		=func(A1,A1-1)	=[]
3		for B2	=A1.(B3.to(#-1)|A1|B3.to(#,))
4			>C2=C2|C3
5		return C2	
6	=func(A1,4)		=A6.len()

When A1 is 1, directly return the result [[1]], and pay attention to return it as a two-layer sequence. When A1>1, first prepare C2 to be an empty sequence to store the results, recursively call this function to calculate the full permutation of A1-1, and then loop it. For each member, generate A1-1 new permutations in C3 to arrange A1 before the first, second,..., (A1-1)-th positions and append it to the last to get A1 new permutations, and then concatenate these new permutations after C2. At the end of the loop, C2 stores the full sorting of A1 and returns it.

Let's change the problem again, calculating the m-permutation of n, that is, select m different numbers from 1,2,..., n to arrange. There are two parameters in this case, and the situation is a little more complicated than just now. Similar to the Fibonacci sequence, we need to call the recursive function twice.

1) When m = 1, there are n types, namely [[1],..., [n]];

2) When n>m, after we already have the (m-1)-permutation of n-1 and the m-permutation of n-1, which are recorded by p and q respectively, then as long as n is inserted into each member of p by the positions mentioned earlier, new m permutations can be obtained (each p member corresponds to m new permutations, which all contain n), and then merging them with q (which do not have n), thus getting m-permutation of n.

3) When n = m, just deal with p in step 2, which is equivalent to the full permutation.

	A	B	C
1	func		
2		if B1==1	return A1.([~])
3		=func(A1,A1-1,B1-1)	=[]
4		for B3	>C3=C3|B1.(B4.to(#-1)|A1|B4.to(#,))
5		if A1>B1	>C3=C3|func(A1,A1-1,B1)
6		return C3	
7	=func(A1,5,3)		=A7.len()

This section of code is a little complicated, but the difficulty is not the writing of the code itself, but to come up with this calculation method, that is, how to solve the problem mathematically. Let's recall what we said at the end of the loop chapter. Programming language can't help us find a solution to a problem, it can only help us implement the solution that we have already thought of.

In order to see the process clearly, we wrote the steps separately. After we are proficient, the code can be more compact.

	A	B	C
1	func		
2		if B1==1	return A1.([~])
3		=func(A1,A1-1,B1-1)	=B3.(B1.(B3.~.to(#-1)|A1|B3.~.to(#,)))
4		return C3.conj()|if(A1>B1, func(A1,A1-1,B1),[])	
5	=func(A1,5,3)		=A5.len()

The relatively complicated is C3, which is a two-layer loop function. The expression uses the inner # and the outer ~, resulting in a multi-layer sequence. B3 itself will return a two-layer sequence (each member is a permutation). C3 will expand each member permutation in B3 into a sequence composed of B1 permutations, so as to get a three-layer sequence (each member's member is a permutation). The conj() function in B4 is used in a multi-layer sequence, concatenates the member sequences, and it is equivalent to performing | operation among all members. C3.conj() is a sequence composed of B1*B3.len() permutations, and the expression to the right of | is easy to understand.

But it's really hard to understand. Sometimes it's not a bad thing to write longer code.

6.3   Reusable script

Until now, we've been writing code in a cellset. This cellset can be saved as a file with the extension .dfx, which we call a **script**.

Now we have learned to write custom functions that are called repeatedly, but this function can only be used in one script. After creating a new script, we have to copy it again. Unlike library functions, it can be used in any script.

How to achieve this effect of a library function?

SPL provides a function to call another script in a script. Let's take the example of the code that calculates the outliers to illustrate how to do this.

First, create a new script, and then use the parameter function under the program menu to pop up such a dialog box:

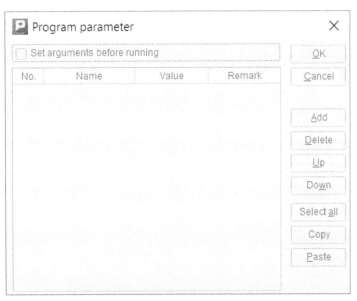

First fill in the parameters of the script to be called here. Suppose that this script will receive the coordinates of a batch of points as parameters, calculate the sequence of outliers and return it. We design three parameters: X is a sequence, storing abscissas; Y is a sequence of the same length as X, which stores ordinates; ratio is a proportion, which indicates how many proportion of the points (sequence numbers) with the largest distance are taken as outliers.

The completed dialog box will look like this:

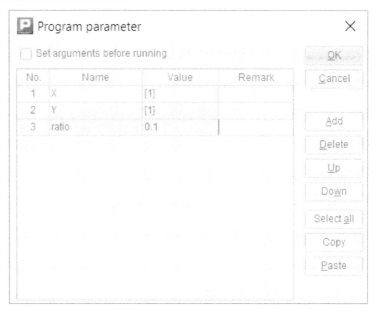

The value column refers to the default value. When calling this script, if no parameter is input, this default value will be used. Here we just write a few.

Now write the code in the cell:

	A	B	C	D
1	=X.(Y.sum(func(A3,X(X.#),X(#),Y(X.#),Y(#))))			
2	return A1.psort@z().to(int(X.len()*ratio))			
3	func			
4		return sqrt((A3-B3)*(A3-B3)+(C3-D3)*(C3-D3))		

The script also uses the return statement to return the result. In the script, the parameters can be directly used as the variable names. In fact, if we execute it, we can see the parameters in the variable table at the bottom right. For SPL, script parameters and named variables are the same thing.

Cell A1 uses the variable name of the parameters to determine the level of # in a multi-layer loop function.

Save the script and give it a name, such as outlier.dfx. Now, with a new script, we can call the script we just wrote.

	A
1	100
2	>rand@s(0)
3	=call("outlier.dfx", A1.(rand()),A1.(rand()),0.1)
4	>rand@s(0)
5	=call("outlier.dfx", A1.(rand()),A1.(rand()))

Use the call() function to call another script and get the return value.

It should be noted that this new script needs to be saved and stored in the same path as outlier.dfx. SPL will generally look for the called script in the path of the current script. If the script has not been saved, there will be no path. If the path is wrong, it is likely that it will not be found.

We have a default value when writing outlier.dfx, so A5 can omit one parameter, and because we've used the rand@s(), A3 and A5 will return the same result.

If the script still reports an error that it cann't find the outlier.dfx, it may be because the searching path or main path is not written correctly. Use the options function under the tools menu to open the dialog box and switch to the environment page. The searching path may have been filled with inappropriate content, and the called script will be searched under this path first.

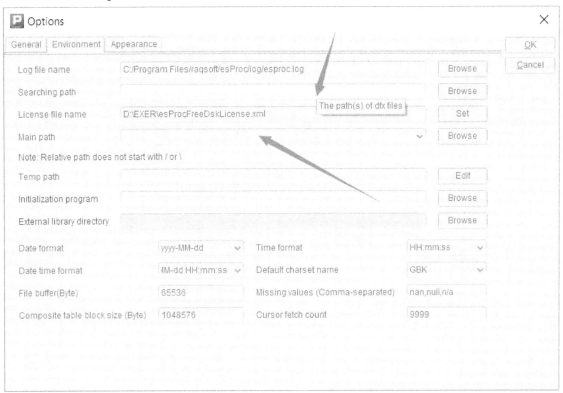

The advantage is that we can write some common scripts and put them in this path, so a script stored in any path can call these common scripts, and there is no need to copy the called scripts to the path of the calling scripts.

If the called script still can not be found when the searching path is empty, there may be an error in the main path. For file names (including script names) that use relative paths, esProc first searches the main path. When the main path is filled with blank, it will search the path of the current script. This rule is a bit complicated, and it is set for developing complex applications with many scripts.

SPL also provides a register() function to register a script as an ordinary function.

	A
1	>register("outlier","outlier.dfx")
2	100
3	=outlier(A2.(rand()),A2.(rand()),0.1)

When registering a self writing script as a function, it is better to use the absolute path or put the script into the searching path, otherwise it may not be found because of the different paths to call the script. Registered functions are valid for all scripts, not only for the current script. Repeated registration will replace the original.

We can use a script to register other scripts that are commonly used to be called as our own functions. In the future, every time we start esProc and execute this script to register other scripts, it is equivalent to adding many library functions.

The contents of the first three chapters, together with this chapter, constitute the vast majority of process control mechanisms of modern programming languages (object-oriented languages also have overload mechanisms, but the content is abstruse, which is not covered in this book). These are the ways to control the flow of a program. Different programming languages may use different reserved words, but there is not much difference. When learning a new programming language, these flow control statements and data types are the basic contents.

After this, the focus will shift to richer data types and corresponding functions, such as the sequences we've been exposed to before. Different programming languages have different usages, and they have different emphases in data types and functions. Different programming languages have little difference in process control ability, but the difference in data types and functions may be very huge. It can be said that data types and related operations (functions are also operations) constitute the fundamental style of a programming language.

7 STRING AND TIME

7.1 String

Up to now, the data we have processed in the program, except for a small amount of text in output(), are numerical values or sequences of numerical values. In fact, the computer can also easily process texts. In the programming language, we call these texts **string**. String is another data type different from integer and floating-point number.

In SPL, write text directly in a cell, if it cann't be identified as other meaningful data type or statement, it will be regarded as a string constant by default. In an expression, we can also use double quotation marks to enclose text to represent a string constant.

	A	B
1	esProc	SPL
2	="esProc"	="SPL"
3	3+5	="3+5"
4	=3*4	'=3*4
5	2020-1-1	'2020-1-1
6	for 10	'for 10

A1 is the string constant "esProc", A2 is a normal calculation cell, and its calculation result is also "esProc", which is the same as A1; Similarly, the cell values of B1 and B2 are "SPL"; A3 starts with a number, but cannot be interpreted as a numeric value, so it is also a string. Like B3, it is "3+5".

A4 is a calculation cell that can calculate a numerical value, so it is not a string. If we want to write a string constant starting with =, we should add a single quotation mark ' at the beginning of the cell. This extra single quotation mark is not part of the string, and the cell value of A4 is "=3*4". Note that only one single quotation mark is needed, do not write another one on the right. If it is written, the single quotation mark on the right will also be regarded as a character of the string.

Similarly, A5 is a date constant that can be identified, and it is not a string. If we want to generate such a string, a single quotation mark ' should also be used at the beginning of the cell; And also, A6 is a legal statement and will not be recognized as a string. To obtain such a string constant, a single quotation mark ' should also be used at the beginning of the cell.

String is also a data type and can be operated. Its most common operation is concatenation, that is, concatenating two strings to form a longer string.

	A	B
1	esProc	
2	=A1+"2020"	esProc 2020
3	=A1+2020	2020
4	=A1+string(2020)	esProc2020
5	=A1/2020	esProc2020
6	=A1/"2020"	esProc2020

Use the + sign to concatenate two strings (A2); However, it should be noted that the string part (A3) will be ignored when adding a string and a value. This is a special stipulation of SPL. Most other programming languages do not stipulate like this. Instead, they will either report an error or convert the value into a string and then concatenate. The value can be normally concatenated with other strings by converting it into a string with the string() function (A4). If the slash / is used to concatenate the string and the value, the value will be automatically converted into a string (A5). The slash / can also concatenate two strings directly (A6).

Now, we can use the string to transform the code of prime factorization and display the result as a complete expression.

	A	B	C
1	7215	=2	=string(A1)+"=1"
2	for A1>1	if A1%B1==0	>C1=C1+"*"+string(B1)
3			>A1=A1\B1
4			next
5		>B1+=1	

After the execution of this program, a string will be obtained in cell C1: 7215=1*3*5*13*37, and the result of prime factorization is written out. If you carefully interpret the execution process of the program, you can imagine how it is concatenated step by step.

If there is a concatenation, there is a split. SPL also provides the following functions:

	A	B
1	SPL2020	
2	=len(A1)	'7
3	=left(A1,2)	'SP
4	=right(A1,3)	'020
5	=mid(A1,3,2)	'L2
6	=A2.(mid(A1,~,1))	["S","P","L","2","0","2","0"]

The len() function returns the number of **characters** constituting the string, also known as the **length** of the string. Note that the name of this len() function is the same as that of the function getting the sequence length, but the writing method is different. The string should be regarded as a parameter here instead of writing as A1.len(). It should also be noted that SPL adopts unicode, and a Chinese character or a number or an English letter is only one character. In some early programming languages, a Chinese character will be two characters.

The left(), right() and mid() functions of A3, A4 and A5 will get a part from the string to form a new string and return. The function name has reflected the part to be taken. Then observe the operation results. It is easy to understand the meaning of its parameters, and we won't elaborate here. Almost all programming languages that can handle strings have these functions, and the naming and parameter rules are the same.

68

A6 split a string into a sequence of characters with a loop function, and you can understand the mid() function again. A single character is also a string, that is, a string with a length of 1.

The result of prime factorization will always be written with a 1* in the front, this is because we concatenate a * and a factor to the result string every time in the loop. If we don't write the first 1, there will be a result of 7215=*3*5*13*37, which is wrong.

But in any case, this 1* is a little redundant. What can we do?

It can be solved by splitting the string.

	A	B	C
1	7215	=2	=string(A1)+"="
2	for A1>1	if A1%B1==0	>C1=C1+if(right(C1,1)=="=","","*")/B1
3			>A1=A1\B1
4			next
5		>B1+=1	

When concatenating the factor, judge whether the current string ends with =. If so, it means that it is the first factor, do not concatenate the * sign, otherwise it will be concatenated. Now we can get the desired result 7215=3*5*13*37.

We can also do it later and remove the redundant 1* part:

	A	B	C
1	7215	=2	=string(A1)+"=1"
2	for A1>1	if A1%B1==0	>C1=C1+"*"+string(B1)
3			>A1=A1\B1
4			next
5		>B1+=1	
6	=pos(C1,"=1*")	>C1=left(C1,A6+1)+mid(C1,A6+3)	

We encounter another function pos() here, which will find another string in a string. The former is called a **substring**. After finding the substring, it will return the position, that is, starting from this position, the character of the original string will be this substring. If it cannot be found, it will return null. This is very similar to the pos() function of the sequence, but it also needs to write the string as a parameter rather than the object syntax.

We know for sure that there must be a substring =1* in the calculated result string now (there will only be one after adding =, otherwise there may be a prime factor in the middle ending with 1, but pos only finds the first one and it's not wrong, but we are more rigorous here). After finding its position, we can remove the 1* part by splitting and concatenating.

We can also use the replace() function to directly replace: =replace(C1,"=1*","="). Similarly, replace =1* with =, not 1* with an empty string.

SPL provides many string processing functions, which are not listed here one by one. You can check the help documents when necessary.

We just used == to compare strings. Of course, we can also use !=. Then, are the symbols like >, < meaningful to strings?

Yes.

In essence, computers can only process numerical values. When processing characters, they should also be represented by numerical values, which is the encoding method. As we said earlier, the encoding method adopted by SPL is called unicode.

Since it is a numeric value, it can be compared with the value. When the strings are compared, it is compared with the character code. The comparison rule is very similar to the sequence, that is, the first character of the two is compared first. If it is different, the bigger one will be bigger. If it is the same, then compare the second character,...,, until it is different or one of them is not long enough. In fact, this is the real source of the term dictionary order.

So, how do we know which of the two characters is bigger and which is smaller? Like "1" and "2", or "1" and "A"?

Simply put, we can write a code and compare it. However, it's too tiresome to memorize all by rote. Let's see if these codes have any rules. SPL provides asc() function to return the code of a character.

	A	B
1	=asc("0")	=9.(asc(string(~)))
2	=asc("A")	=asc("C")
3	=asc("a")	=asc("z")

We won't explain it one by one. Please execute these codes to see the results. Here we directly write the coding rules:

1) The coding of "0"-"9" is continuous, from 48 to 57;

2) The coding of "A"-"Z" is continuous, from 65 to 90;

3) The coding of "a"-"z" is continuous, from 97 to 112;

This coding standard was originally called ASCII, and unicode is extended on the basis of ASCII, so this function is also called asc().

In reverse to the asc() function, SPL also has a char() function that can convert the coding into a character.

We can use the char() function and the rules just found to write a function: given two integers r and c, calculate the name of the cell in row r and column c in Excel.

	A	B	C	D
1	>r=2,c=123			
2	>rc=""	=1	=26	
3	for c>C2	>c-=C2	>C2*=26	>B2+=1
4	>c-=1			
5	for B2	>rc=char(65+c%26)+rc	>c\=26	
6	return rc/r			

The main difficulty in calculating the cell name is to calculate the column name. First calculate the number of letters needed(B1), and then calculate the letter string corresponding to the column.

Conversely, the asc() function can be used to inversely calculate the row number and column number from the cell name rc:

	A	B	C	D
1	>rc="PG45"			
2	=len(rc).(upper(mid(rc,~,1)))			
3	>r=c=0	=-1	=1	
4	for A2	if A4>="A"	>c=c*26+asc(A4)-65	
5			>B3+=C3	>C3*=26
6		else	>r=r*10+asc(A4)-48	
7	return [r,c+B3+1]			

The upper() function is used to capitalize letters.

The rule of Excel cell name looks simple, but it is not easy to come up with the correct calculation logic. As we said earlier, the program code will not help us solve the problem, but will only help us realize the solution.

7.2 Split and concatenate

We have used the loop function and mid() to split the string into a sequence of single characters. Because this is very common, SPL provides the split() function. s.split() is equivalent to len(s).(mid(s,~,1)).

Split() also has more string splitting capabilities.

However, before we talk about split, let's learn a clipboard() function.

Just find a text editing program, such as Notepad, enter some text, select it, and then press Ctrl-C, which is the familiar copy action. Now switch to esProc, create a new cellset, enter =clipboard() in cell A1, and then execute to see the value of cell A1.

The text just copied in Notepad is now here. The clipboard() function can take out the text copied to the system clipboard.

Then enter in A2

>clipboard("Hello,esProc")

After execution, switch back to Notepad and press Ctrl-V to paste. What do you see?

The clipboard() function with a parameter will copy the string used as a parameter to the system clipboard, and then it can be pasted in other programs.

Now let's use this clipboard() function to help Excel do something.

Suppose a column in Excel, such as column A, has some names. For example, the first few rows are as follows:

	A
1	James
2	Andrew
3	Sanders
4	Mike
5	John
6	Alice
7	Selina

Now we want to know how many times the letter e is used in these names.

It's not easy for Excel to calculate this. Let's use SPL to cooperate.

1) Select this column in Excel, press Ctrl-C and copy it to the clipboard.
2) Switch to esProc and write the following code:

	A
1	=clipboard()
2	=A1.split("\n")
3	=A2.(~.split())
4	=A3.conj()
5	=A4.count(lower(~)=="e")

Execute it, A5 is the result we want.

Let's look at each cell value in the script after the code is executed. A1 is as follows:

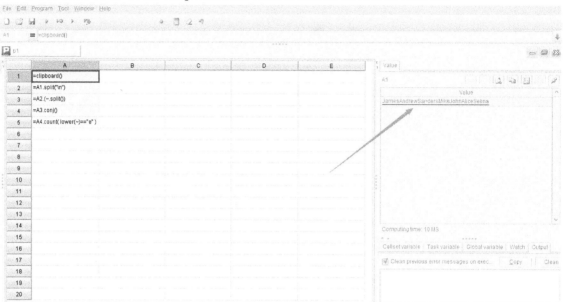

It takes out the content just copied in Excel from the clipboard. It seems to squeeze the text in the column of Excel together. Look at A2:

This is a sequence. Each member is exactly every row of text in the Excel column. How does this happen?

In fact, what we copied from Excel is a large string composed of these texts, separated by return between the two rows. The return character is a non displayable character, which can not be seen in esProc, so it looks like squeezing the text of these rows together. A1.split("\n") means that the return character is used as the separator to split the large string into a sequence, so it returns to the case where each member exactly corresponds to each row in Excel.

The "\n" here is the return character. The backslash \ in the string constant is called the **escape character**. Its

72

function is to help us write some characters that are inconvenient to write. For example, return is represented by \n and tab is represented by \t. These are non displayable characters, but they also have codes and are two characters. \n is only one character in the string, although it is written in quotation marks as \ and n (two characters), \t is also similar.

Because \ is regarded as an escape character, if we really want to have a \ in the string constant, it will be escaped. It will be written twice, that is, the actual content of "a\\b" is a\b, and the length is 3; In addition, double quotation marks are used as the delimiter of a string, but it is still possible that a string contains double quotation marks. In this case, it should also be written with an escape character. The actual content of "a\"b" is a"b with a length of 3.

The following statements are simple. A3 is a loop function. Its inner ~.split() will split the string of each member into a sequence of single characters, so A3 is a two-layer sequence:

       [["J","a","m","e","s"],["A","n","d","r","e","w"],...]

We have encountered the conj() function when we talked about recursion. Its function is to concatenate the member sequences of a multi-layer sequence and return the result of | operation among these members. Therefore, A3.conj() in A4 will get:

       ["J","a","m","e","s","A","n","d","r","e","w",...]

The lower() function turns the character into lowercase. Now it can be compared with the string "e", and then count it.

It is written in this way to disassemble the steps and facilitate the interpretation of the code. In fact, these operations can be written continuously:

	A
1	=clipboard()
2	=A1.split@n().conj()
3	=A2.count(lower(~)=="e")

s.split@n(x) is s.split("\n").(~.split(x)), because it is common to split by return first and then split again, SPL adds the @n option to the split function.

Let's take another example.

A batch of email addresses are stored in a column in Excel. As we know, the email addresses are x@y format. We hope to sort these email addresses so that the mailboxes of the same enterprise can be arranged together, that is, we hope to arrange them in the order of y first and then x, for example, abc@google.com and xyz@google.com should be arranged together instead of putting abc@google.com and abc@apple.com together, but the latter situation will occur if they are sorted directly in Excel.

We still use the clipboard, first copy this column of data in Excel, and then switch to esProc to write code:

	A
1	=clipboard()
2	=A1.split@n("@")
3	=A2.sort([~(2),~(1)])
4	=A3.concat@n("@")
5	>clipboard(A4)

Execute it, then switch back to Excel and paste it in that column with Ctrl-V. It has been arranged as we want.

We've understood A1. The split@n in A2 first split the string into a sequence of strings according to the return character, and then split each member with the separator "@". There is and will only be one @ in an email address, so each member string will be split into a sequence of two members, which are the parts before and after @ respectively. Then, when sorting with the sort function, write the sequence members in reverse. In this way, according to the sequence comparison rules, the later part of @ will be compared first and then the front part of @, that is, the order we want.

concat() in A4 is the opposite function of split(). split() is responsible for splitting and concat() is responsible for concatenating. The @n option indicates doing concat for the 2-layer sequence. Each member is restored to the original email address string and assembled into a large string separated by return, but now the order is reasonable. Then use the clipboard() function to copy it to the clipboard. In Excel, just paste it.

A4 can also be directly written as A3.sort(~(2),~(1)). The sort() function also supports multi parameter form, which means comparing the previous parameter first and then the following parameter. For a sequence with single values, multi parameter sort() is of little significance, but it will be more convenient for a two-layer sequence. After learning structured data in the future, multi parameter sort() will be more common.

Now we are dealing with a single column data in Excel, how about multiple columns?

Of course, there's no problem.

For example, in Excel, we want to sort the data of each row from small to large.

	A	B	C	D	E	F	G
1	49	18	16	19	99	34	49
2	84	30	64	33	87	74	95
3	96	73	15	59	17	0	47
4	32	87	23	8	94	16	32
5	58	5	81	74	98	37	5
6	81	47	87	62	34	33	68
7	60	13	40	44	22	10	67
8	59	12	94	8	25	27	41
9	30	1	63	19	31	72	31
10	50	57	5	58	42	54	62

Excel usually sorts by row, and it is difficult to sort in the column direction. It is easy to implement with SPL. Select and copy this piece in Excel, and then switch to esProc to execute such code:

	A
1	=clipboard()
2	=A1.split@n("\t")
3	=A2.(~.sort())
4	=A3.concat@n("\t")
5	>clipboard(A4)

Then paste it back.

The piece of data copied from Excel is a large string after being received by the clipboard function. Each row is separated by return, that is, \n, and the columns in each row are separated by tab(\t). So A1.split@n("\t") in A2 can split this large string into a two-layer sequence, and its inner member is just the data of each cell in Excel; Then sort each row in A3, concatenate it back into such a \n and \t separated string in A4, and paste it into Excel.

Look carefully at the results in Excel. It seems that there is something wrong. It ranks 42 in front of 5. Is the size wrong?

In fact, it's not wrong, because the result that is split by the split function is still a string, and as a string, "42" is smaller than "5".

So how can we compare by value? We need to change A3 to:

    =A2.(~.sort(number(~)))

Corresponding to string(), number() can convert a string parameter into numeric type, and then it can be compared and sorted according to numerical rules. Look now, there's no problem.

Under the previous operating system, there was a command called grep, which can find the file containing a string and the line number in many text files. This is a very useful command, which was cancelled by Windows. Let's implement it by ourselves now.

Assuming that the string to be found is in A1, let's specify all text files under the path:

	A	B	C	D
1	abc	=directory@p("D:/data/*.txt")		
2	for B1	=file(A2).read@n()		=filename(A2)
3		for B2	if pos(B3,A1)	>output(D2/"\t"/#B3/"\t"/B3)

We're going to learn a few new functions.

The directory() function in B1 will return all .txt file names under the specified path (it is better to use the absolute path, otherwise the file may not be found because the startup path of esProc is uncertain). These file names will be returned as a string sequence, @p indicating that the returned file name is also a full path. A2 loops this sequence, B2 reads out each file, and the file() function generates a file object with the file name, read@n() function reads the text file into a sequence of strings, one member per line. filename() takes out the part of the path in the full path file name.

B3:D3 is easy to understand. Loops through each line of text, if A1 is found, output the file name, line number and the content of this line.

Here we assume that the files are small and can be read in at one time. If the file is large, we need to use the cursor technology mentioned later.

Counting the number of words in a batch of articles is also a common exercise. After learning to read files, we can also practice:

	A
1	=directory@p("D:/book/*.txt").sum(file(~).read().words().len())

The read() function without options will read the whole text file into a large string, and the words() function will disassemble the words in the large string to form a sequence. Then, just count the length and add it up. One line is enough.

Let's do another task that may be useful in daily work: merge a batch of Excel files into a large one.

We may often collect Excel files of various periods or departments. The Excel format is the same. These files need to be combined into a complete file to facilitate further statistics. But manual copy and paste is very troublesome. If there are dozens or hundreds of files, it will be very tiresome. This kind of thing is just for the program to do.

Let's assume that the Excel to be merged is row type, the first row is the title, and then each row is data, such as:

	A	B	C	D	E	F
1	ID	Company	Area	OrderDate	Amount	Phone
2	10248	Shantai	North	2012-07-04	428	(030) 26471510
3	10249	Dongdiwar	East	2012-07-05	1842	(0251) 1031259
4	10250	Shiyi	North	2012-07-08	1523.5	(0211) 5550091
5	10251	Qiangu	East	2012-07-08	624.95	(071) 8325486
6	10252	Fuxing	West	2012-07-09	3559.5	(030) 23672220
7	10253	Shiyi	North	2012-07-10	1428	(0211) 5550091
8	10254	Haotian	Center	2012-07-11	545.4	(030) 30076545
9	10255	Yongda	North	2012-07-12	2450	(089) 7034214

This is a very common Excel file format.

Add a requirement to spell the original Excel file name into the last column of the merged Excel, so as to distinguish which file the data comes from.

	A	B
1	=directory@p("D:/data/*.xlsx")	
2	for A1	=file(A2).xlsimport@w()
3		=filename@n(A2)
4		=B2.to(2,).(~|B3)
5		=@|B4
6		=if(#A2==1,B2(1)|"File",@)
7	=file("D:/all.xlsx").xlsexport@w([B6]|B5)	

filename@n() in B3 will disassemble the part of the file name with the extension removed, and it can also be done by splitting a string. xlsimport@w() in B2 will read an Excel file into a two-layer sequence. Each row of Excel corresponds to one member, and each column in each row corresponds to the member of its member. B4 removes the title of the first row and spells the file name to the end of each row. B5 combines these data, while B6 needs to keep one title and spell one more column.

Finally xlsexport@w() in A7 write the summarized two-layer sequence [B6]|B5 into a new Excel file (it is better to use the absolute path when exporting the file).

xlsimport() without @w option can actually read an Excel file into more convenient data type, and the code to complete this task will be simpler, but it will be introduced after we talk about structured data.

With the in-depth study, we will gradually enter the phase of handling practical tasks. Processing file data is a very common task. In the examples of this section, we all use absolute paths to locate files. Here is a brief introduction to the file search rules of esProc when using relative paths (absolute paths can be found directly):

If the main path is set in the environment (Chapter 6, section 3), esProc will start from this main path; If the main path is empty, search from the path where the currently used script file is located. The current script may have just been created and have not been saved. In this case, there is no path, so it can not determine where to find it, and it is likely that it will not be found. Therefore, either set the main path, or the current script is saved and has the path.

The searching path that was set at the same time as the main path is used to search the called script, and it has nothing to do with the data file. Placing the data file in the searching path will not enable it to be found automatically.

Do some experiments by yourself, and it's easy to figure it out.

When we give examples later, we will use a simple relative path. Please adjust the appropriate system configuration and the path in the code according to the above introduction.

7.3 Date and time

Time related processing and calculation are also common. SPL has three data types: **date, time** and **datetime.**

Date data has only date information but no time information; Time data has only time information and no corresponding date information; Datetime has both date and time, which is equivalent to a certain moment.

It is necessary to provide a time type without date information. Some events that occur on an uncertain date do not have date information, and it is more appropriate to use a time type, an extra date may cause confusion. For example, calculate the interval between 8:00 and 9:00. If there must be a date information, we have to pay attention to whether it is 8:00 and 9:00 of the same day, which is easy to be neglected.

But with a more precise datetime type, why should there be an imprecise date type?

This is similar to integer and floating-point number, because for many events, we only care about the date of occurrence and no longer care about the time. If only datetime type is used, the amount of storage and calculation will become larger. Moreover, when comparing whether the two dates are equal, we should also pay attention to whether the attached time information is also equal, and errors are likely to occur.

Not all programming languages provide these three data types, and most databases have only datetime and no date.

The most basic operation related to date and time is the splitting and combination of components:

	A	B	C
1	2020-12-20	=date(2020,12,2)	
2	=year(A1)	=month(A1)	=day(A1)
3	22:3:5	=time(22,3,5)	
4	=hour(A3)	=minute(A3)	=second(A3)
5	2020-12-2 10:3:5	=datetime(2020,12,2,10,3,5)	=datetime(A1,A3)
6	=year(A5)	=month(A5)	=day(A5)
7	=hour(A5)	=minute(A5)	=second(A5)
8	=date(A5)	=time(A5)	

These functions are very simple. Just look at the examples, and there is no need to explain them in detail.

SPL also supports putting the month and year together as a component, that is, a six-digit number.

	A	B	C
...	...		
9	=date(202012,20)	=month@y(A9)	

Sometimes you will find this kind of processing very convenient.

The conversion between date time and string is troublesome, and there are many kinds of formats. For example, 2020-12-20 may also be written as 2020/12/20, 12/20/2020, 20-12-2020, Europeans and Americans may also use the format Dec/20/2020 or 20-Dec-2020. The formats of time are relatively less, but it may also be written as 10:03:05 PM or 22:3:5.

Therefore, a program language that can handle date and time usually provides the ability of format parsing and conversion.

	A	B
1	2020-12-2	22:3:5
2	=string(A1,"yyyy/MM/dd")	=string(B1,"hh:mm:ss")
3	=string(A1,"MM/dd/yyyy")	=string(B1,"HH:m:s")
4	=string(A1,"MMM-d-yy")	=string(B1,"h:m:s a")
5	=string(A1,"d/MMM/yyyy")	
6	=date("2020-12-20")	=time("22:3:5")
7	=date("DEC/20/20","MMM/d/yy")	=time("10:3:5 pm","h:m:s a")
8	=datetime(A1,B1)	=string(A8,"MM mm")

The writing method of these format strings can be found in the function help. It is almost a common rule all over the world, and we will not explain in detail here. You only need to know this usage. It should be emphasized that since the starting letter of month and minute are both m, it is necessary to distinguish them by uppercase and lowercase. You can observe B8.

By the way, numerical values also have format problems,

	A	B
1	12345.23456	12345678
2	=string(A1,"#.00")	=string(B1,"# ")
3	=string(A1,"#.0")	=string(B1,"#,###")
4	=string(A1,"#,###.0000000000")	

These are not explained in detail. Just try it yourself.

As we said earlier, there are only numbers in the computer, and other data types are actually numbers by some kind of coding. For example, the string in SPL is encoded by unicode, so how is the date and time encoded?

The internal codes of date and time data types are long integers. Let's observe their rules:

	A	B	C
1	2020-12-1	2020-12-2	
2	=long(A1)	=long(B1)	=B2-A2
3	0:0:0	0:0:1	
4	=long(A3)	=long(B3)	=B4-A4
5	=date(0)	=time(0)	

First observe C2, two dates with a difference of 1 day, after converting to long integer, the difference is 86400000. What is this number?

Readers who often do date calculation will sensitively find that 86400=24*60*60, and it is exactly 1000 times the number of seconds of a day. Observe C4. The difference between two dates with a difference of 1 second is 1000 after converting to a long integer. This confirms our idea that the long integer corresponding to date and time is the number of milliseconds from a certain moment.

Then, from which moment? We can't figure it out by observing A1, B1, A4 and B4 directly, we can simply reverse it and observe A5 and B5. It turns out that the date is counted from January 1, 1970. This is an agreement of the International Computer Standards Organization. Dates earlier than 1970 should be expressed as negative numbers. Interestingly, several days in history are not exactly 86400 seconds, and the long integer value corresponding to a date is not always the number of days from January 1, 1970 multiplied by 86400000. Interested readers can program to find out which days (with the skills we have learned till now readers should be able to do this), and then search the Internet to see why these dates are not 86400 seconds.

Let's look at the time, the result of B5 is strange. I calculate it here as 8 o'clock. Why not start from 0 o'clock?

Because I am writing this book in Beijing, China. The time zone of Beijing is East Zone 8, and 8:00 Beijing time is exactly 0:00 GMT. The time is counted from 0:00, but it is Greenwich mean time, not the local time zone. If you happen to be in the UK now, the calculated B5 will be 0.

There are so many interesting things about date and time.

Let's continue to learn about date and time operations. The most common requirement is to calculate the gap between two moments and the time after a period of time from a certain moment.

For example, if we want to see how effective the optimization method used in the calculation of Narcissus number is, we need to calculate the execution time of this program:

	A	B	C	D	E	F
1	=now()					
2	for 1000	=0	=[]			
3		for 9	=100*B3	=B3*B3*B3		
4			for 0,9	=C3+10*B4	=D3+C4*C4*C4	
5				for 0,9	=D4+D5	=E4+D5*D5*D5
6					if E5==E5	>C2.insert(0,E5)
7	=now()		=interval@ms(A1,A7)			

Here we need to use the code that generates the result sequence, because the output method will involve screen display. In fact, this action is very complex, and it may take longer than completing these calculations, and it is not the test of calculation time. Moreover, we repeated this action 1000 times, because the CPU of modern computers is so fast that we can't see the difference by only executing it once.

now() of A1 will return the time when this statement is executed, that is, record the start time of the program in A1. At A7, use now() to get the time when the program ends, and then use inteval@ms() to calculate the gap between the two moments, and write the two parameters in chronological order, so as to get the execution time of the program.

now() returns the datetime type, which can be accurate to milliseconds. The @ms option of interval() means that the calculated time gap is accurate to milliseconds. Because the program executes very fast, even if it is repeated 1000 times, if it is not accurate to milliseconds, we still can not see the gap.

Now do the same transformation to the optimized code and execute it:

	A	B	C	D	E	F	G
1	=now()						
2	for 1000	=0	=[]				
3		for 9	=100*B3	=B3*B3*B3			
4			for 0,9	=C3+10*B4	=D3+C4*C4*C4		break
5				for 0,9	=D4+D5	=E4+D5*D5*D5	
6					if E5==E5	>C2.insert(0,E5)	
7					else if E5<F5	break	
8	=now()		=interval@ms(A1,A8)				

Comparing these two time gaps, we can know whether optimization works. On my computer, the optimized code is about 25% faster, which is pretty obvious.

The interval() function has various options and can return the time gap of different accuracy. In daily work, the most common task is to calculate the number of days between two dates, which is also the default return value of the interval() function when the option is not used. Moreover, because it is too common, SPL simplifies this calculation to be expressed directly by subtraction, that is, interval(d1,d2)==d2-d1.

Someone borrowed 25000 yuan on December 4, 2018, with a daily interest of 0.013%. If he pays it back today, how much interest should he pay?

	A
1	=25000*0.013/100*interval(date(2018,12,4),now())
2	=25000*0.013/100*(now()-date(2018,12,4))

The results of A1 and A2 are the same. now() contains date information, and can be used as today.

Let's make the case a little more complicated. If the interest is added to the principal at the end of each year and the following interest is calculated on this basis, how much should be paid in total when it is returned today?

In other words, on January 1 of each year, the interest at that time shall be calculated and added to the principal, and the following interest shall be calculated on this basis. We use a clumsy way to calculate, looping day by day from the loan date to today.

	A	B	C	D
1	2018-12-4	0.013%	=25000	=0
2	for now()-A1	if month(A1)==1 && day(A1)==1	>C1+=D1	>D1=0
3		>A1=elapse(A1,1)	>D1+=B1*C1	
4	=C1+D1			

The current interest is stored in D1. The initial value is 0. For every day of the loop, the interest will be increased by one day. If the current date is January 1, add the current interest to the principal and then clear the interest. At the end of the loop, add the principal and interest at that time.

It should be noted that in cell B3, the elapse(d,n) function returns the date n days after a date d, with this action, the loop can run normally.

Like interval(), elapse() has many options to control accuracy. Moreover, when the accuracy is days, it can be expressed directly by addition. That is, cell B3 can be simply written as >A1=A1+1, or even >A1+=1.

The percentage constant can be directly expressed by % in a cell, but not in the expression, % will be regarded as the operator of remainder.

8 DATA TABLE

8.1 Structured data

From this chapter, we begin to learn the tabular data and its processing methods that we deal with every day in our daily work.

In the previous example of merging Excel files, we have seen this kind of table:

	A	B	C	D	E	F
1	ID	Company	Area	OrderDate	Amount	Phone
2	10248	Shantai	North	2012-07-04	428	(030) 26471510
3	10249	Dongdiwar	East	2012-07-05	1842	(0251) 1031259
4	10250	Shiyi	North	2012-07-08	1523.5	(0211) 5550091
5	10251	Qiangu	East	2012-07-08	624.95	(071) 8325486
6	10252	Fuxing	West	2012-07-09	3559.5	(030) 23672220
7	10253	Shiyi	North	2012-07-10	1428	(0211) 5550091
8	10254	Haotian	Center	2012-07-11	545.4	(030) 30076545
9	10255	Yongda	North	2012-07-12	2450	(089) 7034214

The first row is the title, explaining what is stored in each column. Each row is an item of data, which may correspond to a person, an organization, an order, an event, ...

This kind of data has a professional term, which is called **structured data**. This is the most common data type in modern data processing.

The data of the whole table is referred to as a **data table**, in which each row (except the title) is called a **record**, the column is called a **field**, and the string in the title is called a **field name**. There are 9 records in the visible part of the above table, corresponding to row 2 to 10 of the Excel; There are also six fields. The field names are ID, Company, Area, OrderDate, Amount and Phone. Field names are different from each other and can uniquely identify a column. These fields (including name and order) are called the **data structure** of the data table, or **structure** for short.

Structured data is data with data structure.

A2:F9 in the table is the data in the data table. We will say what is the value of a field of a record. For example, the ID field of the second record is 10248, and the area field of the eighth record is "Center". Each field of each record in the data table will have a value.

Note that only fields in the data table have names, and records have no names. We will talk about how to identify and distinguish records later.

There can be various data tables, and the data structure of different data tables can of course be different. A data table must have a set of data structure, and there can only be one. Sometimes we also say the record structure, which means the structure of the data table where the record is located.

Because structured data is often presented in the form of this row-column style table, we will also intuitively call records and fields **rows** and **columns**. This is a common term in the database industry, not a popular term invented in this book. Even, sometimes there are no obvious rows and columns when the data table is presented (we will talk about such an example soon), people still use the terms row and column to represent record and field.

Structured data in the form of tables is very common in reality, and most readers will have this experience. It is not difficult to understand the concepts of records and fields by looking at a table. We won't give more examples here.

However, structured data is not always presented in the form of the above table, it may also be something else.

For example:

	No	Item Code	Item Name	Unit	Quantity	SumOfMoney (yuan)	
						Price	Sum
1.1.2	NJSJ		Internal scaffolding	term			
1.1.2.1	11001004001		Internal scaffolding	term	1.00	1006577.54	1006577.54
1.1.2.1.1.1	A22-28		Steel pipe	100m²	137.88	912.07	125756.21
1.1.2.1.1.2	A22-28		Base of internal scaffolding	100m²	71.83	912.07	65513.99

The data from row 5 can be regarded as a data table, but what are the fields? It seems that the contents in row 3 and 4 are the field names, but the string with a space in the middle, Item Code, is usually not suitable for the field name (in fact, SPL supports it, but it is rarely used, and this book does not intend to cover it), and it is unclear whether the field names in columns F and G on the right are the contents of F4 and G4.

In fact, the contents of row 3 and 4 here can only be regarded as a description of the fields. The real data structure (mainly the field name) is not necessarily the content of the title row seen in the table, but can also be described and set separately.

There is also this form:

	B	C	D	E	F
ID:	1				
Name:	Yin Zhang	Sex	F		
Position	Sales				
Birthday	1968-12-08				
Phone:		(010) 65559857			
Address:	No. 236 of Fuxingmen Beijing				
PostCode:	100098				
ID:	2				
Name:	Wei Wang	Sex	M		
Position	Sales Manager				
Birthday	1962-02-19				
Phone:		(010) 65559482			
Address:	No. 890 of Luoma Garden Beijing				
PostCode:	109801				

This is no longer in the form of row-column table, but it can still form a data table with 2 records. The fields can be ID, Name, Sex, Position, Birthday, Phone, Address and Postcode.

So, what is structured data and data table?

Look at the above examples. The data in the same Excel describes the same kind of things, such as a person, an order, etc. These things have the same attributes. For example, people have common attributes such as Name,Sex,Birthday, and orders also have common attributes such as customer, date and amount. Each thing is a record, and these attributes are fields. A batch of things with the same attributes constitute a data table, that is, the data table has multiple records and fields.

Data table, record and field are abstract concepts, which essentially correspond to something and its attributes. They are not the same as the Excel table. The data table does not have a fixed rendering style that must be observed, but for easy recognition, it is usually rendered as a row-column table and filled with field names in the title.

For the data in Excel table, as long as the attributes used to describe a certain kind of things can be extracted, and if there are multiple similar things with the same attributes, it can be considered as structured data. As for what the title content of the table is, whether there is a title, or even whether the table is in row-column form, it is not an important factor. The key is only whether a class of things with (common) attributes is described.

Look at another table:

	A	B	C	D	E	F	G	H
1			Employee Information					
2	company	XX company				date:	1982-06-25	
3	Name	San Zhang	Sex	M	Birthday	1982-06-25	Nation	han
4	IDCard	510121198206253112			Phone	13612345678	Depart	Research
5	Home	No. 25 Xisanqi			Marital	Married	Entry	2002-02
6		Name	Relation		Workplace		Phone	
7	Family	Zhou Zhang	farther		retired		15313231568	
8		Yin Hu	wife		XX company		13718826593	
9		Wuji Zhang	son		XX school			

Can we find structured data from here? In other words, can we extract things described by attributes?

Yes, but there are two data tables here. The first is in the upper part, describing the basic information of an employee, and the fields include Name, Sex, Birthday, Nation, IDCard, ...; The second is in the lower part, describing the employee's family members, and the fields include Name, Relation, Workplace, Phone. Employees themselves and family members are two different things with different attributes. A data table can only have one set of data structure and can only describe one kind of things. To fully describe the information of an employee, two data tables (employee and family members) are required.

There is another case like this:

	Area	West	East	Center	North	South	Northwest	Southwest
Type \ Amount								
Urgent express		20	70	1	97	23	2	35
Unified parcel		25	89	1	148	39	3	27
Federal cargo		15	79	52	108	29	2	23
Air transport		5	1	12	1	1	9	6
Cash on Delivery		8	2	4	1	6	7	9
General express		32	41	36	48	26	22	18

Orders Statistics

This looks like a row table, and it should be easy to extract structured data. But what is the data structure?

Simply put, we can take each column as a field name, that is, Type, West, East, ... This is indeed a method, but it is not convenient. The computing ability of structured data in the direction of rows and columns (records and fields) is different. When we want to calculate the sum of various regions, it is troublesome to list the fields one by one, while the statistics on records is much easier.

In order to facilitate statistics, for this cross table, we usually design a data table with three fields: Type, Area, Amount. In this way, the statistics in both directions will be relatively simple, and if necessary, the table can be displayed in another way. For example, put Area on the row and Type on the column, which does not affect the data structure.

However, to design the structure like above is not inevitable. It should be determined according to the calculation objectives of the next step. Sometimes it is still designed as Type, West, East, ..., which will be more convenient.

To find out structured data from chaotic tables, we call this work **structure analysis.** It is not a very obvious and easy task. We need to design a reasonable data structure according to different conditions and objectives. Structure analysis is also a very important work. If the data is not structured, it is difficult to implement further calculation, and the data that cannot be calculated is meaningless.

Of course, structured data is not always stored as Excel files (conversely, the data stored in Excel is not always structured data). In fact, the most structured data is stored in the database. However, the knowledge of database is too professional to be covered in this book.

In daily work, in addition to Excel files, text files are also commonly used to store structured data. There are two common formats: txt and csv. Text files usually correspond to one record per line. Usually, the first line will be the title, usually the field names. The columns of txt files are separated by tabs(\t), while csv files are separated by commas.

```
orders.txt - Notepad                                                    —    □    ×
File  Edit  Format  View  Help
O_ORDERKEY      O_CUSTKEY       O_ORDERSTATUS  O_TOTALPRICE      O_ORDERDATE      O_ORDERPRIORITY
1       36901   O       173665.47       1996/1/2 5-LOW
2       78002   O       46929.18 1996/12/1      1-URGENT
3       123314  F       193846.25       1993/10/14      5-LOW
4       136777  O       32151.78 1995/10/11     5-LOW
5       44485   F       144659.2 1994/7/30      5-LOW
6       55624   F       58749.59 1992/2/21      4-NOT SPECIFIED
7       39136   O       252004.18       1996/1/10       2-HIGH
```

A txt file separated by tab

```
O_ORDERKEY,O_CUSTKEY,O_ORDERSTATUS,O_TOTALPRICE,O_ORDERDATE,O_ORDERPRIORITY
1,36901,O,173665.47,1996/1/2,5-LOW
2,78002,O,46929.18,1996/12/1,1-URGENT
3,123314,F,193846.25,1993/10/14,5-LOW
4,136777,O,32151.78,1995/10/11,5-LOW
5,44485,F,144659.2,1994/7/30,5-LOW
6,55624,F,58749.59,1992/2/21,4-NOT SPECIFIED
7,39136,O,252004.18,1996/1/10,2-HIGH
```

A csv file separated by comma

The text file is obviously not as neat as Excel in display, but it will not cause the field dislocation of the record.

8.2 Table sequence and record sequence

With the basic concept of structured data, let's learn how to process this data, that is, the second half of the book mentioned in the preface.

Among the programming languages used to process structured data, SQL is the most widely used at present. The full name of SQL is structured query language, which means the language specially used for structured data query. It is the common language of relational database.

Except for SQL related materials, most programming books do not talk about structured data. After talking about the content equivalent to the first half of this book, they begin to turn to more advanced object-oriented content. For non professionals, this book can be said to have ended. However, learning to this level, except for doing some math problems of primary and secondary schools (just like the examples mentioned above) to practice our brains, it will not be of any substantive help to our daily work. Only after learning the knowledge and skills of structured data can we really use programming to improve work efficiency, which is also an important goal of this book.

However, this book is not going to talk about SQL. There are a lot of materials in this area. If readers are interested, you can learn it yourself. SQL usually can only be used in the database, and the skill requirements for installing and adminstrating a database are a bit high, which is not suitable for the readers of this book.

We continue to use SPL. Compared with SQL, SPL has much richer structured data processing capabilities. In most cases, the code is more concise than SQL, and the environment does not rely on the database, which is more suitable for non professionals.

In fact, the full name of SPL is structured process language, which is also invented to process structured data. Structured data is very common. Most data processing tasks in daily work are related to structured data, and it is necessary to invent a more efficient program language.

Actually, SQL is allowed to be used for file data in esProc. The basic SQL function is realized as a special statement of SPL. You can also learn SQL with esProc without installing the database.

Back to the subject, let's first look at how to create a data table.

	A
1	=create(name,sex,weight,height)

The create() function creates an empty data table. The data table must have a data structure, that is, field names, and fill them in the parameters of the create() function in turn. The newly created data table has no records. When viewing the data, we will see that there is only a header on the right.

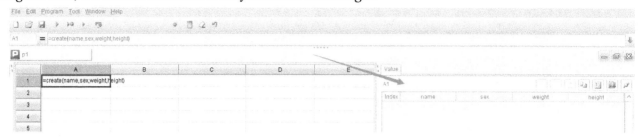

Let's write the code more completely and add some data.

	A	B	C	D
1	Zhang San	Male	80	1.75
2	Li Si	Male	60	1.68
3	Wang Hua	Female	51	1.64
4	Zhao Ting	Female	49	1.6
5	=create(name,sex,weight,height)		=A5.record([A1:D4])	

Create a data table in A5, and then use the record() function to fill in the data in C5. We talked about the writing method of [A1:D4] earlier. The record() function is used to fill the members of the sequence(parameters) into the data table as field values. The sequence members will be filled in according to the field order in the data structure. After filling in a record, if there are remaining sequence members, a new record will be created for the data table to continue to fill in the remaining sequence members.

Now view the data (the record function still returns the data table. To view A5 or C5 is the same).

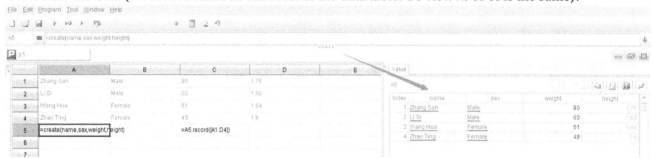

This looks very similar to the sequence values, only that a sequence is displayed as one column, and the data table is displayed as multiple columns, and each column has a name (field name). esProc will also automatically display an index column on the left to faciliate counting. It seems to be a more complex sequence?

We can indeed understand the data table in SPL as a sequence with records as members (it is still a little different, and we'll talk about it later). In fact, the formal name of the data table in SPL is **table sequence**, because SPL places great emphasis on the order of records in the table. For people who are used to Excel, it is natural for records (that is, rows) to have order; But for database programmers, the records in the data table are orderless. SPL emphasizes order to distinguish it from SQL.

A data table is called a table sequence, but records are still records and fields are also fields.

Since a table sequence is a sequence composed of records, can records be obtained by referencing members in the sequence?

Yes, we can continue to write the code:

	A	B	C	D
...	...	...	...	...
5	=create(name,sex,weight,height)		=A5.record([A1:D4])	
6	=A5(1)	=A5(3)	=A5.m(-1)	=A5.len()

Look at the value of A6 after execution:

name	sex	weight	height
Zhang San	Male	80	1.75

It is still displayed as a table with header, but there is only one row of data, and there is no index column on the left.

This is a record. It has a data structure (that is, the data structure of the table sequence), i.e., fields. Each of its fields has a value, which is listed above.

A5 is really like a sequence. It can correctly execute code such as A5.m(-1), and A5.len() is OK.

Let's study the record. Can we get the field value of the record to participate in the operation? Continue writing:

	A	B	C	D
...			...	
6	=A5(1)	=A5(3)	=A5.m(-1)	
7	=A6.weight/A6.height*A6.height			
8	>output(if(B6.height>C6.height,B6.name,C6.name) + " is taller")			

Use the . operator followed by the field name to get the field value. The BMI of the first person Zhang San is calculated in A7, and the height of the third and fourth person is compared in A8, and the name of the taller person is displayed.

Can we change the field value? it's OK too.

	A	B	C	D
...			...	
6	=A5(1)	=A5(3)	=A5.m(-1)	
7	=A6.weight/A6.height*A6.height			
8	>output(if(B6.height>C6.height,B6.name,C6.name) + " is taller")			
9	=C6.height=1.8		=A5(4).name="NewZhaoTing"	
10	>output(if(B6.height>C6.height,B6.name,C6.name) + " is taller")			

Field values can be referenced and modified by using the extracted record variable (C6) and the direct table sequence member (A5(4)).

For the field F of record r, r.F is equivalent to a variable with slightly complex name, which can be freely referenced in the expression or assigned.

We can see that in SPL, we can get a record from the table sequence to view and calculate separately. Don't take this for granted. This is not allowed in SQL. A SQL record cannot be calculated independently outside the data table.

Review the object concept we talked about earlier. Complex data types are not stored directly in variables,

87

but only one address. A record has multiple fields, which seems a little complex. Is it the same?

	A	B	C	D
...		...		
6	=A5(1)	=A6	=A5(1)	
7	>A6.name="Test"	=B6.name	=C6.name	

Just do some experiments. The record is also an object. Not only the address of the record is stored in the record variable, but also in the table sequence without copying the record value. Modifying the field value of a record will affect all subsequent codes that reference this record field.

As for the table sequence, it is obviously an object.

Moreover, a record has more special features:

	A	B	C	D
1	Zhang San	Male	80	1.75
2	Li Si	Male	60	1.68
3	Wang Hua	Female	51	1.64
4	Li Si	Male	60	1.68
5	=create(name,sex,weight,height)		=A5.record([A1:D4])	
6	=A5(1)>A5(2)	=A5(2)==A5(4)	=A5(2)>A5(4)	

We deliberately fill the data in row 4 and row 2 exactly the same, and then observe the calculation results of the three logical expressions in row 6.

The results of A6 and C6 are unpredictable, and multiple executions may get different results. B6 is always false.

What's going on?

The fields of a record are not always the same kind of things like the members of a sequence. It is usually meaningless to use the field order to compare two records. For example, the name field precedes sex here, but there is no reason that name should take precedence over sex in comparison. However, it is not necessary to return an error, so SPL specifies that the internal address value is used for record comparison, so A6 and C6 will get unpredictable results. As for two records of the same table sequence, even if the contents are exactly the same, they will be allocated memory space respectively, and their address values are also different, so the two different records will never be equal.

Then, what can we do if we just want to compare whether the field values of two records are equal, or we just want to compare the records according to the field order?

SPL provides special functions for such comparison:

	A	B	C	D
1	Zhang San	Male	80	1.75
2	Li Si	Male	60	1.68
3	Wang Hua	Female	51	1.64
4	Li Si	Male	60	1.68
5	=create(name,sex,weight,height)		=A5.record([A1:D4])	
6	=cmp(A5(1),A5(2))	=cmp(A5(2),A5(4))		

We'll get a definite result now. The difference is that the cmp() function does not return true or false, but an integer. If it is equal, it returns 0; If the former is smaller, it returns -1; If the former is larger, it returns +1. There are three cases in a comparison.

Why doesn't SPL directly stipulate the comparison of records as the calculation result of cmp() function?

Comparing the records according to the rules of cmp() function is not a common operation. It doesn't matter if it's a little troublesome. Comparing whether the address stored in a record variable is the same (to determine whether it is physically the same record) is a relatively common operation, which is often performed implicitly (such as the grouping operation to be discussed later). If the record comparison is stipulated as the result of cmp() operation, the action of comparing addresses will be much more troublesome or inefficient. Therefore, the SPL convention of the current rule is the result of weighing the computational efficiency and code complexity.

A table sequence is like a sequence composed of records. Can we use the insert() and delete() functions to add and delete members like a sequence?

delete() is OK, but insert() is different. This is the key difference between a sequence and a table sequence.

As we said, a data table has only one set of data structure. When adding a record to the table sequence, it must be a record with the same data structure. If it is allowed to grab a record and insert it into the table sequence, we need to check it in detail to avoid this situation. Moreover, this may cause a record to belong to two different table sequences. When one table sequence adjusts the data structure for some reason, it may lead to the inconsistency of the data structure in the other table sequence. This is too troublesome and seriously affects the efficiency of the program.

Therefore, SPL stipulates that a record must be generated from a table sequence and cannot be inserted into other table sequences. In this way, the records of a table sequence are all under the control of the table sequence. There will be no record that comes to another table sequence, and there will be no record that comes from others. Therefore, we will find that SPL provides a function to create a table sequence, but there is no function to create a separate record. After a record is created, it can participate in other operations outside the table sequence, but it must be attached to a table sequence when it is created. A single record created is essentially a record in a table sequence with only one record. This table sequence can continue to insert new records.

This can also explain the above: different records will never be equal.

The insert() function of the table sequence is made as follows:

	A	B	C	D
...	...	...	...	...
5	=create(name,sex,weight,height)		=A5.record([A1:D4])	
6	>A5.insert(0,"Mary","Female",55,1.7)			
7	>A5.insert(2,"John","Male",75,1.8)			

The first position parameter of insert() has the same meaning as that of sequence insert. A record can be inserted in the middle or appended at the end. Then write each field value of the record to be inserted in the remaining parameters. SPL will create a new record in the appropriate position of the table sequence and fill in the field value.

The purpose of assembling members into a sequence, that is, a set, is to facilitate operation and processing together, for example, we can use the loop function mentioned above. If the records of the table sequence must exist in the table sequence, can the records of different table sequences be put together for operation? Moreover, even if it is the same table sequence, not all the members may participate in the operation at one time, and a sequence has a method to get a subsequence. Is this still valid for the table sequence?

These operations are allowed in SPL. Records are only attached to the table sequence when they are created to ensure the consistency of their data structure. Once created, they can be referenced and combined freely like ordinary data.

It is very common for a sequence composed of a batch of records from different table sequences, or a sequence composed of partial records of a table sequence. This sequence has a special name in SPL called **record sequence.**

Of course, a record sequence is also an object.

For the loop functions of table sequence and record sequence, we will talk about them later. Now we will manually create several record sequences:

	A	B	C	D
...	...	...	...	...
5	=create(name,sex,weight,height)		=A5.record([A1:D4])	
6	=A5.to(2,)	=[A6(1),A5(4),A5.m(-1)]	=A5.step(2,2)	
7	=A6.len()	=B6(2)==B6(3)	=C6(1)==A6(1)	

At present, we have only one table sequence at hand, and can only create record sequences composed of the records of this table sequence. Note B6 that the member of a record sequence can be referenced from another record sequence, not necessarily directly from the table sequence. Moreover, its members can be repeated, and B7 will calculate true; The members of the table sequences cannot be equal to each other because they are newly created every time; while different record sequences can of course be composed of the same record, and C7 also calculates true.

A record sequence can be understood as an ordinary sequence, because it may have same members, and the set operations are also meaningful:

	A	B	C	D
...	...	...	...	...
5	=create(name,sex,weight,height)		=A5.record([A1:D4])	
6	=A5.to(2,)	=[A6(1),A5(4),A5.m(-1)]	=A5.step(2,2)	
7	=A6&B6	=A6^C6	=A5\C6	

The result of these set operations is still a record sequence, and the table sequence itself can be regarded as a record sequence composed of all its records, and can also participate in these set operations, but the calculation result will no longer be a table sequence, but just a record sequence.

Now let's do the problem of merging Excel again, since we haven't learned to change the data structure, we reduce one requirement: only merge the data without adding the file name to the end.

	A	B
1	=directory@p("data/*.xlsx")	
2	for A1	=file(A2).xlsimport@t()
3		=@|B2
4	=file("all.xlsx").xlsexport@t(B3)	

We have understood A1. This time, B2 uses the xlsimport() function without @w, which will read the file into a table sequence, @t indicates that the first row of the file is the field names of the table sequence. B3 in the loop body concatenates the table sequences read each time, which will form a sequence composed of records from multiple table sequences, that is, a record sequence composed of records from multiple table sequences. After the concatenation, just write it in A4 with xlsexport() function, @t also means to write the field names to the first row as the title.

This code is much simpler than the previous string processing, and there is no need to deal with the disassembly and assembly of the title. In fact, using loop function can be simpler:

	A
1	=directory@p("data/*.xlsx").(file(~).xlsimport@t()).conj()
2	>file("all.xlsx").xlsexport@t(A1)

Multiple record sequences can also form a two-layer sequence, and then concatenate into one using conj() function.

This code requires that the merged Excel files have the same data structure (i.e. the same columns). In fact, a record sequence does not require that all member records have the same data structure. There will be no problem as long as there is no error when referencing fields. However, this situation is very rare, and we won't give an example.

8.3 Generation of table sequence

In order to further learn the operations of record sequence, we need a table sequence with a little more records, such as the table sequence with four fields we used earlier: name, sex, weight, height. It is much more convenient to generate hundreds of records and do experiments again.

Obviously, it is too troublesome to manually fill in the field values of many records. We use a program to generate them. The specific values of the fields do not affect learning. They can be generated randomly.

We can already do this with the code technology we have learned now.

	A	B	C
1	=create(name,sex,weight,height)		
2	for 100	=string(A2)	=if(rand()<0.5,"Male","Female")
3		=50+rand(50)	=1.5+rand(40)/100
4		>A1.insert(0,B2,C2,B3,C3)	
5	=A1.len()		

The meaningful name is troublesome, so we use the number string instead. C2, B3, C3 are easy to understand, and then in B4, insert the generated fields into the empty table sequence created in A1. After the code is executed, we can get a table sequence with 100 records.

There's nothing wrong with this code, but it's still a little troublesome. We've learned loop functions, and it's easy to think that there should be a loop function to solve this task. However, the loop function 100.(x) used to generate a new sequence can only return a sequence, which is not what we need.

SPL provides a loop function to return a new table sequence. The above code can be simplified into one statement:

	A
1	=100.new(string(~):name,if(rand()<0.5,"Male","Female"):sex,50+rand(50):weight,1.5+rand(40)/100:height)

It's a little long, so it's written in two lines. The statements related to structured data are often very long. This is also the advantage of using a cell to write code. It won't let too long code in a cell to write out of the cell and affect the code reading on the right and below.

Similar to A.(x) returning a sequence with the same length as A, A.new(…) will return a table sequence with the same number of records as A.len(). It also generates a record for each member of A, and these records will form a table sequence and return.

The new() function is a little different in the way the parameters are written.

It is obvious that each field is separated by a comma. The calculation formula of the field value is before the colon and the field name is after the colon. Is this colon a special provision of the new() function?

Yes, and no.

After we are dealing with structured data, we often face more complex function parameters. For example, to execute the new() function correctly, we need to know the value calculation formula and field name of each field in the table sequence to be generated, and the field value calculation formula and field name are a pair and cannot be misplaced. With the current new() function, the field value formula and field name are always a group of two. If we still use the comma separated writing method, we can still use the position of the parameter to determine the corresponding relationship, but it already looks dizzy. If the number of parameters in each group is uncertain, there is no way to correspond at all. In fact, the new() function does allow that field names are omitted. In many cases, it can automatically identify a reasonable field name. If the field names are to be written every time, it will be very troublesome.

In this case, one way is to use the set as a parameter. For example, this new function can be written as:

```
=100.new({string(~),name},{if(rand()<0.5,"Male","Female"),sex},
{50+rand(50),weight},{1.5+rand(40)/100,height})
```

The parameters here are divided into four groups. Each field is a group, and each group has two members, namely, the calculation formula and the field name. In this way, the corresponding relationship between parameters can be described clearly. If the field name is not written, the result is that a group has only one member and will not be misaligned with the parameters of other groups.

This is the concept of **multi-level parameters.** The parameters written in the function should be divided into multi-level groups to ensure a clear description of the corresponding relationship between these parameters.

Theoretically, there may be more levels, so {} may be nested, which still looks a little messy.

SPL does not adopt the writing method of nested {}, but the convention only supports three-level parameters, separated by semicolons, commas and colons respectively. Semicolons are the first level. The semicolon-separated parameter is a group. If there are lower-level parameters in this group, they are separated by commas, and the next-level parameters are separated by colons. There are three levels in total.

Practice shows that three levels are basically enough, and there is rarely any parameter relationship that cannot be described clearly with this method. While using commas only is often ambiguous.

In fact, we have seen semicolons when we talked about the top() function, but we haven't analyzed them carefully.

Multi-level parameter syntax is also the invention of SPL. It is not designed only for structured data calculation. It will also be involved in conventional numerical operations, but it often appears due to the complexity of structured data processing.

If you have learned SQL, you can compare it. Each part of SQL separated by keywords can also be understood as multi-level parameters. Only that pretending to be English will have better readability, but its universality is much worse. You should select special keywords for each statement. The complexity of structured data will force multi-level parameters to appear (in different forms).

After understanding the multi-level parameters, the new() function above is easy to understand. The colon is indeed required for the new() function parameters, because it has two levels of parameters, but it is not deliberately specified for the new() function, but a general rule in SPL.

The insert() function of the table sequence also has multi-level parameters. Field names can be specified during insertion. Fields not listed in the parameters will be filled with null after insertion.

For example, we need to add 100 records just created with the new function to the previous table sequence with 4 manual records, but only fill in weight and height, and let the others be null.

	A	B	C	D
...	...	...	...	...
5	=create(name,sex,weight,height)		=A5.record([A1:D4])	
6	for 100	>A5.insert(0,50+rand(50):weight,1.5+rand(40)/100:height)		

In practice, structured data often has many fields, and it will be more troublesome if the default writing method is not allowed.

Similar to the sequence, the insert() of the table sequence can also insert multiple records in batch at one time:

	A	B	C	D
...	...	...	...	...
5	=create(name,sex,weight,height)		=A5.record([A1:D4])	
6	>A5.insert(0:100,50+rand(50):weight,1.5+rand(40)/100:height)			

Multi-level parameters can easily express various intentions in one pattern.

Now we have a table sequence with 100 records, and each record corresponds to one person. We want to get a new table sequence with one more field to store the BMI of each person.

With the new() function, it is easy:

	A
1	=100.new(string(~):name,if(rand()<0.5,"Male","Female"):sex,50+rand(50):weight,1.5+rand(40)/100:height)
2	=A1.new(~.name:name,~.sex:sex,~.weight:weight,~.height:height,~.weight/~.height/~.height:bmi)

As a loop function, ~ in A1.new() is defined as the current member when the sequence loops, that is, a record of table sequence A1. Then we can use the syntax of ~.F to refer to the field of record ~.

However, A2 written in this way is a little long.

SPL stipulates that in the loop function of a table sequence or a record sequence, the field name can be directly used to refer to the field of the current member without writing ~., that is, name is ~.name, sex is ~.sex, ... Moreover, as we said earlier, the new() function can sometimes omit the field name, and it can be omitted when the current formula and the field name of the target table sequence are the same. In this way, A2 can be written as:

	A
1	...
2	=A1.new(name,sex,weight,height,weight/height/height:bmi)

This makes it look much clearer and less error prone.

This kind of appending fields to the end is very common in structured data processing. SPL simply provides a function to process, and the code can be simplified to:

	A
1	...
2	=A1.derive(weight/height/height:bmi)

The derive() function will append new fields based on the data structure of the original table sequence, and all the fields of the original table sequence will be copied.

It should be noted that the derive() function will create a new table sequence without changing the original table sequence. It will copy all the fields and values of the original table sequence, and the original table sequence is still there. In fact, the derive() function can be executed for a record sequence, not necessarily for a table sequence.

The new() function will of course create a new one, and it can even be executed for a sequence rather than a record sequence.

Now, we can restore the problem of merging Excel to the previous requirement: append the file name to the end.

	A
1	=directory@p("data/*.xlsx")
2	=A1.(file(~).xlsimport@t().derive(filename@n(A1.~):File))
3	>file("all.xlsx").xlsexport@t(A2.conj())

The statement is a little long, and we wrote one more line. Actually all actions can be written in one statement.

For the table sequence read out by each file, use the derive() function to append a File field to the end, and the value is the current file name. It should be noted that derive() is a loop function, and the ~ written directly in its expression refers to the current record of the table sequence (record sequence). Here, when adding a file name, we should use the upper layer ~, that is, A1.~.

8.4 Loop functions

Since record sequences (a table sequence is also a record sequence) can be regarded as sequences, we should also be able to use loop functions for these objects. We have used new() and derive(). Let's try the loop functions we learned before and continue to use the table sequence of 100 records created with new().

Calculate the average height, maximum weight and minimum BMI of these people.

	A	B
1	=100.new(string(~):name,if(rand()<0.5,"Male","Female"):sex,50+rand(50):weight,1.5+rand(40)/100:height)	
2	=A1.(height).avg()	=A1.avg(height)
3	=A1.(weight).max()	=A1.max(weight)
4	=A1.min(weight/height/height)	

Taking a record sequence as a sequence, the A.(x) operation can be performed normally. It is often used to get the sequence composed of values of a field. Structured data has multiple fields, so it is easy to form some expressions with business significance. Therefore, aggregation functions based on record sequence will often be calculated directly with an expression (B2, B3 and A4 here).

The selection function for structured data will also be more business meaningful than for conventional data.

Find the person with the largest weight and the person with the smallest BMI:

	A	B
1	...	
2	=A1.maxp(weight)	=A1.maxp@a(weight)
3	=A1.minp(weight/height/height)	

A2 only finds the first and return, and B2 uses @a to find all the records that maximize the weight.

This is often what we are more concerned about, that is, the record corresponding to the maximum and minimum value, rather than the maximum and minimum value itself.

The records selected by conditions can also perform various set operations, as well as further aggregation and selection operations:

	A	B
1	...	
2	=A1.select(height>=1.7)	=A1.select(sex=="Female")
3	=A2^B2	=A1.select(height>=1.7 && sex=="Female")
4	=A2\B2	=A1.select(height>=1.7 && sex!="Female")
5	=A2.maxp@a(weight)	=B2.minp(weight/height/height)
6	=A3.avg(height)	=A4.max(weight)

A2 selects the persons whose height is not less than 1.7 and B2 selects the females. A3 calculates the intersection of the two, B3 uses logical operation to express the same calculation result as A3. It is the similar case with A4 and B4. A5 and B5 do further selection to the selected record sequence, and A6 and B6 continue to do aggregation to the selected record sequence.

Sorting is also a common operation:

	A	B
1	...	
2	=A1.sort(height)	
3	=A1.select(sex=="Female")	=A3.sort(-weight)
4	=A1.sort(height,-weight)	
5	=A1.top(-3,weight)	=A1.top(-3;weight)
6	=A1.ranks(height)	=A1.derive(A6(#):hrank)

We know that the default sorting direction of the sort() function is from small to large, and we can use @z to reverse the order. However, when it comes to structured data, there are often multiple fields to sort, and the sorting directions of these parameters are different. In this case, there is no way to use only one @z to control. The method given by SPL is to write the parameters as opposite numbers (plus a negative sign), so that if we continue to sort from small to large, we will realize the reverse order of the original values. The method of writing negative signs into opposite numbers is also applicable to string and date time data.

In this way, A2 sorts by height from low to high, and B3 sorts females by weight from large to small. A4 will sort by height from small to large first, and those with the same height will be sorted by weight from large to small.

Using negative numbers in the top() function is another way to represent the reverse order, which is equivalent to getting the last few after sorting (if positive numbers, the first few). A5 and B5 will calculate the three largest weights and the three individuals with largest weights respectively. The calculation result of A5 is a sequence composed of three numbers, while B5 returns a record sequence composed of three records. SPL also supports ranking function. A6's ranks function can calculate everyone's ranking by height.

We feel that using Male and Female to represent gender is too long. Just use one letter M and F. In the future, it will be shorter when writing comparative expressions. It can be done with the run() function.

	A
1	...
2	>A1.run(sex=left(sex,1))

When using the loop function to assign a value to a field, we can also directly use the field name to represent the field of the current record instead of writing as ~.sex.

derive() can be used to append fields to generate a new table sequence. Sometimes we need to append multiple fields, and the field to be appended later needs to be calculated from the field to be appended first. For example, we need to add a BMI field, and then add a flag field for obesity according to the value of BMI. With derive(), it will be written as follows:

	A
1	...
2	=A1.derive(weight/height/height:bmi)
3	=A2.derive(if(bmi>25,"FAT","OK"):flag)

However, the calculation of derive() is very complex. It needs to create new records and table sequence and copy the original data. The performance is poor. In principle, it should be used as little as possible. A better way is to use derive() and run() to complete the task:

	A
1	...
2	=A1.derive(weight/height/height:bmi,:flag)
3	=A2.run(flag =if(bmi>25,"FAT","OK"))

Append both fields at one time in A2, and then use run() in A3 to calculate the value of flag field. The derive() function is executed only once, and the actions of creating and copying table sequence are reduced, and the operation performance can be improved a lot.

From these examples, we can realize once again that multiple fields of structured data are easy to form many calculation expressions with business significance. There are many operations on field expressions in loop functions, but they are relatively uncommon in single value sequence calculation.

Combined with the functions of reading and writing Excel files, we can now use program code to merge, filter, add calculation results, sort and perform other operations on a batch of Excel files.

Similar to the loop function of a sequence, the record sequence will also have multi-layer nesting.

For example, we want to calculate the minimum height difference between males and females in this group:

	A	B
1	...	
2	=A1.select(sex=="Male")	=A1.select(sex=="Female")
3	=A2.min(B2.min(abs(height–A2.height)))	

When the inner layer needs to reference the record field of the outer loop, the corresponding variable name of the outer loop function should also be written to represent the current record, still it is not necessary to write ~.

To find out which pairs of male and female make the minimum height difference true, it is more troublesome.

	A	B
1	...	
2	=A1.select(sex=="Male")	=A1.select(sex=="Female")
3	=A2.conj(B2.([A2.~,~]))	=A3.minp@a(abs(~(1).height-~(2).height))

Here, we need to use ~ to keep the record, form a male and female pair, and then find it with the selection function. A3 in B3 is no longer a record sequence, and it is meaningless to reference field names if ~ is omitted.

The members of a record sequence are records with multiple fields, and the information content is relatively rich. The result obtained by the selection function is also a record sequence composed of these records. Therefore, the information contained in the position returned by positioning functions such as pselect, pmax and pmin is seldom needed, but the position still needs to be obtained when it comes to order related calculations.

Now let's discuss the loop functions related to order and regenerate a date related table sequence.

	A
1	=100.new(date(now())-100+~:dt,rand()*100:price)
2	=A1.select(day@w(dt)>1 && day@w(dt)<7)

Randomly generate a price table of a stock from 100 days ago to today. dt field is the date and price field is the price. Because there is no transaction on weekends, filter out the weekend dates after generating the data, and use this A2 in the future. The day@w() function returns the weekday of a date, but note that its return value is 1 on Sunday and 7 on Saturday. For historical reasons, the computer system uses the habit of Westerners. Sunday is the first day of the week.

First, we want to calculate the daily increase and moving average price:

	A
...	...
3	=A2.derive(price-price[-1]:gain)
4	=A2.derive(price[-1:1].avg():mavg)

In the loop functions of a record sequence, we can add [±i] after the field to refer to the field of an adjacent record, and add [a:b] to refer to the sequence composed of the field values of adjacent records. These are the same as the loop functions of the sequence.

Calculate the maximum consecutive rising days of this stock:

	A
...	...
3	=0
4	=A2.(if(price>price[-1],A3+=1,A3=0)).max()

According to natural thinking, first fill in 0, add 1 if it rises one day, and clear to 0 if it does not rise. We can calculate the days of continuous rise to one day, and then get the maximum value.

Calculate the increase on the day when the stock price is the highest:

	A
...	...
3	=A2.pmax(price)
4	=A2(A3).price-A2.m(A3-1).price

Here, use the positioning function pmax() to calculate the sequence number where the maximum value is located, and then use this sequence number to calculate the increase. If we need to consider that the highest price may appear on multiple dates, use the @a option.

	A
...	...
3	=A2.pmax@a(price)
4	=A3.new(A2(~).dt,A2(~).price-A2.m(~-1).price:gain)

First calculate the sequence composed of the record sequence numbers where the maximum value is located, and then generate a two field sequence with new() based on this sequence, taking the date and gain as the fields. In this case, new() can also omit the field name. You can see what the field names of the generated table sequence will be.

Similarly, calculate the average increase on the days when the stock price exceeds 90 yuan:

	A
...	...
3	=A2.pselect@a(price>90)
4	=A3.new(A2(~).dt,A2(~).price-A2.m(~-1).price:gain)

For this cross-row calculation for a certain position, SPL provides a positioning calculation function. The previous code can also be written as follows:

	A
...	...
3	=A2.pmax(price)
4	=A2.calc(A3,price-price[-1])

The positioning calculation function calc() allows the syntax of ~, #, [] and so on in the loop function to be used in the non loop function.

	A
...	...
3	=A2.pmax@a(price)
4	=A2.calc(A3,price-price[-1])
5	=A3.new(A2(~).dt,A4(#):gain)

The calc() function can also be used for sequences, but there are few business-meaningful scenarios when structured data is not involved, so we give some examples here.

8.5 Calculations on the fields

As we said earlier, the ability of structured data in row and column directions is asymmetric. Convenient batch operations are usually only provided for row direction, and columns always appear as independent individuals. However, we also need to perform some overall operations in the column direction sometimes, that is, to process a batch of fields together as a set.

Let's do the problem of merging Excel again. Change the requirement to: spell the file name in front of all columns.

The derive() function can only append fields to the end. To change the order of fields, we can only recreate with new() function for the present, and we need to know what fields are already in the table sequence and copy them again.

The fname() function can return a sequence of field names in the table sequence, that is, a sequence of strings. But this is not enough. Even if we concatenate the new field to the front, we still don't know how to write this new() function, such as the following code:

	A
1	=10.new(rand(10):a,rand(20):b,rand(30):c)
2	=A1.fname()
3	=A1.new(0:NewField, A2)

A1 is a table sequence, A2 gets its field name sequence, but A3 is meaningless. SPL will generate a field named A2, and its value is the current cell value of A2, that is, the field name sequence of A1. When SPL executes here, it does not know to concatenate the value of A2 into this code, but will execute the two characters A and 2 as part of the code.

What should we do?

SPL provides the syntax of dynamic program. The above code is written as follows, and it can be executed correctly:

	A
1	=10.new(rand(10):a,rand(20):b,rand(30):c)
2	=A1.fname().concat(",")
3	=A1.new(0:NewField, ${A2})

We have used the concat() function. It will concatenate a string sequence with the specified separator, and here we use commas. Here A1 has three fields a,b,c, and the calculation result of A2 is the string "a,b,c".

The meaning of ${} in A3 is to tell SPL to calculate the expression in braces (it will be a string), then spell the string as part of the statement, and then execute it. A2 is now "a,b,c", ${A2} will spell this string into the statement in A3. As a result, the actual statement to be executed by A3 is

    =A1.new(0:NewField, a,b,c)

That's what we want.

The syntax of ${} is called a **macro**. Using macros, we can dynamically spell some code to execute, and achieve a very flexible operation effect. Calculations related to uncertain number fields often use macros.

Using macros, we can solve the problem of spelling the file name to the front in merging Excel:

	A	B
1	=directory@p("data/*.xlsx")	
2	for A1	=file(A2).xlsimport@t()
3		=B2.new(filename@n(A2):File,${B2.fname().concat@c()})
4		=@|B3
5	=file("all.xlsx").xlsexport@t(B4)	

concat@c() means to separate by commas. A calculation expression can be written in ${} as long as the calculation result is a string.

Using macros, we can easily generate the student score table:

	A
1	[English,Maths,Science,Arts,PE]
2	=A1.("rand(100):"+~).concat@c()
3	=100.new(string(~,"0000"):id, ${A2})

The calculation result of A2 will be a string:

"rand(100):Engligh,rand(100):Maths,rand(100):Science,rand(100):Arts,rand(100):PE"

After spelling into A3, we will get a score table of 100 students, and the id field is the student number of the student.

Now we want to calculate a total score field Total for each student and append it to the end.

	A
...	...
4	=A3.derive(English+Maths+Science+Arts+PE:Total)

Of course, it's OK, but if there are many subjects, it's hard to write.

SPL provides a method to convert record fields into a sequence, and it is much more convenient when field values need to be processed in batch:

	A
...	...
4	=A3.derive(~.array().to(2,).sum():Total)

r.array() gets the field values of record r to form a sequence and return. In this way, no matter how many subjects, the code is like this. It should be noted that since the data types of each field value may be different, the return value of array() may not be a sequence composed of members of the same data type.

With macros, we can also complete more complex tasks.

All of the Excel files we have previously processed are in row format. However, just as we talked about the concept of structured data, many Excel files storing structured data are not in row format, such as:

	A	B	C	D	E	F
1	ID:		1			
2	Name:		Yin Zhang	Sex	F	
3	Position		Sales			
4	Birthday		1968-12-08			
5	Phone:			(010) 65559857		
7	Address:		No. 236 of Fuxingmen Beijing			
8	PostCode:		100098			

(This is part of the previous example. There is only one record to simplify the problem.)

Suppose there are a batch of such files, each file stores a person's information. Now we hope to extract these data and make a row table, using the field names in this table: ID, name, sex, postion, birthday, phone, address, postcode.

If there are hundreds of such files, it will obviously be too tiring to do it manually. We use a program to do it.

To do this, we also need to use two Excel related functions xlsopen() and xlscell().

xlsopen() can open an Excel file to form an Excel object, and xlscell() can read the content of a cell from the Excel object. With them, we can finish the work.

	A	B	C
1	=create(ID,Name,Sex,Postion,Birthday,Phone,Address,PostCode)		
2	=directory@p("data/*.xlsx")		
3	for A2	=file(A3).xlsopen()	
4		=B3.xlscell("C1")	=B3.xlscell("C2")
5		=B3.xlscell("F2")	=B3.xlscell("C3")
6		=B3.xlscell("C4")	=B3.xlscell("D5")
7		=B3.xlscell("C7")	=B3.xlscell("C8")
8		=A1.insert(0,B4,C4,B5,C5,B6,C6,B7,C7)	
9	>file("all.xlsx").xlsexport@t(A1)		

The code logic is not complex, and we will not explain it in detail.

However, it is still a little troublesome to write, and if the table style and data structure change, it needs to be changed a lot.

We use macros and loop functions to simplify it.

	A	B	C
1	[ID,Name,Sex,Postion,Birthday,Phone,Address,PostCode]		
2	[C1,C2,F2,C3,C4,D5,C7,C8]		
3	=directory@p("data/*.xlsx")		
4	for A3	=file(A4).xlsopen()	=B2.(B4.xlscell(~))
5		=@|C4	
6	=create(${A1.concat@c()}).record(B5)		
7	>file("all.xlsx").xlsexport@t(A6)		

The fields and corresponding cells are made into two sequences, and it is much easier to get data from each Excel file and do concatenation. The code is not only shorter, but also more general. If we encounter a new format, just modify the first two lines.

101

Conversely, we may use the data of a row table to generate multiple such free-style Excel. Obviously, doing it manually will be very tiring.

We still use a program to complete this task. We need to learn a little more knowledge: the xlscell() function can also fill data into a cell of an Excel object; and then learn an xlswrite() function, which can write the processed Excel object into a file.

	A	B	C
1	[ID,Name,Sex,Postion,Birthday,Phone,Address,PostCode]		
2	[C1,C2,F2,C3,C4,D5,C7,C8]		
3	=file("temp.xlsx").xlsopen()		
4	=file("all.xlsx").xlsimport@t()		
5	for A4	=A1.(A5.field(~))	>A2.(A3.xlscell(~;B5(#)))
6		=file(A5.ID/".xlsx").xlswrite(A3)	

First make a template Excel file in this format, read it into an Excel object, and then fill the relevant values into the Excel object for each record, and then write it into a file. Fill them in and write it out repeatedly, and it's done.

When doing artificial intelligence tasks, we often encounter the problem of filling in missing values, that is, filling in the missing data according to certain rules, such as mode (the most frequent of other non missing values) or average (calculated from other non missing values).

Let's try this task. Suppose data.xlsx stores the original data:

	A	B	C	D	E	F	G	H	I	J	K	L	M	N
1	CRIM	ZN	INDUS	CHAS	NOX	RM	AGE	DIS	RAD	TAX	PTRATIO	B	LSTAT	MEDV
27	0.84054	0	8.14	0	0.538	5.599	85.7	4.4546	4	307	21	303.42	16.51	13.9
28	0.67191	0	8.14	0	0.538	5.813	90.3	4.682	4	307	21	376.88	14.81	16.6
29	0.95577	0	8.14	0	0.538	6.047	88.8	4.4534	4	307	21	306.38	17.28	14.8
30	0.77299	0	8.14	0	0.538	6.495	94.4	4.4547	4	307	21	387.94	12.8	18.4
31	1.00245	0		0	0.538	6.674	87.3	4.239	4	307	21	380.23	11.98	21
32	1.13081	0	8.14	0	0.538	5.713	94.1	4.233	4	307	21	360.17	22.6	12.7
33	1.35472	0	8.14	0	0.538	6.072	100	4.175	4	307	21		13.04	14.5
34	1.38799	0	8.14	0	0.538	5.95	82	3.99	4	307	21	232.6	27.71	13.2
35	1.15172	0	8.14	0	0.538	5.701	95	3.7872	4	307	21	358.77	18.35	
36	1.61282	0	8.14	0		6.096			4	307	21	248.31	20.34	13.5
37	0.06417	0		0	0.499	5.933	68.2	3.3603	5		19.2	396.9	9.68	18.9
38	0.09744	0	5.96	0	0.499	5.841	61.4	3.3779	5	279	19.2	377.56	11.41	20
39		0	5.96	0	0.499	5.85	41.5	3.9342	5	279	19.2	396.9	8.77	21
40	0.17505	0	5.96	0	0.499	5.966	30.2	3.8473	5	279	19.2		10.13	24.7
41	0.02763	75	2.95	0	0.428		21.8	5.4011	3	252	18.3	395.63	4.32	30.8
42	0.03359	75	2.95	0	0.428	7.024	15.8	5.4011	3	252	18.3	395.62	1.98	34.9
43	0.12744	0	6.91	0	0.448	6.77	2.9	5.7209	3	233	17.9	385.41		26.6
44	0.1415	0	6.91	0	0.448	6.169	6.6	5.7209	3	233	17.9	383.37	5.81	25.3
45	0.15936	0	6.91	0	0.448	6.211	6.5	5.7209	3	233	17.9	394.46	7.44	24.7
46	0.12269	0	6.91	0	0.448	6.069	40	5.7209	3	233	17.9	389.39	9.55	21.2
47	0.17142	0	6.91		0.448	5.682	33.8	5.1004	3		17.9	396.9	10.21	19.3
48	0.18836	0	6.91	0	0.448	5.786	33.3	5.1004	3	233	17.9	396.9	14.15	20
49	0.22927	0	6.91	0	0.448	6.03	85.5	5.6894	3	233	17.9	392.74	18.8	16.6
50	0.25387	0	6.91	0	0.448	5.399	95.3	5.87	3	233	17.9	396.9	30.81	14.4
51	0.21977	0	6.91	0	0.448	5.602	62	6.0877	3	233	17.9	396.9	16.2	19.4

The blank part indicates missing. Our rule is: if this column is an integer, fill it with the mode scheme; If it is a floating-point number, it is filled with the average scheme.

	A	B	C
1	=file("data.xlsx").xlsimport@t()		
2	for A1.fname()	=A1.field(A2)	
3		=B2.sum()	=B2.sum(int(~))
4		=if(B3==C3,B2.mode(),B2.avg())	
5		=B2.(if(~,~,B4))	>A1.field(A2,B5)
6	>file("dataNew.xlsx").xlsexport@t(A1)		

Read the data into table sequence A1, A2 loops through each field. The field() function in B2 will get all the values of a certain field of all records to form a sequence. It is a bit like A1.(x), but the difference is that the parameter of the field() function here is a string, while x in A1.(x) is a field name. If it is written in A1.(x), a macro needs to be used and it should be written as A1.(${A2}).

Calculate the sum of the whole column, compare it with the sum of the integerized members, if it is equal, it can be regarded as all integers, then execute the mode scheme, otherwise execute the average scheme. The mode() function can return the mode of the sequence.

Then calculate the field value sequence after filling in the missing values in B5. The field() function can also fill the sequence into the field. Here, it can also be written as A1.run(${A2}=B5(#)) in macro, but it is obviously clearer and simpler using the field() function.

9 GROUPING

9.1 Grouping and aggregation

When there are many things, people will be used to divide these things into several categories according to their attributes, and then investigate some aggregate information of each category. This operation is called **grouping** on structured data. The specific action of grouping is: divide the records in a data table into several small sets according to a field, and those with the same field values are divided into the same small set, which is called a **grouped subset** or a **group**, and then calculate some statistical values of each group of records to study the pattern of these data.

For example, in the previously generated personnel table, we can calculate the average height and maximum weight by gender.

	A
1	=100.new(string(~):name,if(rand()<0.5,"Male","Female"):sex,50+rand(50):weight,1.5+rand(40)/100:height)
2	=A1.groups(sex;avg(height):avg_height,max(weight):max_height)

The groups() function can implement the above actions. Here, the multi-level parameters are also used. Before the semicolon is the field used for grouping, and here is sex; After the semicolon are the aggregate operations to be done. There are two of them, average height and maximum weight, separated by comma.

The return value of the groups() function is a table sequence, which takes the field used for grouping and the aggregate expressions as the data structure; Because the returned is a table sequence, the field names need to be set. Write them after each parameter of the groups() function, separated by a colon. For the record sequence to be grouped, the number of records in the returned table sequence depends on the number of values of the grouping field, and they are exactly the same.

Index	sex	avg_height	max_height
1	Female	1.7115517241379308	99
2	Male	1.5642857142857148	98

(Because the data is generated randomly, the statistical values will change every time, and they are not in line with common sense. But it does not affect understanding.)

The aggregate operation in the second half of the groups function cannot be written casually. It can only support several aggregate functions made in advance. There are five common aggregate operations: sum, count, avg, max and min. Writing these operations in the parameters is equivalent to executing the aggregate functions for these subsets (also a record sequence).

Aggregation can also be done for an expression, such as:

	A
1	...
2	=A1.groups(sex;min(weight/height/height):min_bmi)

It is not necessarily to do grouping by field, but also by the result calculated by field.

	A
1	=100.new(date(now())-100+~:dt,rand()*100:price)
2	=A1.select(day@w(dt)>1 && day@w(dt)<7)
3	=A2.groups(day@w(dt)-1:wday;min(price):min_p,max(price):max_p)

Group and aggregate the stock data, and calculate the highest and lowest stock prices of all Mondays, Tuesdays,... and Fridays. The calculation results are 5 records (weekends have been excluded).

For the grouping field or expression, we have a term called **grouping key**. We will understand why we use the word "key" when we've learned the later content.

There can also be multiple grouping keys:

	A
1	=1000.new(date(now())-1000+~:dt,rand()*100:price)
2	=A1.select(day@w(dt)>1 && day@w(dt)<7)
3	=A2.groups(month(dt):m,day@w(dt)-1:wd;avg(price):price)

A3 can calculate the average stock price on each weekday of each month. When there are multiple grouping expressions, the data table will be split in more detail, and the number of groups will roughly be the same as the product of the number of value types of these grouping keys. For example, the above operation will divide into 12*5=60 groups, because there are 12 types of months and 5 types of weekdays (excluding weekends). The returned table sequence has 60 records.

However, this is not absolute. Because in this set of data, there are data on any weekday in any month, these 60 groups will all have corresponding aggregate data. Sometimes the data is incomplete, and some groups will no longer exist. For example, we do a sampling in A2, randomly getting 100 records and then observe the grouping results (we learned how to sample before) to see whether there are always 60 records in the returned table sequence. Please try it yourself.

Because there may be multiple grouping keys, the groups function uses a higher-level semicolon to separate the expression used for grouping keys and the expression used for aggregation in the parameters. Here you can experience the convenience of multi-level parameters.

In fact, group aggregation can also be done without grouping key at all.

	A
1	...
2	=A1.groups(;min(weight/height/height):min_bmi)

This means that all members are divided into one set, that is, no splitting. For this whole set, calculate some aggregate values, and the returned table sequence has only one record.

However, this operation is not common because it can be done directly with aggregate functions.

Similarly, group aggregation can also have no aggegate value part:

	A
1	...
2	...
3	=A2.groups(month(dt):m,day@w(dt)-1:wd)

A3 will calculate the months and weekdays when these stock transactions occur (we can try the results by reducing the amount of data with sampling we just mentioned), that is, we only care about the groups that can be divided, not the aggregate value of each group.

This is a common operation. It will calculate the possible values for grouping keys in a data table and list all the possible values without repetition. The database industry has a special name for this operation, which is called getting the **DISTINCT** values.

SPL also gives a function id() to calculate DISTINCT.

	A
1	...
2	...
3	=A2.groups(month(dt):m)
4	=A2.id(month(dt))

Different from the groups() function that returns a table sequence, id() returns a sequence that has no data structure and no field name parameter.

The id() function with multiple parameters does not calculate DISTINCT for multiple grouping keys, but calculates multiple groups of DISTINCT values respectively. If we want to calculate the DISTINCT values for the combined multiple grouping keys, we need to use a sequence expression.

	A
1	...
2	...
3	=A2.groups(month(dt):m,day@w(dt)-1:wd)
4	=A2.id(month(dt),day@w(dt)-1)
5	=A2.id([month(dt),day@w(dt)-1])

You can observe the return results of A3, A4 and A5, especially the length of these return values (as table sequence or sequence).

Again, it's easier to see the difference by sampling the data and then executing these codes.

Now give us some Excel files, and we can already make various classification statistics on the data in them. For example, we have used this data for many times:

	A	B	C	D	E	F
1	ID	Company	Area	OrderDate	Amount	Phone
2	10248	Shantai	North	2012-07-04	428	(030) 26471510
3	10249	Dongdiwar	East	2012-07-05	1842	(0251) 1031259
4	10250	Shiyi	North	2012-07-08	1523.5	(0211) 5550091
5	10251	Qiangu	East	2012-07-08	624.95	(071) 8325486
6	10252	Fuxing	West	2012-07-09	3559.5	(030) 23672220
7	10253	Shiyi	North	2012-07-10	1428	(0211) 5550091
8	10254	Haotian	Center	2012-07-11	545.4	(030) 30076545
9	10255	Yongda	North	2012-07-12	2450	(089) 7034214

It is very easy to calculate sales amount and order quantity by area or month:

	A
1	=T("data.xlsx")
2	=A1.groups(Area;sum(Amount),count(Amount))
3	=A2.groups(month@y(OrderDate);sum(Amount),count(Amount))

file(…).xlsimport@t() can be simplified into a T() function. Note that SPL is a case sensitive language, and the field names should be written correctly.

It's easy to calculate the companies that have done business with:

	A
1	=T("data.xlsx")
2	=A1.id(Company)

DISTINCT lets us know that there are groups that do not need to be summarized. In fact, there are groups that should not be summarized.

For example, in a group of people, we want to know who has the same birthday as others. It's very simple, after grouping by birthday, just see which groups have more than one member. However, the groups() function will force a summary action, and we will lose those divided groups.

Grouping is not always forced to summarize. Sometimes we are also interested in the subset after grouping. In fact, the word grouping has only the meaning of splitting in the dictionary, and does not continue to summarize. Because this operation was invented by SQL, and the set data type of SQL is relatively weak, it is unable to maintain the intermediate results of grouping, so a summary is forced. Over time, the whole industry felt that grouping must be accompanied by summary, and forgot the original intention of grouping.

SPL restores this operation. The group() function without s just group without summary. The s in the name of groups() function means summary.

	A
1	=200.new(string(~):ID, date(now())-10000+rand(3000):Birthday)
2	=A1.group(month(Birthday),day(Birthday))
3	=A2.select(~.len()>1).conj()

Randomly generating the birthdays of 200 people, and then group by birthday (not counting years). The group() function returns the divided groups, that is, a sequence composed of some record sequences, which is equivalent to a two-layer sequence. Then, we just need to see which group has more than one member, and this is the syntax we have learned. Finally, concatenate these groups.

Grouping without summary has practical business significance. Finding someone with the same birthday is just a game. Let's take another practical example, for the previous Excel file, we want to split it into multiple files according to the Area field for different managers to deal with.

It is reasonable to use grouping operation to split it, but obviously we can't summarize any more.

	A	B
1	=T("data.xlsx")	=A1.group(Area)
2	for B1	>T(A2.Area/".xlsx",A2)

T() function can also write a record sequence directly into an Excel file. After grouping by Area, write each group into a corresponding file. A2.Area is the abbreviation of A2(1).Area. According to the SPL convention, getting a field from a record sequence is equivalent to getting a field from its first member.

Sometimes, even if we want to get an aggregation result of the grouped subset, it is not easy to calculate, and there is no simple aggregation function to use. In this case, we also need to keep the grouped subsets for further calculation.

For example, we want to group the personnel table by gender, concatenate the names (now some number strings) of people of the same gender into a comma separated string. This is indeed an aggregation result, but SPL does not have such an aggregation function, it can be written with an expression:

	A
1	=100.new(string(~):name,if(rand()<0.5,"Male","Female"):sex,50+rand(50):weight,1.5+rand(40)/100:height)
2	=A1.group(sex).new(~.sex,~.(name).concat@c():Names)

Just do new() for the subset sequence after grouping.

This operation is common. SPL also allows it to be simplified into the parameters of the group() function:

	A
1	...
2	=A1.group(sex;~.(name).concat@c():Names)

Note that this is easily confused with groups(). The calculation after the semicolon of group() is equivalent to a simplified new(), and we need to write ~ to represent a grouped subset. But we don't need to write ~ in groups(). In fact, its calculation method is different. It doesnot calculate the subset first and then calculate the summary value.

As mentioned earlier, there are five common aggregate operations. SPL also provides other aggregate functions that can be used in grouping and aggregation, but most of them do not need to be specifically mentioned. You can check the documents when necessary. There is only one icount() to mention here.

icount(x) returns the number of DISTINCT values of x in each group. This is roughly equivalent to another grouping in the group, but the inner grouping only counts and does not do other summaries.

For example, we want to calculate how many companies each area has done business with:

	A
1	=T("data.xlsx")
2	=A1.groups(Area;icount(Company))

If you understand the iterative function mentioned earlier, SPL also allows you to spell out new grouping and summary operations. Moreover, after fully understanding the iterative function, you will also realize that groups()

and group() use different methods in calculating the summary value. Groups() use the iterative function method to calculate the summary value, and each grouping subset will not be maintained in the process, which will be more efficient and use less memory. This is also the main reason why groups() is designed separately (its syntax is sometimes slightly simpler than group(), but it is only a secondary reason).

In addition, grouping operation is not only valid for structured data, but also for numerical or string sequences.

	A
1	=100.(rand(100)).groups(~%2;sum(~))
2	=directory("*.*").group(filename@e(~))

A1 will group integers by parity and calculate the sum of each group; A2 divides the file names under the path into several groups according to the extension.

However, grouping for sequences is relatively uncommon, so we talk about this operation in the structured data section.

9.2 Enumeration and alignment

Members with equal grouping keys are divided into a group, which is called **equivalence grouping**. Equivalence grouping meets the following two characteristics:

1) All members of the original set are in and only in a unique group;

2) No group is empty;

Grouping satisfying these characteristics is also called **complete partition** in mathematics.

Then is there an incomplete partition?

Yes, the two requirements of complete partition may not be satisfied. For example, there may be an empty subset in the result, or some members of the original set may not be in any group or in multiple groups.

In this section, we will talk about this kind of grouping.

We have made statistics on grouping personnel table by gender. Generally speaking, we expect the returned table sequence to have two records, that is, one for male and one for female, and even ensure the order, so that we can know exactly which record to use to obtain the summary result of male or female.

However, equivalence grouping can not guarantee this result.

Because there are not necessarily two genders in this personnel table. If there is only one gender, there is only one record in the returned table sequence. In this case, we must compare again to know whether this record is male or female.

This is very inconvenient. We want to make sure that there are two records returned, and the order is also determined. If there is only one gender in the data to be grouped, let the summary value of the other gender be 0.

This kind of grouping is called **alignment grouping**. It is not completely divided because empty set may appear.

	A
1	=100.new(string(~):name,if(rand()<0.5,"Male","Female"):sex,50+rand(50):weight,1.5+rand(40)/100:height)
2	[Male,Female]
3	=A1.align@a(A2,sex)
4	=A3.new(A2(#):sex,~.avg(height):avg_height,~.max(weight):max_height)

Before alignment grouping, there need to be a criterion sequence, such as A2 here. The align@a function in A3 divides the set to be grouped (A1) into several subsets, and the grouping key of each subset corresponds to the criterion sequence members one by one, that is, the records(members of the sequence to be grouped) with the same grouping key value as the criterion sequence member are divided into the same group, so that the number and order of the obtained grouping subsets are determined by the criterion sequence. If a criterion sequence member does not correspond to the grouping key value of any sequence member to be grouped, it will correspond to an empty subset.

With the grouped subset sequence, it is very easy to calculate the table sequence composed of grouping key values and summary values. Note that for the new() function in A4, A2(#) should be used to obtain the grouping key value, because some grouped subset may be empty and this information cannot be obtained from the grouped subsets.

SPL only provides the method of generating grouped subsets, and does not further provide simplified functions to calculate the summary values at one time. On the one hand, it is not difficult to write. On the other hand, alignment grouping is less commonly used than equivalence grouping.

Let's take another example: in the previous order data, we want to calculate the sales amount by month in the last two years, regardless of whether there are no orders in a certain month or not.

	A
1	=T("data.xlsx")
2	=to(202001,202012)|to(202101,202112)
3	=A1.align@a(A2,month@y(OrderDate))
4	=A3.new(A2(#):ym,~.sum(Amount),~.count(Amount))

In this grouping, not only empty sets may appear, but also some records of the original set may not be divided into any subset (those orders that are not in the past two years).

Careful readers may find that the align() function has an option @a, so what is the operation when there is no option?

It is used for sorting.

Similar to alignment grouping, we sometimes need to arrange a batch of data in the order we want, rather than the conventional alphabetic or coding order.

In this order table, we want to calculate sales amount by region, but the results should be arranged in the order of East, West, North, South, Center. Of course, we can use align@a that we just learned.

	A
1	=T("data.xlsx")
2	[East,West,North,South,Center]
3	=A1.align@a(A2,Area)
4	=A3.new(A2(#):Area,~.sum(Amount),~.count(Amount))

If we know for certain that there is at most one item in each group, we can write it in another way:

	A
1	=T("data.xlsx")
2	[East,West,North,South,Center]
3	=A1.groups(Area;sum(Amount),count(Amount))
4	=A3.align(A2,Area)

In the table sequence obtained after group aggregation in A3, there is at most one record (maybe no record) in each region. The align() function without option can rearrange these records in A2 order.

Aligned sorting is more common than alignment grouping. People have many conventional fixed sorting orders. For example, China's provincial rankings usually rank Beijing first, rather than Anhui first according to the unicode order. Americans do not have such a fixed notion of sorting regions, but they also have conventions such as Sunday, Monday, Tuesday,... and Low, Medium, High that cannot be sorted directly in alphabetic order.

There is also a very common alignment grouping. The grouping key values are positive integers starting from 1, and the target order is to arrange the numbers from small to large. For example, the months are numbers 1-12, and weekdays are also integers of 1-7. This situation is also called **serial number grouping**. SPL provides an option @n to support serial number grouping in the group() and groups() functions.

	A
1	=T("data.xlsx")
2	=A1.groups@n(month(OrderDate):M;sum(Amount),count(Amount))

When used, it is very similar to groups() without @n, but it is an alignment grouping, allowing the generation of emplty sets. If the grouping key value is less than 1, it will also be discarded. Try the stock data we generated earlier:

	A
1	=100.new(now()-100+~:dt,rand()*100:price)
2	=A1.select(day@w(dt)>1 && day@w(dt)<7)
3	=A2.groups@n(day@w(dt):wday;min(price):min_p,max(price):max_p)

The table sequence returned by A3 will have 6 records, of which the first one corresponds to the grouped subset of Sunday is an empty set (its grouping key value should be 1), because the data of Sunday has been filtered out in A2, and the largest grouping key value in the remaining data is 6 (Saturday data has been filtered out, and 7 cannot be calculated out), so the result table sequence has 6 records. The first record corresponds to an empty grouped subset, and both aggregation fields are null, but the grouping key value field still has a value.

The grouping key value here does not decrease by 1, and will be 2,..., 6, corresponding to Monday,..., Friday, which is different from the previous calculation result.

We can also change this to subtract 1 from the grouping key.

	A
1	=100.new(now()-100+~:dt,rand()*100:price)
2	=A1.select(day@w(dt)<7)
3	=A2.groups@n(day@w(dt)-1:wday;min(price):min_p,max(price):max_p)

Only Saturday data is filtered out in A2, and the grouping key value is subtracted by 1 when grouping in A3, thus the grouping key value of Sunday data will be calculated as 0 and discarded. A3 will calculate 5 records (without Saturday data, the maximum is 5), and this is the same result as before.

It can be seen from these two examples that serial number grouping is not an ordinary grouping with serial number as the grouping key value. Its behavior is more like alignment grouping. Empty sets may appear and members without corresponding grouping subset will be discarded.

The effect of using @n for group() is similar to that of groups(), and we won't elaborate here.

Another advantage of serial number grouping is fast calculation speed, because the correct grouping subset can be found directly with serial number without comparison operation.

In addition to regular alignment grouping, conditional grouping will also occur, and the most common is grouping by segment. For example, people are divided into several groups according to age, or orders are divided into different groups according to amount.

For example, we divide the previous personnel table into four groups according to BMI value: <20, UnderWeight; 20-25, Normal; 25-30: OverWeight; >30, Obesity. Then calculate the average height of each group.

	A
1	=100.new(string(~):name,if(rand()<0.5,"Male","Female"):sex,50+rand(50):weight,1.5+rand(40)/100:height)
2	[?<20,?>=20 && ?<25,?>=25 && ?<30,?>=30]
3	[UnderWeight,Normal,OverWeight,Fat]
4	=A1.enum(A2,weight/height/height)
5	=A4.new(A3(#):Grade,~.avg(height):avg_height)

The conditions of different levels are written into strings to form a sequence, in which ? represents the grouping key value to be substituted into the calculation. The enum() function will use the grouping key of each member in the set to be grouped to calculate these conditions in turn. If it gets true, the member will be divided into the corresponding group. The final grouping subsets will also correspond to these criterion conditions in quantity and order.

This grouping is called **enumeration grouping**. Obviously, enumeration grouping may also get empty sets, and some members may not be divided into any groups.

Similarly, SPL only provides the enum() function to return the grouped subsets. To get the summary value, we need to further calculate it ourselves. Unlike alignment grouping, enumeration grouping usually has another sequence to identify the name of each group (A3 here).

Because segment grouping is very common, this case can also be converted into serial number grouping with the pseg() function described earlier, which is simpler to write and faster to execute.

	A
1	...
2	[20,25,30]
3	[UnderWeight,Normal,OverWeight,Fat]
4	=A1.group@n(A2.pseg(weight/height/height)+1)
5	=A4.new(A3(#):Grade,~.avg(height):avg_height)

group@n() is used here to calculate the grouped subsets first. Because the pseg() function will return 0 for the case that is less than the first member, it needs to add 1 as the grouping key value, otherwise this segment will be discarded.

It is also OK to calculate the summary value directly with groups(), but we need another step to fill in the segment ID correctly, otherwise we will see the grouping key value itself, that is, 1, 2, 3, . . .

	A
1	...
2	[20,25,30]
3	[UnderWeight,Normal,OverWeight,Fat]
4	=A1.groups@n(A2.pseg(weight/height/height)+1:Grade;avg(height):avg_height)
5	=A4.run(Grade=A3(Grade))

In fact, alignment grouping can be regarded as a special enumeration grouping. All alignment grouping can be written by enumeration grouping.

	A
1	...
2	[?=="Male",?=="Female"]
3	[Male,Female]
4	=A1.enum(A2,sex)
5	=A4.new(A3(#):sex,~.avg(height):avg_height,~.max(weight):max_height)

The enum() function also supports **repeated grouping** (that is, a member may be divided into multiple grouping subsets), but we won't talk about it because it is less common. You can use help when necessary.

SQL has only equivalence grouping, and it is very troublesome when encountering the calculation requirements of the enumeration grouping (including alignment grouping).

9.3 Order-related grouping

As we said, record sequences and sequences are ordered, and the positioning information of members often participates in the calculation. Grouping is no exception, and grouping keys may also be related to sequence numbers of members.

For example, we want to divide the personnel table into groups of every three records:

	A
1	=100.new(string(~):name,if(rand()<0.5,"Male","Female"):sex,50+rand(50):weight,1.5+rand(40)/100:height)
2	=A1.group((#-1)\3)

The grouping in A2 does not use any information of records in A1, but only the sequence number, which is also a reasonable and even common grouping. After all, the essence of grouping is to split a large set into small sets. As long as there is a clear splitting method, it is reasonable.

To divide the personnel table into three groups, we can use the step() function mentioned before or directly use group.

	A
1	...
2	=A1.group(#%3)

By the way, the grouping key values of these two examples are integers. We can also modify the serial number grouping mentioned earlier (need to ensure that the grouping key value is a natural number starting from 1):

	A
1	...
2	=A1.group@n((#+2)\3)
2	=A1.group@n(#%3+1)

In addition to directly using the sequence number as the grouping key value, the grouping may also be related to adjacent members.

For example, given a string composed of letters and numbers, it should be split into consecutive letters and numbers, such as abc1234wxyz56mn098pqrst, and into small strings abc, 1234, wxyz, 56, mn, 098, pqrst.

	A
1	abc1234wxyz56mn098pqrst
2	=A1.split().group@o(isdigit(~)).(~.concat())

The group@o() function will scan the whole sequence in turn. When the grouping key value is the same as that of the previous member, the member will be added to the current grouping subset. If the grouping key value changes, a new grouping subset will be generated and the current member will be added to it. After scanning, a batch of grouping subsets will be obtained to complete the grouping operation.

isdigit(x) returns true when x is a numeric character, otherwise false. We have learned A1.split() and it will split this string into a sequence of single characters. Thus, the grouping key value expression isdigit(~) will be calculated successively for this single character sequence as

false fasle false true true true true false ...

That is, it is false when encountering a letter and true when encountering a number. Changing from number to letter or from letter to number will cause isdigit(~) to change, resulting in a new grouping subset, so the return value of group@o() will be

[[a,b,c],[1,2,3,4],[w,x,y,z],[5,6],....]

That is, divide the adjacent letters or numbers into a group, and then use concat() to concatenate each group into a string.

This grouping is difficult to describe with the grouping operation we learned earlier.

This is another example of doing grouping directly to a sequence.

If we know that the grouping key value itself is orderly, the ordinary equivalence grouping can also be done with @o. For example, if the order data is orderly by date, and we want to group and summarize it by month, we can write this:

	A
1	=T("data.xlsx")
3	=A2.groups@o(month@y(OrderDate);sum(Amount),count(Amount))

@o also works for groups(). There is no difference in the result whether we use @o or not here, but if we use @o when the data is orderly, groups() only need to compare the grouping key value with adjacent member, and the calculation speed is much faster.

@o has another variant @i, with which the grouping key is a logical expression, and a new grouping subset is generated whenever true is calculated out.

Let's review the previous problem of calculating the maximum consecutive days of stock rise. Another way of thinking is to sort the transaction data by date (often already in order), and then scan these data in turn for grouping. If the price of one day is higher than that of the previous day, it will continue to be divided into the same group as that of the previous day; If there is no rise, a new group is generated. After scanning, we will get some subsets. In each subset, the stock price rises continuously. Then we just need to see which subset has the most members.

	A
1	=100.new(date(now())-100+~:dt,rand()*100:price)
2	=A1.select(day@w(dt)>1 && day@w(dt)<7)
3	=A2.group@i(price<=price[-1]).max(~.len())

By the way, the easiest way for SQL to complete this task is also to use this idea, but the code is like this (only corresponding to code in A3):

```
SELECT max(consecutive_day)
FROM (SELECT count(*) consecutive_day FROM
            (SELECT sum(rise_or_fall) OVER(ORDER BY dt)
                    day_no_gain FROM
                    (SELECT dt, CASE
                            when price>lag(price)
                            OVER(ORDER BY dt)
                            then 0 else 1 end rise_or_fall
            FROM T ) )
      GROUP BY day_no_gain)
```

You can feel the difference.

The grouping operation that needs to use order and position information is called **order-related grouping**. Order-related grouping is very useful in parsing text.

Some text files are not in very neat TXT or CSV format, but have regular text strings, in which there will be structured data, which needs to be parsed by programming if it needs to be reused, such as:

```
[18-07-19 14:35:06][9416]-[31ms][QQLiveMainModule.dll][CQQLiveModule::ParsCommandLine]
cmd="C:\Program Files (x86)\Tencent\QQLive\QQLive.exe" -system_startup
[18-07-19 14:35:08][9416]-[2266ms][HttpModule.dll][CDownloadMgr::AddTask]keyid = 1,url =
http://182.254.116.117/d?dn=vv.video.qq.com.&ttl=1
```

Generally speaking, a batch of events will be described in the log, and each event will occupy several lines of text. Structure analysis is to extract the field values of each event.

Using order-related grouping, these log texts can be easily divided into small segments with events as units. The log is usually divided into events in the following ways:

1) Each N line corresponds to an event, which can be split by group((#-1\N)) :

	A	B
1	=file("S.log").read@n()	
2	=create(...)	
3	for A1.group((#-1)\3)	...
...		...
...		>A2.insert(...2.

2) The number of lines is not fixed. There will be a fixed starting string before each event, which can be split with group@i :

	A	B
3	for A1.group@i(~=="---start---")	...

3) The number of lines is not fixed. Each line of the same event has the same prefix (such as the user ID of the log), which can be used split with group@o :

	A	B
3	for A1.group@o(left(~,6))	...

After splitting, the code can concentrate on parsing the field values from the string of each segment. Of course, this is usually not a simple task.

9.4 Expansion and transpose

After grouping and then summarizing, we usually get a smaller set than the original set, which is equivalent to aggregation. Then, is there an inverse operation of grouping, using a smaller data table to calculate a larger data table through some rules?

We call this kind of operation **expansion** or **inverse grouping**.

However, the summarized data generally has lost the detailed information, and the reverse calculation cannot be realized. Explicit expansion rules are required for expansion operations.

The table sequence contains loan information of some customers, including loan periods and amounts. Now we need to calculate the monthly repayment amount of these people according to the equal principal and interest method, and the interest rate is a constant.

	A	B
1	=10.new(string(~):id,rand(20):number,rand(100):amount)	>rate=0.05/12
2	=A1.news(number;id,month@y(elapse@m(now(),#)):ym,amount*(1-rate*power(1+rate,number)/power(1+rate,number)):payment)	

The news() function in A2 will generate number records for each member of A1. The field name and calculation formula are described by the following parameters. The calculation formula of this installment loan is copied online. It's not the point.

Think about the # in the parameters. The news() function is essentially a two-layer loop function. First, it loops through the members of A1, and then it loops through the first parameter number. The parameters after the semicolon are actually for the inner loop function, that is, # is for the number layer, i.e., the number of loans, not the member of A1.

The calculation amount of this code is a little large. Because the monthly repayment amount is actually the same in the equal principal and interest method, there is no need to calculate it so many times. Just calculate it once for each A1 member.

	A	B
1	...	...
2	=A1.(amount*(1-rate*power(1+rate,number)/power(1+rate,number)))	
3	=A1.news(number;id,month@y(elapse@m(now(),#)):ym,A2(A1.#):payment)	

Note that A1.# is used here to refer to the sequence number of the outer loop function.

Let's implement the inverse operation of string merging in the previous section.

	A
1	=100.new(string(~):name,if(rand()<0.5,"Male","Female"):sex)
2	=A1.group(sex;~.(name).concat@c():Names)
3	=A2.news(Names.split@c();~:name,sex)

A3 will split the string concatenated in A2 and expand it into records with the same number of rows as A1.

Again, news() is essentially a two-layer loop function. The sex in the parameters is the field of the outer loop function. Because this field cannot be found in the inner layer, SPL will automatically find it in the outer layer, so we don't have to write A2.sex. And ~ is the current member of the inner loop function, i.e., the name after splitting.

There is also a more common expansion operation: expand the columns (fields) of the data table into rows (records).

We need to use the student score table we used before:

	A
1	[English,Maths,Science,Arts,PE]
2	=A1.("rand(100):"+~).concat@c()
3	=100.new(string(~,"0000"):id, ${A2})

A3 will generate a data table with 6 fields. Except for the id field, the others are all one subject (score of one subject).

Index	id	English	Maths	Science	Arts	PE
1	0001	40	10	46	63	63
2	0002	88	78	97	51	2
3	0003	1	33	58	25	16
4	0004	54	33	37	4	56
5	0005	61	70	78	46	37
6	0006	32	74	12	83	68
7	0007	7	76	77	19	32
8	0008	23	16	61	71	64
9	0009	56	51	51	38	18
10	0010	39	77	17	97	81
11	0011	39	47	32	35	8
12	0012	3	15	69	49	50
13	0013	14	68	57	99	51
14	0014	74	53	14	23	71

When we talked about the concept of structured data, we mentioned that since these subjects are of equal status, statistics on these subjects (scores) may occur. Therefore, the more common data structure will be three fields: id, subject, score. Now the field name of the data table will become the field value of the subject field of the new data table, and each record of the original table will become 5 records (there are 5 subjects) of the new table, which leads to expansion operation.

We can write it with news():

	A
...	...
4	=A3.fname().to(2,)
5	=A3.news(A4;id,~:subject,A3.~.field(~):score)

A4 lists all subject fields, and A5 performs the expansion operation. Note the two ~ in A3.~.field(~), the former is A3.~, i.e., the current record of A3, that is, the record being expanded, and the latter ~ is A4, i.e., a subject field.

Now A5 becomes such a data structure:

Index	id	subject	score
1	0001	English	40
2	0001	Maths	10
3	0001	Science	46
4	0001	Arts	63
5	0001	PE	63
6	0002	English	88
7	0002	Maths	78
8	0002	Science	97
9	0002	Arts	51
10	0002	PE	2
11	0003	English	1
12	0003	Maths	33
13	0003	Science	58
14	0003	Arts	25

This kind of operation is very common, and SPL provides a special function to handle it:

	A
...	...
4	=A3.fname().to(2,)
5	=A3.pivot@r(id;subject,score;${A4.concat@c()})

For this case where all fields except id need to be expanded, it can be further simplified as:

	A
...	...
4	=A3.pivot@r(id;subject,score)

Careful readers may find that the pivot() function uses an @r option, so what will be calculated without the @r option?

When there is no @r, it is its inverse operation, which is equivalent to grouping.

	A
...	...
4	=A3.pivot@r(id;subject,score)
5	=A4.pivot(id;subject,score)

We will find that A5 becomes A3 again, but the field order has changed, and the subject fields are arranged in alphabetical order, however there is no problem with the data. If we want to follow the original field order, we need to write the field list into the parameter:

5	=A4.pivot(id;subject,score;${A1.concat@cq()})

concat() plus @q means to spell additional quotation marks, and it will be explained later.

pivot() function is also called **transpose** operation, and with @r it is called inverse transpose.

Transpose is a variant of grouping operation, which can also be realized by grouping:

	A
...	...
4	=A3.pivot@r(id;subject,score)
5	=A4.id(subject)
6	=A4.group(id;${A5.("~.select@1(subject==\""+~+"\").score:"+~).concat@c()})

It can be seen that A6 here also changes back to A3 (the subject fields are also sorted. If the original order is to be used, replace A5 with A1 in the A6 expression).

The macro in A6 expression is complex, but it can be understood through careful study, that is, take the score with the same subject name in the current grouping subset as the value of the subject field in the table sequence after grouping. Because the subject is a string in A4 and the grouping subset is composed of records in A4, quotation marks should also be added during comparison. The same principle is used in the previous code using pivot, so the @q option should be added in concat(). This syntax is really troublesome, so SPL provides the pivot() function to directly implement this grouping and summary.

In other words, transpose is just a grouping and summary operation; Accordingly, inverse transpose is the expansion operation.

It should be emphasized that this transpose is different from the transpose in Excel. The transpose in Excel is equivalent to the transpose of matrix, which is a simple row column exchange (row to column, column to row). The transpose here is actually a pivot in multidimensional analysis. It is an extended variant of grouping operation (inverse transpose is a variant of inverse grouping). Usually, a field is used as a grouping key, and this field is stable and will not be transferred into a column. Transpose is actually a common saying that refers to pivot in the context of this book.

However, the transpose of SPL is slightly different from the ordinary grouping. As can be seen from the expression of A6, it will not aggregate the grouping subset, but simply get the first item. In fact, this operation assumes that there is only one record (or none) in each grouping subset after filtering with the field name of the target table. If there are multiple records at this time (theoretically possible), the pivot() function has no place to describe how to aggregate these records. A better way is to do a round of group aggregation in advance, and then do the pivot() function.

	A
1	[English,Maths,Science,Arts,PE]
2	=100.new(string(rand(10),"0000"):id, A1(rand(5)+1):subject,rand(100):score)
3	=A2.pivot(id;subject,score)
4	=A2.groups(id,subject;sum(score):score)
5	=A4.pivot(id;subject,score)
6	=A2.pivot@s(id;subject,sum(score))

The table sequence we generated in A2 has duplicate id and subject, so that the grouping subset will have multiple records after being filtered by the field name during pivot(). Direct pivot() may not get the desired result (A3); A round of group aggregation (A4) needs to be done first, and then pivot() (A5); If the aggregation method of all fields is the same, it can also be simplified as A6. The option @s indicates that one more step of aggregation is required, and the aggregate function is written in the parameter. If it is different (for example, some calculate sum and some calculate max), we can only do the aggregation of A4 first.

It is very convenient to use the pivot() function without the third segment parameter (after the second semicolon), but some desired fields in the result table sequence may not be generated due to the lack of data.

	A
1	[English,Maths,Science,Arts,PE]
2	=100.new(string(~,"0000"):id, A1(rand(5)+1):subject,rand(100):score)
3	=A2.select(subject!="Arts")
4	=A3.pivot(id;subject,score)
5	=A3.pivot(id;subject,score;${A1.concat@cq()})

A3 filter out the Arts subject and then do pivot(). The result will be one less column, and there will be no Arts subject. To forcibly list all subjects according to A5, the corresponding values of the field with missing data in the result table sequence will be filled with null.

10 ASSOCIATION

10.1 Primary key

When we talked about the concept of structured data, we said that the fields of the data table have names, but the records have no names. So how do we identify the difference between one record and another? We know that each record corresponds to the information of one thing. Which is it? How to determine that the current referenced or operated record is the one corresponding to the expected thing?

It is often unreliable to use the order of a record in the table sequence to identify, because the sequence number will change with the insertion and deletion action.

In the examples of the previous chapter, most of the table sequences we created and referenced have a field with values that are unique in the whole table sequence, such as the id field in the personnel table or the dt field in the stock table. Structured data uses this unique field value to identify a record.

In a data table, if there are one or more fields and the values of any two records in this field (the sequence of values if multiple fields) are different, we can set this field (fields) as the **primary key** of the data table.

Note that the primary key is set manually and not found automatically. There may be multiple fields (or sets of fields) in a data table that meet the condition of primary key (uniqueness), but we will only select one (set) as the primary key. A primary key must be unique, but a unique field may not be a primary key.

The field value of the primary key of a record, also known as the **primary key value** of the record, is also referred to as the **primary key** when the context is unambiguous.

Because the primary key is unique, that is, the primary key value of a record will not be repeated in the whole data table, the primary key can be used to uniquely identify a record. We say that the current referenced or operated record is a record with a primary key of xxx, so there will only be one such record, and there will be no mistake.

For a data table with a primary key already set, in principle, it is not allowed to add new records with the same primary key as existing records. When inserting and deleting records, the primary key will not change. Using the primary key to identify a record is more stable than using the sequence number.

However, primary key is not required (none of the previous examples has one). A data table without a primary key usually only appends records instead of modifying, deleting existing records or inserting new records in front, because these actions will change the sequence number.

In fact, we are not unfamiliar with the concept of primary key in our daily life. All students in the school will have a unique student number. The attribute of student number itself has no effective information, and its function is only to uniquely identify a student. It will not work to directly use students' names. People may often have duplicate names, so it is difficult to accurately identify a student. For things like orders, they don't have a name. They need a (unique) number to identify them. Otherwise, we don't know how to determine which order we are talking about. Other similar ones include flight number, bank account, telephone number, etc., which all play the role of primary key.

The "primary key" in daily life is almost everywhere. The primary key of structured data is only an embodiment of people's daily experience in the programming language. The primary key is the name of the record. Setting the primary key is to give the record a (unique) name.

SPL provides some functions for primary key:

	A
1	=1000.new(string(1000+~):id,if(rand()<0.5,"Male","Female"):sex)
2	=A1.keys(id)
3	=A1(1).key()

A2 uses the keys() function to set the primary key of the table sequence as the id field, and A3 uses key() to calculate the primary key of a record.

Index	id	sex
1	1001	Female
2	1002	Male
3	1003	Female
4	1004	Female
5	1005	Male
6	1006	Male
7	1007	Female
8	1008	Female
9	1009	Female
10	1010	Female
11	1011	Male
12	1012	Male
13	1013	Female
14	1014	Male

For the table sequence with primary key set, a key icon will be drawn on the primary key field when the values are displayed.

However, SPL does not check the uniqueness of the primary key when it is set. Whether the primary key is unique is controlled by the programmers themselves.

Using the grouping operation we have learned, it is easy to judge whether a field is unique in the data table:

	A
1	=1000.new(string(rand(1000)):id,if(rand()<0.5,"Male","Female"):sex)
2	=A1.id().len()==A1.len()

Just see if the sequence after DISTINCT is as long as the original table sequence.

When inserting records, SPL does not check the uniqueness of the primary key. The following code will not report an error.

	A
1	=1000.new(string(1000+~):id,if(rand()<0.5,"Male","Female"):sex)
2	=A1.keys(id)
3	=A1.insert(1,"1002")

SPL only checks the uniqueness of the primary key when it is required. This has the advantage of better computing performance, and each check is a time-consuming action, but the disadvantage is that there may be potential errors. The principle of SPL fully believes in programmers and leaves freedom to programmers.

The main usage of the primary key is to identify records, that is, to find a record with the primary key value.

	A
1	=1000.new(string(1000+~):id,if(rand()<0.5,"Male","Female"):sex)
2	=A1.keys(id)
3	=A1.find("1053")

SPL uses the find() function to return the record whose primary key is its parameter. If it cannot be found, it will return null.

In the table sequence we are using now as an example, the primary key of records is arranged from small to large just like the sequence number. This is to facilitate the generation of a unique field (if they are generated randomly, it is necessary to compare whether they are repeated). However, SPL does not have this requirement for the primary key. It can be out of order:

	A
1	=1000.(string(1000+~)).sort(rand())
2	=1000.new(A1(#):id,if(rand()<0.5,"Male","Female"):sex)
3	=A2.keys(id)
4	=A2.find("1053")

A4 can also normally find the record with the parameter as primary key.

Since SPL does not check the uniqueness of the primary key, if there are records with the same primary key in the table sequence, the find() function will not report an error. It will find the first record and return, which is a bit like select@1().

By the way, find() is similar to pos(). It is not a loop function. Its parameter will be calculated first when being called, and there will be no ~, # and so on.

It is a common action to use the primary key to find a record. If the table sequence is a relatively large, the search speed will be slow, because this search usually needs to compare one by one.

SPL provides a mechanism to index the primary key, and the search speed will be much faster.

	A	B
1	=1000.(string(1000+~)).sort(rand())	
2	=1000.new(A1(#):id,if(rand()<0.5,"Male","Female"):sex)	
3	=A2.keys(id)	
4	=now()	>10000.run(A2.find(string(1000+rand(1000))))
5	=now()	=interval@ms(A4,A5)
6	>A2.index()	
7	=now()	>10000.run(A2.find(string(1000+rand(1000))))
8	=now()	=interval@ms(A7,A8)

The index() function will create an index for the table sequence with a primary key, and the index will be automatically used by find() after the index is created.

When you execute this code and compare the running time before and after indexing, you will find that the performance gap is very large (but it also needs to be executed 10000 times and use interval@ms() to capture). After the index is provided, the method of comparison one by one is no longer used. The specific method is far beyond the content of this book, which will not be explained here.

SPL requires the uniqueness of the primary key when creating an index. When index() is executed, SPL checks whether the primary key is unique. If it is found that the primary key is not unique at this time, an error message of duplicate primary keys will be reported.

SPL seems a little lazy and won't take the initiative to do things until necessary.

Unlike the operations mentioned earlier, primary key and index can only be created for a table sequence, not for a record sequence. They are part of the data structure.

However, find() can be used in a record sequence, only that it can't use the index. It can only compare one by one.

As an aside, if the primary keys are in order, find() also supports a fast search technology called binary search, which is much faster than comparison one by one (close to the index, but still can't catch up). It can be used for a record sequence without index or a table sequence that has not created an index. The select() function and pos() function also support this binary search. Interested readers can refer to the relevant documents of SPL, because high-performance computing is not the focus of this book (we didn't talk about the principle of indexing just now), we won't elaborate here.

Let's review the grouping operation mentioned in the previous chapter. Observing the table sequence returned by groups(), it is obvious that the field corresponding to the grouping key value is unique, that is, this field can naturally constitute the primary key of the table sequence returned by groups(). Therefore, the field value used for grouping is called key. Careful readers may have found that when viewing the returned result of groups(), the small key icon has been drawn on the grouping key.

10.2 Foreign key

With a primary key, we can uniquely identify a record. Then, we can establish the association between the records of different data tables.

First, generate two tables with primary key for experiments. For simplicity, we use integers as primary key, but the order is deliberately disrupted.

	A	B	C
1	[HR,R&D,Sales,Marketing,Admin]	=A1.len().sort(rand())	=100.sort(rand())
2	=A1.new(B1(#):did, ~:name, C1(#):manager).keys(did)		[CHN,USA]
3	=100.new(C1(#):eid,C2(rand(2)+1):nation,rand(5)+1:dept).keys(eid)		
4	=A2.run(A3(manager).dept=did)		

A2 is a department table, each record corresponds to a department, the did field is the department number, which is used as the primary key, and the name field is the department name; A3 is the employee table, each record corresponds to an employee, eid field is the employee number, which is used as the primary key, and the nation field is the employee's nationality. The employee table usually has a name field, but it's useless here, so we won't generate it.

The key points are the dept field of A3 and the manager field of A2. dept stores an integer representing the department to which the employee belongs. The department of the employee corresponding to record e in the employee table is the department corresponding to record d with e.dept as the primary key in the department table. We will also say that record e is **associated** with record d.

The manager field of A2 indicates the manager of the department. The manager is also an employee and will also appear in the employee table. The manager of the department corresponding to record d in the department table is the employee corresponding to record e with d.manager as the primary key in the employee table. We also say

124

that the two records d and e are associated.

Understanding this relationship makes the role of A4 clear. Because the randomly generated data can not guarantee that the manager's department is his own department, it should be adjusted in A4 so that this data can be used.

Now we want to list all the people in the R&D department.

This is a simple selection problem, and we should use the select() function. However, there is no department name in the employee table, and there is only the department number. The selection can only be done by using the number to find the department name in the department table.

	A	B	C
...	...		
5	=A3.select(A2.find(dept).name=="R&D")		

Similarly, we can also list all departments where the manager is American:

	A	B	C
...	...		
5	=A2.select(A3.find(manager).nation=="USA")		

In this way, we associate the employee table with the department table, and can jointly use the information of the two tables for operation. The dept field in the employee table is always the primary key of a record in the department table, and it is also used to represent this record in the department table. We call this field a **foreign key**, and a more complete saying is the foreign key **pointing to** the department table in the employee table. Through the foreign key, we can refer to some fields of the associated record in another table in the operation of a table, and the two tables are associated by the foreign key.

Similarly, the manager field in the department table is also a foreign key pointing to the employee table.

The primary key may consist of multiple fields, correspondingly, a foreign key may also have multiple fields, but it is relatively uncommon, and we won't give an example here.

When there is a foreign key relationship between two tables, for example, a field in table A is a foreign key pointing to table B. We also need to know two terms: table B is the **dimension table** of table A, and table A is called the **fact table**. The relationship between the dimension table and the fact table is relative. When we care about the foreign key dept of the employee table, the department table is the dimension table of the employee table, while when we care about the foreign key manager of the department table, the employee table is the dimension table of the department table.

Dimension table and fact table are often used by programmers when discussing database operations. We don't use this kind of technical vocabulary in daily data processing, but it's better to know.

In the terminology of database, it is also said that foreign key association is **many to one** association, that is, multiple fact table records may be associated with the same dimension table record.

Foreign key is not an unfamiliar concept. Dimension table is the code table we often use. We list some frequently referenced attributes of things in a code table and give a code (i.e., primary key) to identify them. When referencing, we only use this code (i.e., foreign key), for more detailed information, we use this code to query the code table.

For example, the owner's name, address,... and other information will be listed with the phone number, while there is only the phone number in the call record. The phone number is the primary key of the phone book. The phone number in the call record is the foreign key pointing to the phone book. The phone book is the dimension table of call record, and call record is the fact table. In the calculations of call records, it is often possible to use information related to phone numbers, such as querying the number of calls made in Beijing, which uses foreign keys to find the fields of associated records.

There are also others, such as bank accounts and bank transaction records, commodity information and trading records.

It is very common to use dimension table information in the operations of fact table. Why don't we directly copy the dimension table fields to the fact table?

Readers who have experience with this code table will know the answer. There are many information contents in the dimension table. If they are copied into the fact table, the fact table will be very large and occupy a lot of storage space, resulting in low performance; Moreover, the dimension table is likely to change, such as department name and owner's address. If they are copied into the fact table, once they change, the fact table will be updated, and the fact table is usually much larger, and it is very troublesome and inefficient. If it is an independent dimension table, you can always get the latest information by modifying the dimension table and temporarily fetching the dimension table fields during the operation of the fact table.

Having understood the concept, let's continue. Now list the employee id (replaced by the id field without generating the name field) and the department name into a table:

	A	B	C
...	...		
5	=A3.new(eid,A2.find(dept).name:dept)		

This is very similar to the VLookup function in Excel. That's how the code table is used.

However, it is obviously very troublesome to always use find() to write, and the efficiency is very poor to calculate every time. For example, if we want to list the id of the manager of the employee's department, we have to write this find() twice.

	A	B	C
...	...		
5	=A3.new(eid,A2.find(dept).name:dept,A2.find(dept).manager)		

This is more like VLookup. Excel has to write VLookup twice to reference two columns of the associated table.

SPL obviously won't fail to take this problem into consideration. This kind of routine operation for structured data can't be so troublesome. SPL provides the switch() function to realize the association operation of foreign key:

	A	B	C
...	...		
5	>A3.switch(dept,A2)		
6	=A3.new(eid,dept.name:dept,dept.manager)		

The switch() function will switch the foreign key field to the corresponding dimension table record. The A5 code is equivalent to executing the following statement:

```
>A3.run(dept=A2.find(dept))
```

Before executing A5, look at the value of A3 (debugging function can be used). It is as follows, and the dept field is an integer:

After execution, look at A3. The dept field still looks like an integer, but it changes color and is displayed on the left:

Double click the value of a dept, and the following result may appear in the value display area:

The value of dept field has become a record. Double clicking it will display the details of this record. The just displayed value with changed color is actually the primary key of this record.

Since it is a record, of course, its fields can be referenced, and dept.name and dept.manager in A6 can be calculated normally.

The function name switch() is used because it can also switch the field valued as a record back:

	A	B	C
...	...		
5	>A3.switch(dept,A2)		
6	=A3.select(dept.name=="R&D")		
7	>A3.switch(dept)		

A5 switches the foreign key to the record of the dimension table, and A6 can use it to reference the field of the dimension table record. A7 switches the field now valued as the record back. A7 is equivalent to executing

>A3.run(dept=dept.key())

However, switching back is rare.

After being processed by switch(), it seems that the records of the two tables are really connected. The field value of this table is the record of another table. You can reference the fields of another table through this field. This is much more convenient than VLookup.

Accordingly, the manager field in the department table is also a foreign key and can also be switched to the record in the personnel table.

For example, we want to count how many American employees have a Chinese manager:

	A	B	C
...	...		
5	>A3.switch(dept,A2)	>A2.switch(manager,A3)	
6	=A3.count(nation=="USA" && dept.manager.nation=="CHN")		

Foreign key relationships may have multiple layers. In this case, it will be difficult to describe if we still use the find() method (Interested readers can also try to think about how to use VLookup to realize this multi-layer association in Excel). For the foreign key switched by the switch() function, the point operator can be vividly interpreted as "'s". The dept.manager.nation in A6 can be interpreted as the department's manager's nationality of the current employee. You will not find it difficult even if there are many levels. Such a syntax is simple to write and easy to understand.

Generally, the value of the foreign key field must be within the range of the primary key value of the dimension table, but sometimes it may exceed the range. For example, before the department of a new employee is determined, the dept field is filled with 0, and there is no corresponding record in the department table.

	A	B	C
...	...		
4	=A2.run(A3(manager).dept=did)	>C1.to(90,).run(A3(~).dept=0)	
5	=A3.switch(dept,A2)	=A5.count(dept.name==null)	
5	=A3.switch@i(dept,A2)	=A5.count(dept.name==null)	
5	=A3.switch@d(dept,A2)	=A5.count(dept.name==null)	

In the code B4 for generating data, we deliberately find some employees' dept and fill it in as 0, and then we can observe the calculation results of the three A5. Note that it should be executed separately, not sequentially, because A3 will be changed after execution, and it is meaningless to continue to execute another A5.

When the switch() cannot find the dimension table record corresponding to the foreign key, it will fill in the foreign key as null, and the subsequent reference of its field will not report an error, but will return null, and the corresponding B5 will not be 0. The @i option will delete the fact table records that cannot find the record corresponding to the foreign key, ensuring that all the foreign keys of the fact table records after switch are correctly switched to dimension table records, and the corresponding B5 will return 0. While the @d option only retains the fact table records that cannot find the corresponding record of the foreign key, and cannot perform the foreign key switch, and the corresponding B5 will report an error.

Using foreign key to associate two data tables is often used to temporarily concatenate some fields of the dimension table to the fact table (that is, what VLookup does). In most cases, it is not intended to change the field of the fact table. Although the switch() function is convenient for association operation, it will change the foreign key field value of the original fact table. If we only want to append dimension table fields, we need to do another step of switching the foreign key that has become a record back to the foreign key, which is troublesome. Moreover, if we encounter the situation that there is no correspondence that we just mentioned, the foreign key will be filled in as null, and the information has been lost and cannot be switched back.

SPL provides the join() function to achieve this goal:

	A	B	C
...	...		
4	=A2.run(A3(manager).dept=did)	>C1.to(90,).run(A3(~).dept=0)	
5	=A3.join(dept,A2,name:deptname,manager:manager)		

A5 will add deptname and manager fields on the basis of table sequence A3, and fill in the employee's department name and manager id respectively. The dept field will remain the same. If the corresponding dimension table record cannot be found, the newly added fields will be filled with null.

The join() function will generate a new table sequence, and the original A3 will not change.

The join() function can also support multi field primary keys and foreign keys. Because they are not common, we won't give examples here. When you need to use them, you can consult the relevant SPL documents and understand the necessity of multi-layer parameters.

The switch() function does not support a dimension table with multi field primary keys. It can only switch single field foreign key.

It is very common to use a foreign key to find the corresponding record in the dimension table to reference some fields of the associated record. However, the business is complex. Sometimes the associated records cannot be determined simply by a foreign key, but need a condition related to the interval.

Go back to the personnel table often used in the previous chapter and create a BMI comparison table:

	A	B
1	=100.new(string(~):name,if(rand()<0.5,"Male","Female"):sex,50+rand(50):weight,1.5+rand(40)/100:height)	
2	=A1.derive(weight/height/height:bmi)	
3	[null,20,25,30]	[UnderWeight,Normal,OverWeight,Fat]
4	=A3.new(~:low,~[1]:high,B3(#):type)	

Now we want to add a field to the personnel table A2 with BMI information to list everyone's weight type.

If the BMI comparison table A3 is used as a dimension table (with fields to be referenced), it has low and high fields to represent the BMI interval of a weight type, but does not have a field suitable for primary key (although low and high are unique). It also appears that there is no field in personnel table A2 that can act as a foreign key. However, it is obvious that there is an association between A2 and A4, and each record of A2 will correspond to a record of A4.

Interval association is also a common association. How should it be implemented?

We can of course simply use the select() function, just like using find() at the beginning of this section.

	A	B
...	...	
5	=A2.derive(A4.select@1(low<=bmi && (!high || high>bmi)).type)	

Here, we need to judge whether high is null (indicating the last segment), and low does not need to be judged, because SPL stipulates that null is the smallest, and null<=bmi will always get true.

In fact, interval association can also be understood as foreign key association. If we modify the BMI comparison table and add the BMI segment number calculated by pseg() function to the personnel table, we can see the foreign key relationship.

	A	B
...	...	
3	[null,20,25,30]	[UnderWeight,Normal,OverWeight,Fat]
4	=A3.new(#:no,~:level,B3(#):type).keys(no)	
5	=A2.derive(A4.(level).pseg(bmi)+1:bmitype)	
6	=A5.switch(bmitype,A4)	

The modified BMI comparison table A3 has a primary key and can be used as a dimension table. The bmitype field added in A5 is the foreign key pointing to A3. We can also use switch() to establish association.

Interval association is also a foreign key association in essence.

It's really troublesome to create a foreign key for the personnel table. Actually, we wrote the code as above to help you understand that the concept of foreign key can be extended to this situation. In fact, we can directly spell the target field with pseg().

	A	B
...	...	
3	[null,20,25,30]	[UnderWeight,Normal,OverWeight,Fat]
4	=A3.new(~:level,B3(#):type)	
5	=A2.derive(A4(A4.(level).to(2,).pseg(bmi)+1).type)	

Generally, interval association processe does not generate a foreign key, but the concept of dimension table and fact table can still be used.

If, like this example, only the type field needs to be referenced, we will not even generate the comparison table, but directly use the sequence and pseg() to calculate and reference.

	A	B
...	...	
3	[20,25,30]	[UnderWeight,Normal,OverWeight,Fat]
4	=A2.derive(B3(A3.pseg(bmi)+1):type)	

Like all foreign key associations, interval association is also many to one relationship. Even if the dimension table is not generated, this association relationship still exists logically.

10.3 Merge

If there are two Excel files, such as the order table mentioned before, they may be made by two persons respectively, and there may be some duplicate records. We need to pick out these duplicate records and merge them into a table without duplicate records.

Originally, this is a very simple task of set union. We have learned set operations and can directly use operators such as intersection and difference. However, we also know that different records in the table sequence will never be equal, and the records in different table sequences will never be equal. Of course, the table sequences read from Excel files are different table sequences. In this case, they are not suitable for set operations.

SPL provides merge operation function to complete this task:

	A	B
1	=T("data1.xlsx")	=T("data2.xlsx")
2	=[A1,B1].merge@uo()	>T("data.xlsx",A2)

Quite simply, the merge() function compares the contents of the records. The @u option indicates to get the union. Without this option, it will directly concatenate the two table sequences, that is, to get the concatenation (i.e. |). We'll talk about @o later.

Similarly, the merge() function can also get the intersection, that is, to get the duplicate records, just replace @u with @i.

	A	B
1	=T("data1.xlsx")	=T("data2.xlsx")
2	=[A1,B1].merge@io()	>T("data.xlsx",A2)

The merge() function will compare all fields of the whole record. If any field is different, it will be considered that the two records are different. Such comparisons are time-consuming and sometimes unnecessary. For example, for this order problem, we believe that the producer is conscientious and responsible. As long as the order number is correct, the order content will not be wrong. However, there may be duplication and omission in the order collection process, resulting in duplicate order numbers in the two files. And we only need to pick out the records of duplicate order numbers.

	A	B
1	=T("data1.xlsx")	=T("data2.xlsx")

By adding a parameter to the merge() function, we can make it compare only this field.

Or for records with primary key set, the merge() function will only compare the primary key.

	A	B
1	=T("data1.xlsx").keys(ID)	=T("data2.xlsx").keys(ID)
2	=[A1,B1].merge@uo()	>T("data.xlsx",A2)

The operation is same for intersection, just replace @u with @i.

If the situation is more complicated, both producers may make mistakes. We need to see if the records with the same order number in the two files have different contents. Therefore, we need to select the records with the same order number and compare the whole contents to see if they are the same.

	A	B
1	=T("data1.xlsx")	=T("data2.xlsx")
2	=[A1,B1].merge@io(ID)	=[B1,A1].merge@io(ID)
3	=[A2,B2].merge@do()	=A3.(ID)

A2 will calculate those records in A1 with duplicate order numbers as B1, but retain the record sequence composed of A1 records. Correspondingly, B2 will retain the records in B1 that duplicate the order number of A1. A2 and B2 are both the intersection of A1 and B1, but they are only the intersection in the sense of comparing the order number, and the whole contents are not necessarily the same. Then use merge@d() in A3 to calculate the full content difference set between A2 and B2, so that we can get the records in A2 that have different content with that of the corresponding orders in B2, and get the order numbers of these orders in B3, that is, the orders to be reviewed.

This complexity occurs when set operations involve structured data. The same primary key (or a relatively critical field) does not mean that the whole record is the same. When we need to judge that the records are the same when doing intersection, union or difference, we may use only the primary key or the whole record. If only the primary key is used, the exchange law will not be satisfied. This is not only that the order of members may be different, but also the content may be totally different. Pay special attention when writing code.

Now let's talk about this @o option. By default, the merge() function assumes that the data is ordered (for example, from small to large), thus the comparison speed is very fast, and no sorting is needed. The @o option tells the merge function that the data is out of order and needs to be sorted first. In our current example, the orders are arranged in order according to the order number. It doesn't matter if @o is not written.

Another note is that the merge() function is preceded by a sequence ([A1,B1]), which can calculate the union or intersection results of multiple record sequences at the same time. However, it is relatively uncommon, and we won't give examples here.

The merge() function is also valid for sequences, but single valued sequences generally use the set operator directly, and rarely use the merge() function.

10.4 Join

Let's continue to see the above order example. After picking out the records with the same order number but different contents in the two files, we want to spell the fields (except the order number) together and compare them. That is to form a data table with twice the number of fields (except the order number).

We usually use the join() function to accomplish this task.

	A	B
1	=T("data1.xlsx")	=T("data2.xlsx")
2	=[A1,B1].merge@i(ID)	=[B1,A1].merge@i(ID)
3	=join(A2:a,ID;B2:b,ID)	
4	=A3.new(a.ID:ID,a.Company:CompanyA,b.Company:CompanyB, a.Area:AreaA,b.Area:AreaB,a.OrderDate:OrderDateA,b.OrderDate:OrderDateB, a.Amount:AmountA,b.Amount:AmountB, a.Phone:PhoneA, b.Phone:PhoneB)	

The join() function of A3 returns a table sequence with two fields, a and b respectively. It will concatenate the records in A2 and B2 according to the ID field value, that is, fill the A2 record and B2 record with the same ID into field a and field b respectively as a record in the returned table sequence. The value of field a or field b is also a record, which is a bit like the result of a foreign key being switched. After we understand the calculation result of A3, although A4 is long, it is easy to understand.

Unlike merge(), the task of join() is often to make the data table wider, and merge@u will make the data table longer (more records).

A bigger difference from merge() is that the data tables targeted by merge() are generally of the same data structure. While the common scenario of join() is two (or more) data tables with different data structures.

Let's continue to use the personnel table generated earlier, we now have a personnel table with gender, height and weight, as well as an employee table with nationality and department. We want to make the two tables into a wider table. If the name field of the personnel table is the same as the eid field of the employee table, it means that it is the same person.

Let's sort out the code used to generate data. We don't use the department table at the moment, just discard it.

	A	B	C
1	=100.sort(rand())	[HR,R&D,Sales,Marketing,Admin]	[CHN,USA]
2	=100.new(A1(#):eid,C1(rand(2)+1):nation,B1(rand(5)+1):dept)		
3	=100.new(string(~):name,if(rand()<0.5,"Male","Female"):sex,50+rand(50):weight,1.5+rand(40)/100:height)		

The eid in employee table A2 is disordered.

Let's finish the task:

	A	B	C
...	...		
4	=join(A3:P,int(name);A2:E,eid)		
5	=A4.new(P.name,P.sex,P.weight,P.height,E.nation,E.dept)		

Because the name of A3 is a string type, which is different from the eid of A2, it needs to be converted and written as int(name). We can also convert A2 and write A4 as:

=join(A3:P,name;A2:E,string(eid)) .

The calculation result of A4 is as follows:

Index	P	E
1	[1,Female,57, ...]	[1,USA,Admin]
2	[2,Female,78, ...]	[2,CHN,Sales]
3	[3,Male,65, ...]	[3,USA,R&D]
4	[4,Male,60, ...]	[4,USA,Sales]
5	[5,Female,51, ...]	[5,CHN,Marketing]
6	[6,Male,62, ...]	[6,USA,Sales]
7	[7,Male,72, ...]	[7,CHN,HR]
8	[8,Female,95, ...]	[8,CHN,Marketing]
9	[9,Female,94, ...]	[9,USA,HR]
10	[10,Female,68, ...]	[10,CHN,HR]
11	[11,Male,82, ...]	[11,USA,Marketing]
12	[12,Male,82, ...]	[12,USA,Sales]
13	[13,Male,72, ...]	[13,USA,R&D]
14	[14,Female,54, ...]	[14,USA,Admin]

A table sequence with two fields. The field values are A3 record and A2 record respectively. Because we did not set the primary key for A2 and A3, the development environment will display the fields of the record as a sequence. It can be seen that the first field of the records on the left and right sides of the same line, that is, name and eid, are the same. This is the result of the join() operation. It will spell together the records with the same name in A3 and eid in A2 (Actually, int(name) and eid are the same, but they look the same).

Then A5 can easily get the desired results, which will not be explained in detail.

Two data tables can generate a data table with two fields through the equal relationship between certain fields (or expressions). Based on this new data table, the fields of two original data tables can be referenced for operation at the same time, so as to complete the association of the two tables. The field (expression) used to determine association is called **association key**, and records with equal association key values are called **associated records**. This association operation is called **join**.

The foreign key association mentioned in the previous section is also a join operation. It uses the foreign key of the fact table and the primary key of the dimension table as the association key. However, we rarely express the operation result of foreign key association as a table sequence using two fields with records as values as a data structure. Instead, we are used to using the previous method to switch the foreign key with the switch() function or spell the dimension table fields into the fact table with join() (not the join() we are talking about).

If we already set the primary key for A2 and A3 tables, we do not need to write the association key during join().

	A	B	C
1	=100.sort(rand())	[HR,R&D,Sales,Marketing,Admin]	[CHN,USA]
2	=100.new(A1(#):eid,C1(rand(2)+1):nation,B1(rand(5)+1):dept).keys(eid)		
3	=100.new(~:name,if(rand()<0.5,"Male","Female"):sex,50+rand(50):weight,1.5+rand(40)/100:height).keys(name)		
4	=join(A3:P;A2:E)		

We need to change the generation statement in A3 to directly use integers as the values of the name field, so that the primary keys of the two tables do not need a conversion and directly serve as the association key.

The join using the primary key as the association key is called the **homo dimension association**, and the two tables are also called the **homo dimension table** to each other. In database terminology, the homo dimension association is a **one-to-one** association, that is, a record in an association table will only be associated with one record in another association table, not multiple, because the primary key is unique.

Let's continue with this code and change it a little bit. A2 randomly selects 80 integers between 1 and 100 as the primary key to generate 80 records; A3 directly selects 1-90 as the primary key to generate 90 records. In this way, the primary keys of A2 and A3 still have a lot in common, but they also have a small number of primary key values that the other does not have(Because of random generation, the result of each running may be different, but it does not affect our discussion).

	A	B	C
1	=100.sort(rand())	[HR,R&D,Sales,Marketing,Admin]	[CHN,USA]
2	=80.new(A1(#):eid,C1(rand(2)+1):nation,B1(rand(5)+1):dept).keys(eid)		
3	=90.new(~:name,if(rand()<0.5,"Male","Female"):sex,50+rand(50):weight,1.5+rand(40)/100:height).keys(name)		
4	=join(A3:P;A2:E)		
5	=A4.len()	=A2.(eid)^A3.(name)	=B5.len()

Look at the result of A4:

A4		
Index	P	E
1	1	1
2	2	2
3	3	3
4	4	4
5	5	5
6	6	6
7	7	7
8	8	8
9	9	9
10	10	10
11	12	12
12	13	13
13	14	14
14	16	16

The left and right are still equal, but there are obviously missing sequence numbers (that is, primary key).

Looking at A5, of course, it will not be 100, but it is not 80 or 90, but smaller.

The join() function will find records with equal association keys in both tables to associate. If the association key value of one table does not exist in the other table, the corresponding record of this table will also be discarded. This join is called **inner join.** The association key set in the result of the calculated table sequence is the intersection of the association key sets of the two associated table sequences, that is, B5 in the above code, and A5 is bound to be equal to C5, which is usually less than the length of A2 or A3.

Let's try again after changing the last two lines of code:

	A	B	C
...	...		
4	=join@1(A3:P;A2:E)		
5	=A4.len()	=A3.(name)	=B5.len()

Execute again, and then look at A4

Index	P	E
1	1	1
2	2	2
3	3	3
4	4	4
5	5	5
6	6	6
7	7	7
8	8	8
9	9	9
10	10	10
11	11	11
12	12	(null)
13	13	13
14	14	(null)

The record primary key in the values of the P field is complete, ranging from 1 to 90, and corresponds to the records of A3 one by one. Some records of the E field are filled with null. A5 is also 90, the same length as A3.

The join() with @1 will be based on the association table on the left (the first parameter). If there are records with the same association key as the left in the right table, it will be associated. If there is no record, it will be filled with null. The association key value of the result table sequence is the same as that of the left table, and its length is also the same as that of the left table.

This join based on the left is called **left join.**

Some database systems also have right join, that is, join based on the right. However, SPL does not provide it. It is not necessary because it can be done by swapping the parameter position.

And this @1 is the number 1, not the letter l. It means that the join() is based on the first parameter.

Continue:

	A	B	C
...	...		
4	=join@f(A3:P;A2:E)		
5	=A4.len()	=A2.(eid)&A3.(name)	=B5.len()

Then look at A4:

Index	P	E
82	82	82
83	83	83
84	84	(null)
85	85	85
86	86	86
87	87	87
88	88	88
89	89	89
90	90	90
91	(null)	92
92	(null)	93
93	(null)	94
94	(null)	96
95	(null)	97

Because the primary key of A3 is from 1 to 90, the records in the front exist. Pull the table to the end, and the last few records can be seen.

Now there are null field values on the left and right sides, and A5 is greater than 90, but it is often not 100.

The join() with @f will consider both tables. If the association key value exists in either side, a record will be generated in the result table sequence. If both sides have records with association key value, the records will be filled in the corresponding field to realize association. For an association key value, if only one table has a corresponding record, fill it in the corresponding field and fill null in the corresponding field of another table. Finally, the associated key value set in the result table sequence will be the union of the associated key sets of the two table sequences involved in the association, or B5 in the code, and A5 will be the same as C5, usually greater than the length of A2 or A3.

This two-sided join is called **full join**.

Inner join, left join and full join are very important concepts. When performing join operation, we must make sure which kind of join to use. The results of different joins will be very different.

Foreign key association is usually left join, that is, based on the fact table. If the switch() function cannot find the associated record in the dimension table, it will fill the foreign key field with null. While switch@i() is equivalent to inner join. When the associated record cannot be found, the relevant record of the fact table will also be filtered out.

join() and join@f() are a little similar to merge@i() and merge@u(). In fact, join operation can be used to realize the intersection and union of two table sequences according to the primary key.

A piece of data may have multiple production sources, and then spliced into complete data. It may be divided into multiple parts by row (record), which will be combined with merge(), and the duplicated parts will be processed in the process. It may also be divided into multiple parts by column (field), and join() is used to combine them. These data also need to be concatenated reasonably without dislocation.

Let's look at another association case:

	A	B	C
1	=100.sort(rand())	[HR,R&D,Sales,Marketing,Admin]	[CHN,USA]
2	=100.new(A1(#):eid,C1(rand(2)+1):nation,B1(rand(5)+1):dept).keys(eid)		
3	=A2.news(12;eid,~:m,5000+rand(5000):salary).keys(eid,m)		

Based on the employee table, a 12-month salary table is generated for everyone. A3 needs two fields as the primary key (to ensure uniqueness).

Now we want to calculate the total income of each department.

The department information is in the employee table, while the income information is in the salary table, and this task requires the association of the two tables.

Using the foreign key association we have learned, the employee table is regarded as the dimension table of the salary table, and we can solve the problem:

	A	B	C
...	...		
4	=A3.switch(eid,A2)	=A4.groups(eid.dept;sum(salary))	

There is no problem with this code. However, we can also use join() to deal with this association that uses a part of the primary key as a foreign key.

	A	B	C
...	...		
4	=join(A2:E;A3:S,eid)	=A4.groups(E.dept;sum(S.salary))	

The same correct result is calculated as just now.

Look at A4. The result is as follows:

A4		
Index	E	S
1	1	[1,1]
2	1	[1,3]
3	1	[1,5]
4	1	[1,7]
5	1	[1,9]
6	1	[1,11]
7	1	[1,12]
8	1	[1,10]
9	1	[1,8]
10	1	[1,6]
11	1	[1,4]
12	1	[1,2]
13	2	[2,1]
14	2	[2,3]

A2 records are repeated in E field. Each A3 record is associated with an A2 record, while each A2 record is associated with 12 A3 records. The length of A4 is the same as that of A3.

This association, which uses part of the primary key fields as a foreign key, is also called **primary-sub association**. The table with fewer primary key fields is called primary table, and the table with more primary key fields is called sub table. A primary-sub association is a **one-to-many** association, which is the opposite of a foreign key association. From the standpoint of the sub table to look at the primary table, it is a foreign key relationship, while from the standpoint of the primary table to look at the sub table, it is a primary-sub association.

We will also use this join() to handle the primary-sub association, instead of always using switch() and the join()

mentioned in the previous section. Sometimes, we'll do a groups() to the sub table first and then join() with the primary table. For example, for the previous problem:

	A	B	C
...	...		
4	=A3.groups(eid;sum(salary):salary).keys(eid)		
5	=join(A2:E;A4:S)	=A5.groups(E.dept;sum(S.salary))	

After A4 performs group aggregation, a table sequence with grouping key as the primary key is formed, which has the one-to-one homo dimension relationship with A2.

Theoretically, in foreign key association, we can also perform a groups() to the fact table using the foreign key as a grouping key to form a table that has the homo dimension relationship with the dimension table, but we usually don't do that, because a fact table often has multiple foreign keys. If we perform a groups() according to a foreign key, other foreign keys can't be processed. In most cases, the sub table will only have one primary table, so it is no problem to perform a groups() according to the association key and then do a homo dimension association with the primary table.

Of course, in foreign key association, we can also directly perform join() operation just like in primary-sub association, and put together the records of the dimension table and fact table. One dimension table record may be associated with multiple fact table records. In fact, the join() function mentioned in the foreign key section is doing this, but it also does the action of referencing the dimension table field after association, because this combination action is more common. The length of the result table sequence is also the same as that of the fact table (sub table in the concept of primary-sub association), so the function is also named join().

Now we have encountered several join modes: one-to-one, one-to-many and many-to-one. Is there a many-to-many mode?

There is almost no business meaningful many-to-many join in structured data operations. Many-to-many join only exists in theoretical analysis or mathematical operations. There are basically no associations unrelated to the primary key in daily data processing, so we don't have to pay attention to them.

SPL provides the xjoin() function to handle join of any conditions, and can also realize many-to-many. But we can only give a mathematical example to illustrate it.

xjoin() will calculate the Cartesian set of the sets involved in the association (note that we say set instead of table sequence, because it is too difficult to find reasonable business examples for structured data). The process can filter the Cartesian product under specified conditions.

For the concept of Cartesian set, unfamiliar readers can search on the Internet. Let's give a simple example to understand it.

	A	B	C
1	[1,2,3]	[HR,R&D,Sales,Marketing,Admin]	[CHN,USA]
2	=xjoin(A1:a;B1:b)	=xjoin(A1:a;B1:b;C1:c)	=xjoin(A1:a;C1:c)

It is not difficult to understand the calculation results of A2,B2,C2. Take a member from each set to form a record, and all possible combinations are included, which is Cartesian product. It can also be understood as a multi-layer loop, and each layer loops through a set. In the innermost loop, the loop variables of each layer are collected to form a record. The set of these records is the result table sequence, and its length is the product of the lengths of the sets involved in the calculation.

In fact, all the associations we mentioned earlier can be defined as follows: take a subset that meets a certain condition from the Cartesian product of the data tables participating in the association (all the join operations we have learned can use the condition of "equal association key value"), and SQL defines the join operation in this way. This definition is very simple, but it does not reflect the associated characteristics between data, which is not helpful to simplify syntax or improve performance.

SPL does not adopt this definition, but describes the common association modes separately. You can use different operation methods in different scenarios.

Let's use xjoin() to realize the generation of permutations previously realized by recursive program:

	A	B
1	5	3
2	=to(A1)	=B1.("A2:_"/~).concat(";")
3	=xjoin(${B2}).(~.array()).select(~.id().len()==~.len())	

A3 will calculate the permutations of all three members from 1,2,3,4,5.

xjoin() first calculates the Cartesian product of three to(5), and then filters out those with duplicate members (id.len()≠len()), and gets a reasonable permutation.

A1 and B1 can be changed to obtain the permutations of other values.

This code looks much simpler than recursion, but the amount of computation is much larger. We can only try it with smaller values.

We spent three chapters on structured data and its operations. These contents have far exceeded the query and calculation ability of SQL, that is, relational database. Only recursive association in the most common operations has been abandoned because of its difficulty and less application.

In other words, having learned these contents and being able to combine them flexibly, you'll have a stronger ability to handle structured data than professional database programmers who can only use SQL. Combining with Excel and other tabular software to achieve beautiful presentation, you can easily solve almost all the problems of daily data processing.

11 BIG DATA

11.1 Big data and cursor

We'll talk about how to deal with big data in this chapter.

The so-called big data here refers to the data that cannot be loaded in the memory. It is generally stored on the hard disk in the form of file or in the database (also on the hard disk). This book does not involve the database, but only the big data in the file.

Excel files are generally not too large (it has the maximum number of rows). Large files are usually in the txt or csv format mentioned before. According to the memory of modern computers, it takes tens of millions or even hundreds of millions of lines (number of records) of data to be big, and the file size will be several G or dozens of G or more.

In fact, we rarely encounter such a large amount of data in our daily desktop work, so the operation methods mentioned before are sufficient in most scenarios. However, as a complete book, we still introduce the processing methods of big data.

Is there any difference between big data and the data we processed earlier? Can't the methods we learned earlier be used?

The processing methods described in the previous chapters are all for data in memory. The file data used is also processed after being read into memory.

Because the CPU can only directly process the data in memory, it can not directly process the hard disk and other non memory data.

Can we do this: give an address for all the data on the hard disk, temporarily read it into the memory from the hard disk when we need to use it, throw it away when it has been used, and write it back to the hard disk if we need to change it, and this way it looks like directly operating a large piece of memory.

In theory, it is possible. Indeed, there are programs in some scenarios that do this (Windows has a system cache to do this). But it is hard for structured data operation to do this.

Is that because there is any essential difference between memory and hard disk?

Yes, in IT terms, memory allows **random small-piece accessing**, that is, the data under an address can be retrieved by randomly giving the address of a piece of memory. For example, when using a sequence, we can access any member with a sequence number.

The hard disk can't do that.

The hard disk is more suitable for **continuous batch accessing**. It can only read and write the whole block, at least one minimum unit at a time (the specific size is related to the operating system. At present, most computers are 4096 bytes, and bytes are used to measure the space occupied by data. It doesn't matter if you don't understand it, and it doesn't affect your understanding), and to only read an integer (only 4 or 8 bytes, and it will be smaller if compressed) will have to read in the whole block. If a large number of small pieces of data at various addresses are read (many places are accessed, and each place has a small piece of data, which is actually a very common situation), the amount of data read is actually very large, resulting in poor performance. The old mechanical hard disk can not support high-frequency random access (even reading the whole block), and the performance degradation is very serious.

Because of these troubles, for the scenario of structured data operation, no one simulates the hard disk as memory. Moreover, what's more troublesome is that the operating system does not do any special work for structured data. It only reads and writes file for the data on the hard disk, while operating files is a very complex thing, and this will further reduce the performance.

What can we do?

We can't directly access the structured data on the hard disk with the previous method. We usually use **cursor** technology to complete the operation.

When we open a data file, the cursor is like a pointer. First it points to the first record of the file, and then several records can be read into memory for processing. During the reading process, the cursor pointer will also move forward. After the data in memory is processed and discarded, and then read the next batch from the current position of the cursor for processing, ..., it is repeated until all the data are read into memory and processed.

Because the cursor will read a batch of data every time, it usually occupies multiple blocks of the hard disk, and this is actually batch continuous access, and the difficulty of hard disk is avoided.

However, due to the special structure of most data files such as txt and csv, the cursor usually can only move forward, not backward (the cost of moving backward is very high). Even moving forward, it can't jump and can only traverse row by row. In other words, accessing data with a cursor has lost randomness.

Therefore, many of the operation methods mentioned before can not be used. We need to design a set of functions for the cursor.

Let's talk about cursor related functions.

In order to do the experiment, we first generate a large file, a simplified order table.

	A	B
1		[East,West,North,South,Center]
2	for 0,999	=10000.new(A2*10000+~:id,A1(rand(5)+1):area,date(now())-1000+A2:dt,1+rand(10000):amount,1+rand(100):quantity)
3		=B2.select(rand()>=0.01)
4		>file("data.txt").export@at(B3)

The export() function will write the table sequence to the file, @a option means to append when writing. Thus, the file will be appended 1000 times, and less than 10000 records will be written each time (a part will be discarded randomly in B3), with a total of less than 10 million records. @t means that the first line of the file writes the field names as the title, which is the same as @t in xlsimport().

The id field can act as the primary key, but the primary key cannot be really established in the file data. dt is the date. The data generated each time is of the same day and it increases with the loop variable A2, which can ensure that the date is orderly (which will be used later), and the time information of now() needs to be discarded. amount and quantity can be generated randomly.

Note that the original data.txt should be deleted before execution, otherwise a batch of data will be added after the current file. In addition, it's better to add the absolute path of the file in actual use, otherwise you may not find where the file is written because the current path is uncertain.

Let's first count the total number of records in this file.

	A	B	C
1	=0	=file("data.txt").cursor@t()	
2	for	=B1.fetch(10000)	
3		if B2==null	break
4		>A1+=B2.len()	

The cursor() function will open the file and create a cursor (also a complex object), @t indicating that the first line of the file is the title. The fetch() function of the cursor will read out a table sequence composed of a specified number of records (with the title as the field name) and move forward. The next fetch() will be the next batch of records. If the end of the file is encountered in the process of reading, all the remaining records will be read, therefore, the desired number of records may not always be read out. When there is nothing to be read (end of file), null will be returned.

If we understand the above knowledge, this code is easy to understand. Do an endless loop, read 10000 records each time, and jump out of the loop after the reading is finished. In the process, add up the number of records read each time to get the result, which is stored in A1.

On this basis, let's calculate the average order amount:

	A	B	C
1	=0	=file("data.txt").cursor@t()	=0
2	for	=B1.fetch(10000)	
3		if B2==null	break
4		>A1+=B2.len()	
5		>C1+=B2.sum(amount)	
6	=C1/A1		

The sum can also be calculated in the same loop.

To calculate the sum, we only need to read the amount field; and to count the number of records, randomly reading one field is enough. It's not necessary to read all the fields. If we read less, the speed will be faster (as can be seen from the previous discussion, the amount of data read from the hard disk is almost the same, but reading fewer fields will make the processing of file reading easier):

	A	B	C
1	=0	=file("data.txt").cursor@t(amount)	=0
2	for	=B1.fetch(10000)	
3		if B2==null	break
4		>A1+=B2.len()	
5		>C1+=B2.sum(amount)	
6	=C1/A1		

We can write the fields to be read in the parameter of the cursor() function, so that the table sequence fetched will have only a few fields, and the unnecessary fields do not have to be read in. This is an important difference between external storage calculation and in-memory calculation. We never pay attention to this problem in in-memory calculation.

The structure of this endless loop is a fixed pattern. It is a little troublesome to write every time. In addition, it may happen that B3 is forgotten to write or written wrong, which will really become an endless loop. SPL actually supports direct looping against cursor:

	A	B	C
1	=0	=file("data.txt").cursor@t(amount)	=0
2	for B1,10000	>A1+=A2.len()	
3		>C1+=A2.sum(amount)	
4	=C1/A1		

The for statement can loop through the cursor, the following integer is the number of records read out each cycle, and the loop variable is the table sequence read in. When the data cannot be read out, the loop will naturally stop, so there is no need to write fetch() and end conditions, and the code is simpler.

Using loop, the data in the cursor (actually the data in the file used to create the cursor, and we will often use this saying later) is read completely in turn. The process of this operation is called **traversal** of the cursor. Recalling the previous rules, the cursor traversal can only move forward, and can only traverse once. After all the data in the cursor has been read once, the cursor traversal ends, and the cursor is useless and can no longer read data. To read the data from the beginning again, you have to recreate a new cursor.

11.2 Fuctions on cursor

To only count the number of records, SPL also has a skip() function.

	A
1	=file("data.txt").cursor@t()
2	=A1.skip()

skip() is intended to skip several records without reading, and return the number of skipped records. When there is no parameter, it will go to the end, and the number of skipped records returned is the total number of records.

It seems that it will be easier to directly use the functions on cursor. Are there corresponding cursor functions for operations like sum? After all, it's still troublesome to write a loop by yourself. For example, you need to set an initial value for sum and max.

SPL does not have a sum function for cursor, but has groups(). The average order amount in the previous section can be written as follows:

	A
1	=file("data.txt").cursor@t(amount)
2	=A1.groups(;sum(amount):S,count(amount):C)
3	=A2.S/A2.C

We learned that when the first parameter of the groups() function is filled with blank, it means that the whole data table is divided into one group, which is equivalent to summarizing the whole table, so the order amount and quantity of all the records can be recorded. The result set of A2 is a data table with only one row of record, and the average value is obtained by the calculation of A3 (the field of the first member will be selected by default when getting field value from a record sequence).

Why not provide a sum() and count() function for the cursor like for a sequence?

143

Because the cursor traversal is very slow, we should calculate as many results as possible during the traversal. If we provide functions such as sum() and count(), we need to traverse the cursor once for sum() and once again for count(), the performance will be very poor. It is also troublesome to create a new cursor in the code, so SPL does not provide it at all. Directly calculate multiple results in one traversal in groups().

However, if we always use groups() to summarize the whole table, it will always return a table sequence with only one row of record. Although there is no problem in use, it still does not feel good. And we also need to get new field names, it is a little troublesome. Therefore, SPL provides a total function, and it can be slightly simplified:

	A
1	=file("data.txt").cursor@t(amount)
2	=A1.total(sum(amount),count(amount))
3	=A2(1)/A2(2)

The total() function also requires one-time traversal to calculate multiple values, but it returns as a sequence without using the field names.

Since it is the groups() function, it can also be used for group aggregation?

Yes, for example, we can calculate the total order amount and order quantity of each area:

	A
1	=file("data.txt").cursor@t(area,amount)
2	=A1.groups(area;sum(amount):S,count(amount):C)

Note that the area field should also be fetched this time.

It seems that there is no difference in code between doing group aggregation for cursor and for table sequence or record sequence before.

It's true, but the cursor is still special. For example, we want to do another grouping by month. If it's a record sequence, just write another groups(). But if it's a cursor, it can't be used again. It has finished traversing and can't get records. At this time, we need to recreate a new cursor and then do groups().

	A
1	=file("data.txt").cursor@t(area,amount)
2	=A1.groups(area;sum(amount):S,count(amount):C)
3	=file("data.txt").cursor@t(dt,amount)
4	=A3.groups(month@y(dt);sum(amount):S,count(amount):C)

But in this way, the cursor data is traversed twice, and the speed is relatively slow.

There is indeed this problem. SPL also provides a method to calculate multiple sets of aggregate values in the process of one cursor traversal, which is called **traversal reuse**. However, these contents belong to the category of performance optimization, which can only be explained clearly by adding new concepts. They are beyond the design outline of this book, so they are not discussed here. You can refer to other documents of SPL if interested.

If you use SQL, you can only traverse multiple times. It does not support traversal reuse.

There is a groups() function for the cursor, but there is no corresponding group() function (in fact, SPL also has this function, but the use conditions are limited, and it does not correspond to groups(). We'll mention it in the next section). In other words, the groups() function of the cursor does not use the group() function to divide into subsets first, and then summarize them. Why?

Because it is not necessary, actually the groups() function for the table sequence and record sequence also does not divide into grouping subsets first and then perform summary calculation. There are many summary calculations, such as sum, count, max, etc., which can be implemented by accessing the set members in turn in a loop. Each member can be used only once, and there is no need for the random access we mentioned earlier, so the operation efficiency is higher. If you carefully read the iterative function in Chapter 5, you will understand this principle more thoroughly.

Then why doesn't the cursor have a corresponding group() function?

Cursor is introduced to handle large data that cannot be loaded into memory. If the original data table cannot be loaded into memory, it is obviously impossible to load all grouping subsets. If the group() function is provided, it is necessary to keep these grouping subsets in external storage, which has very poor performance and is very troublesome. For the operation that must be realized by grouping subsets, we will think of other better ways to do it, so we do not provide this operation.

Now that we understand the aggregation and grouping operations on a cursor, let's move on to other operations.

What will the select() function look like on a cursor? For example, we want to find orders with an order amount exceeding 5000.

At this time, it is very different from the operation of sequence and record sequence. For the selection function of the record sequence, the result record sequence is calculated directly, and we can view the members. However, it cannot be done for the cursor. Because the cursor corresponds to big data, the selected result may still be big data. We can't calculate it into a table sequence in memory. It has also to be a cursor. Therefore, the select() function on the cursor still returns a cursor.

Then, how do we view the selected result?

We use fetch(). Since the selected cursor is still a cursor, we can also use the fetch() function to fetch data. However, because it is a cursor, we can't fetch all the data, and we can only get part of it at a time.

	A
1	=file("data.txt").cursor@t()
2	=A1.select(amount>=5000)
3	=A2.fetch(100)

A2 conditionally filters the cursor and still returns a cursor. Then A3 can get the table sequence composed of 100 records to examine.

When you execute this code, you can look at the return value of A2 and find that it is a strange thing. You can't see the data in the cursor when it is not fetched. It can't be displayed anyway, so SPL just displays it as the name of the internal object.

However, what exactly does it mean to execute the select() function against the cursor? Will it traverse the data in the cursor once?

It should not. Otherwise, where will the qualified records be placed in the traversal process? As we said, it can't be loaded in memory, shall it be put into the hard disk?

SPL does not do this and there is no need to do so. The select() function of the cursor does not actually do any substantive selection action. It just remembers that there is a selection action to be done on the cursor. Only when fetching data will SPL check that there is a select() action on the cursor, and only then will it really perform condition judgment to select records. After selecting the records required by fetch() (for example, 100 records here), it stops calculating and waits for the next fetch() to calculate again.

The cursor returned by the select() function is called a **deferred cursor.** It will perform substantive calculation only when the data is really fetched. This is different from the groups() just mentioned. groups() will immediately trigger the cursor traversal action, and the returned is no longer a cursor.

When learning a cursor function, you should know its return value and whether it is a deferred cursor.

Deferred cursor technology allows cursor related code to be written much like calculations of a record sequence. For example, we want to group and summarize orders with an amount of more than 5000 by area. If it is a record sequence, we know that we just need to select() and then groups(); The same is true for cursor:

	A
1	=file("data.txt").cursor@t()
2	=A1.select(amount>=5000).groups(area;sum(amount):S)

It is exactly the same as the operation of a record sequence, and is very simple.

Therefore, we can usually not pay much attention to whether the cursors returned by these functions are deferred. It is simply understood that these functions are performing corresponding calculations, and there is generally no problem. However, we still need to know this mechanism, which is necessary when carefully analyzing the running results of some code.

However, cursor still has a key difference from record sequence.

After we execute select() to a certain record sequence, we will get a new record sequence, but the original record sequence will not change, and we can still continue to do various other calculations. The new cursor obtained after executing select() to a cursor is related to the original cursor. In the process of traversing the new cursor, the original cursor will also be traversed at the same time. When the new cursor is traversed and can not be reused, the original cursor will also be traversed and can not be reused. Conversely, traversing the original cursor will also affect the new cursor. After a new deferred cursor is obtained by executing a function on a cursor, in principle, the original cursor should not be used again, otherwise there will be very chaotic consequences.

Cursor and record sequence are essentially different. After all, there are great differences between memory and external storage. SPL just try to make them similar, so it will be more convenient to learn and write code.

Because the cursor cannot be accessed randomly, positioning is meaningless, so there are no functions like pselect() on the cursor. In addition, align() and enum() functions are often only related to small data, so there is no corresponding cursor version.

But the functions new(), run() and derive() are very meaningful. These are also deferred cursors.

For example, we add an average unit price field to orders with an order amount of more than 5000:

	A
1	=file("data.txt").cursor@t()
2	=A1.select(amount>=5000)
3	=A2.derive(amount/quantity:price)
4	=A3.fetch(100)

We can create another deferred cursor based on the deferred cursor. SPL will not calculate immediately, but marks down that there is a select() action and a derive() action on the cursor, which will be executed one by one when fetching.

new() and run() are similar. In fact, news() for expansion can also be executed on cursor. There are no more examples here.

Foreign key related switch() and join() are meaningful to cursor.

Assuming that each region will have its own tax rate, now we want to calculate the total number and amount of orders with tax exceeding 100 by month.

	A
1	[East,West,North,South,Center]
2	[0.05,0.06,0.03,0.04,0.08]
3	=A1.new(~:area,A2(#):taxrate).keys(area)
4	=file("data.txt").cursor@t()
5	=A4.switch(area,A3).select(area.taxrate*amount>100)
6	=A5.groups(month@y(dt):ym;sum(amount):S,count(amount):C)

switch() also returns a deferred cursor. In the process of groups() calculation, only when the data is read in will the switch() be actually processed, that is, converting the foreign key field area into the record of the dimension table.

Similarly, we want to add a tax field to the orders with an amount of more than 5000 and write it to another file.

	A
...	...
5	=A4.select(amount>5000)
6	=A5.join(area,A3,taxrate:tax).run(tax=tax*amount)
7	>file("data.csv").export@ct(A6)

The export() function can write the cursor directly to the file, @c means to write it as a comma separated csv file, @t means to write the field names as the first line as the title. In A6, we first use the join() function to add the tax rate to the cursor data, and then use run to change the tax rate into tax. The functions of deferring cursor can be used at multiple steps, and the writing method is exactly the same as the record sequence in memory.

11.3 Ordered cursor

Let's look at the group() function on the cursor.

As mentioned earlier, for a cursor, we can't keep all the grouped subsets after grouping in memory to continue calculation, but putting them in external storage will be very troublesome and seriously affect the performance, and the losses often outweigh the gains.

However, there is a case where a grouping subset can be placed in memory for processing. If the data in the cursor is in order to the grouping key values (always from small to large or from large to small), and each grouping subset is not large, we can always keep a grouping subset in memory. After completing the relevant summary operation for it, the current grouping subset can be discarded, and then read in the next grouping subset, and so on. In this way, we can complete some operations that must rely on grouping subsets without large memory.

This is the group() function on cursor, which requires that the cursor is ordered to grouping key values.

Moreover, this function returns a deferred cursor!

	A
1	=file("data.txt").cursor@t()
2	=A1.group(dt)
3	=A2.fetch(2)

When generating data before, we ensured that the data in the cursor is orderly to the dt field. Now look at the result of A3:

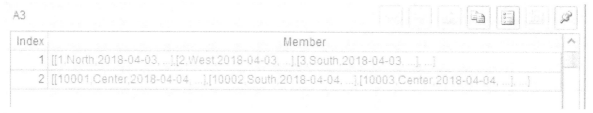

The fetch() result is not a tale sequence, but a sequence with two members (because of fetch(2)). Double click one of them to see:

Index	id	area	dt	amount	quantity
1	10001	Center	2018-04-04	5839	38
2	10002	South	2018-04-04	2343	49
3	10003	Center	2018-04-04	7017	70
4	10004	North	2018-04-04	2171	2
5	10005	Center	2018-04-04	2065	67
6	10006	North	2018-04-04	5811	77
7	10007	North	2018-04-04	3703	73
8	10008	West	2018-04-04	9748	72
9	10009	Center	2018-04-04	9783	75
10	10010	North	2018-04-04	1967	7
11	10011	East	2018-04-04	5478	45
12	10012	West	2018-04-04	4611	33
13	10013	South	2018-04-04	5522	71
14	10014	North	2018-04-04	3543	19

This looks like a table sequence. It's one group, a record sequence composed of records taken from cursor data. In fact, it is a grouping subset.

Different from the sequence, the group() and groups() of the cursor do not correspond. The group() function requires that the cursor data is ordered to the grouping key values, and returns a deferred cursor, it does not calculate immediately; groups() will immediately traverse the cursor for calculation.

A cursor with ordered data for a key value is called an **ordered cursor.**

Using this grouping subset, we will calculate the order amount and number of orders in the region with the largest order amount every day. This requires to do another group aggregation to the grouping subset and get the record where the maximum value is located. Using the code we've learned before, it's easy:

	A
1	=file("data.txt").cursor@t()
2	=A1.group(dt)
3	=A2.(~.groups(area; sum(amount):S,count(amount):C).maxp@a(S))
4	=A3.conj().fetch()

It can be seen that functions such as A.() can also be used for cursor, and it is also a deferred cursor. Moreover, in the next round of calculation based on deferred cursor, ~ can be used to represent the current member like in a loop function, but it can't use # or []. Because the relative position information of the cursor is complex, SPL has not implemented it yet, the subsequent data has not been read out, and forward adjacent reference can't be implemented.

maxp@a() will return a sequence (actually a record sequence here), so A3 will actually be a cursor equivalent to a two-layer sequence. It takes another conj() to become a single-layer sequence. conj() also returns a deferred cursor. It also needs a fetch() to get the result. A fetch() without parameter will fetch all the data. We know that the data has only 1000 days, the final result set will not be very large and can be fetched completely.

Moreover, from the group() itself and here, we can also see that cursor does not always read out a table sequence. It may fetch() out a two-layer sequence. In fact, the cursor corresponds to a sequence, not always a table sequence. The result of the fetch() is also a sub sequence, and its member may be any data that can be member of a sequence.

group() also has the @i option, and same as the group@i() of a record sequence, it is interpreted as to divide into a new group when the condition is true, and it also returns a deferred cursor. In addition, the group(...;...) function of the cursor will also be interpreted as group(...).new(...) like an in-memory record sequence, and will also return a deferred cursor.

groups also has the @o and @i options, which can perform ordered grouping to improve running performance, but groups() always calculate immediately, and will traverse immediately even for ordered cursor.

	A
1	=file("data.txt").cursor@t(dt,amount)
2	=A1.groups@o(month@y(dt);sum(amount):S,count(amount):C)

The result of this code is the same as that without @o, but with @o, the performance is better when using order.

Similar to the previous discussion on ordered grouping, ordered cursor can also be used to assist in log parsing. Usually, the log is really large and cannot be read into memory, so it is more necessary to use ordered cursor. SPL also extends the for statement to directly support fetching one grouping subset from an ordered cursor at a time.

Similar to the case of small data, we also discuss it in three cases:

1) Each N line corresponds to an event :

	A	B
1	=file("S.log").cursor@si()	
2	=create(...r	
3	for A1,3	...
...		...
...		>A2.insert(...)

Note that when reading text with a cursor, add the @si option to the cursor() function, so that it will read out a sequence composed of strings. If there is no option, it will try to interpret it as a table sequence, but the log data is often messy, and it is likely to make errors when directly parsing it as a table sequence.

2) The number of lines is not fixed. There will be a fixed starting string before each event:

3	for A1.group@i(~=="---start---"),1	...

To add parameter 1, it means that one grouping subset is read out at a time, or directly use the extended for statement:

3	for A1;~=="---start---":0	...

Note that it is a semicolon between the cursor and the following condition.

3) The number of lines is not fixed. Each line of the same event has the same prefix (such as the user ID of the log):

3	for A1.group(left(~,6)),1	...

Read in one grouping subset at a time, or use the extended for statement:

3	for A1;left(~,6))	...

You can refer to the previous code that uses ordered grouping to process small data.

11.4 Big cursor

We haven't learned the sorting of big data yet.

Sorting operation is very different. Its calculation result is as large as the source data. If the source data cannot be loaded in memory, the result cannot be loaded for sure, but unlike select() and new(), it cannot be calculated while traversing.

The sorting of big data can only be solved by using external storage as buffer. The general steps are as follows: read in some data, sort in memory and write out the result; Then read the next part, sort and write; . . .; Finally, a batch of ordered intermediate results will be obtained, and then the merging algorithm will be used to concatenate these intermediate results. This process is complex and beyond the design scope of this book, and we won't talk about the detailed principle here.

SPL provides the sortx() function to perform big data sorting. This function implements all the above series of processes. Because the sorting result is still big data, sortx() will also return a cursor, but it is not a deferred cursor. sortx() will calculate immediately, and the returned cursor is based on the intermediate results described above.

For example, we want to arrange the order data according to the average unit price from large to small, and then write it to another file:

	A
1	=file("data.txt").cursor@t()
2	=A1.sortx(-amount/quantity)
3	=file("data.csv").export@ct(A2)

Because sorting is from large to small, sortx() uses negative number as the parameter. A2 after calculation is a cursor, which cannot be viewed directly. You can get data with fetch() or write to another file like A3.

sortx() calculates immediately. When it returns after execution, cursor A1 has been traversed. At this time, even deleting data.txt will not affect the action of A3. This is completely different from functions like select(). The deferred cursor returned by the select() function will be traversed synchronously with its basis cursor in the future.

As a reminder, sortx() may be slow and need to wait for some time after running. It also takes up some hard disk space (used to store intermediate results). esProc will use the operating system temporary directory by default, or you can set the temporary directory yourself in the options.

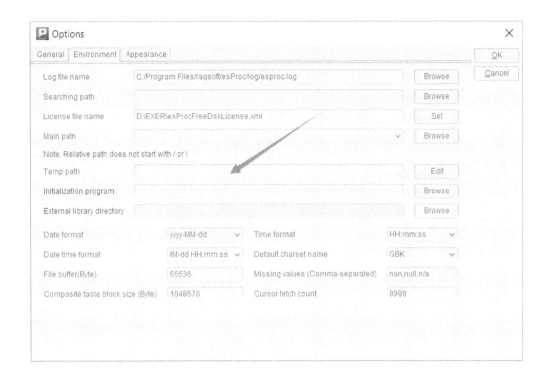

In fact, sorting for big data itself is not commonly used. We usually don't care about the full sorting result of big data, but only the top N. However, sorting is often the basis of other big data operations. Without an orderly result, other operations are difficult to do.

For example, big grouping.

For the groups() function we used before, the returned result is a table sequence, that is, small data. However, there is still some kind of group aggregation operation, and its return result will be so huge that the memory can't fit. At this time, there is no way to use groups(), which will lead to memory overflow.

However, as we said earlier, if the data is in order to the grouping key values, we can use the method of group() function, to summarize at the same time during the traversal process, and there will be no overflow. No matter how large the returned grouping result is, it can be calculated normally.

For example, we want to do a grouping by two fields amount and quantity to see how many orders there are in each group with different amount and quantity. The grouping result may be 1 million lines (it's not big, but we just regard it as big. Suppose it can't be done with groups()).

The current data has no order for the combination of these two fields. After sorting, we can use the group() function.

	A
1	=file("data.txt").cursor@t()
2	=A1.sortx(amount,quantity)
3	=A2.group(amount,quantity)
4	=A3.new(amount,quantity,~.count(1):C)
5	=A3.fetch(100)

In this way, we can calculate out the big grouping, but because the result is large, we can only fetch() a part to view or write to another file.

We can do other calculations based on it. For example, we want to calculate the total amount and quantity for groups with more than 5 orders of the same amount and quantity (that is, the summary field C>5 in A4).

	A
1	=file("data.txt").cursor@t()
2	=A1.sortx(amount,quantity)
3	=A2.group(amount,quantity)
4	=A3.new(amount,quantity,~.count(1):C)
5	=A4.select(C>5).total(sum(C*amount),sum(C*quantity))

The group() function returns a deferred cursor. We can attach another select() operation, and then traverse it with total().

Because big grouping is commonly used, SPL provides a groupx() function, which does sorting and grouping together. The above code can be simplified as:

	A
1	=file("data.txt").cursor@t()
2	=A1.groupx(amount,quantity;count(1):C)
3	=A2.select(C>5).total(sum(C*amount),sum(C*quantity))

The parameter rules of groupx() are the same as those of groups(), but it assumes that the returned result set is large, so it will sort first (actually it is more complex), then do an ordered grouping, and finally return a cursor. Like sortx(), this is not a deferred cursor. When the two actions are executed together, not only the syntax is simpler, but also the execution speed is better. However, like sortx(), it will temporarily occupy hard disk space.

In addition to the big grouping, there is also the big merging calculation.

Similar to the previous example of merging calculation, if we have two large order files on hand, we need to merge them (or calculate the intersection), and the data must be orderly in advance.

	A	B
1	=T@c("data1.txt")	=T@c("data2.txt")
2	=[A1,B1].mergex@u(id)	>T@c("all.csv",A2)

Assuming that the data is ordered by id, we can directly use mergex() to calculate union. The parameters here are the same as those of merge(), but generally we will not establish a primary key on the cursor, so we need to write the association key used in the merge operation.

Because the result set may be large, mergex() also returns a cursor, but it is a deferred cursor and will not traverse automatically. Unlike select() function, mergex() may generate a deferred cursor for multiple basis cursors. After traversing it, it will also traverse all the basis cursors. The previously mentioned select() and other functions only have one basis cursor.

The T() function uses the @c option to generate a cursor, and it will automatically select the opening method according to the file extension. It can also be used to write out, @c means to write out the cursor, and the write out method will also be selected according to the file extension.

Unlike the in-memory merge() function, mergex() requires that the cursor data must be in order to work, and there is no @o option.

After sorting, the operation that can only be realized by random access can be changed into sequential access. Another similar case is the join operation. Finding associated records with associated key values originally requires random access (searching in the data table), but if the data is in order with associated key, sequential access can achieve the goal.

SPL also provides a joinx() function with x to solve the big join.

	A	B
1	=T@c("data1.txt")	=T@c("data2.txt")
2	=joinx(A1:a,id;B1:b,id)	=A2.fetch(100)

joinx() can support the homo dimensional association and primary sub association. It also returns a deferred cursor. The form of the table sequence fetched from it is similar to that of the join() in memory. The value of each field is the record in each associated cursor, and then you can continue to use the new() function to realize further reference calculation.

Similarly, joinx() supports left join and full join with @1 and @f. We won't give detailed examples here. You can generate two data tables with different structures to try to do a big join, and you need to ensure that the association key is orderly, or you should sort with sortx() first.

You may find that there is another situation we have not mentioned, that is, in the case of foreign key association, the dimension table is too large to be loaded into memory. When we talked about switch() and join() related to foreign key on the cursor, the fact table data comes from the cursor, but the dimension table is still a table sequence in memory.

In this case, at present, foreign key can only be understood as join operation and then implemented by joinx(). If the data is disordered to the foreign key of the fact table and the primary key of the dimension table in advance, it needs to be sorted first. Moreover, each joinx() can only resolve one foreign key association, and multiple foreign keys have to do joinx() multiple times. While the switch() and join() for the in-memory dimension table can resolve multiple foreign keys in one traversal.

Unlike select(), groupx() and other functions that only work for one cursor, mergex and joinx work for multiple cursors. So, is it possible to merge and join big data and small data together?

It does exist. The merging and join operations of big data and small data are also big data, and the method of big data should be used. In this case, the small data in memory, that is, the table sequence, should be converted into a cursor, and then the cursor method should be used for operation. SPL provides cursor() function to convert the table sequence or record sequence into a cursor, so that small in-memory data can be simulated into large data and operated together with a file cursor. There are no more examples here. You can refer to relevant help documents when you need them.

We have now learned to use cursor to implement big data operations, but we can only do it right. Another important goal of big data computing is to do it fast, which is also a very complex task, or even a more complex task. Like the traversal reuse technology mentioned earlier, these contents are far beyond the design scope of this book. Here, we just give you an impression. The content of how to improve the performance of big data operation is enough to write another book of the same length. Many calculation methods need to be redesigned, especially to find ways to avoid substantive sorting, because sorting is a very slow action.

In the conventional programming languages for structured data processing, SQL can deal with big data. SQL even achieves data size transparency, that is, users do not need to care about the size of data, which obviously saves people a lot of troubles. This is a huge advantage of SQL. However, using SQL usually needs to load the data into the database, which is too complex and beyond the ability of most non professional programmers.

esProc provides the function of using basic SQL for files and can support most big data operations, so as to avoid the trouble of loading data into the database.

Python is also often used for structured data calculation, but it has no cursor object, and it is very troublesome when processing big data. It is equivalent to implementing the cursor action by yourself, which is basically an impossible task for non professionals.

12 DRAWING GRAPHICS

12.1 Canvas and elements

Programming language can not only help us do data processing, but also draw graphs.

Let's start with a simple example:

	A	B
1	[10,20,40,30,50]	[East,North,West,South,Center]
2	=A1.new(B1(#):area,~:**amount**)	
3	=canvas()	
4	=A3.plot("GraphColumn","categories":A2.(area),"values":A2.(amount))	
5	=A3.draw(600,400)	

Be careful not to write the code wrong. The string contents should be exactly the same. SPL is a case sensitive language.

After execution, click A5 and you will see the following result:

Now click the icon button on the right, and esProc will pop up a graph:

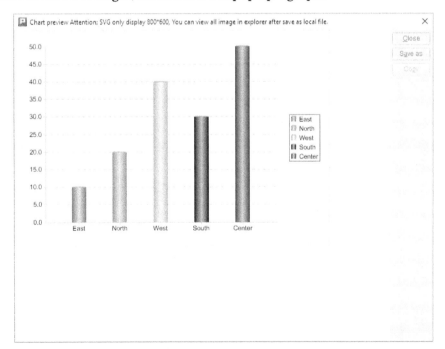

Comparing with the data in table sequence A2, we will find that this graph is a statistical chart drawn with these data.

155

Let's explain this code.

We are already familiar with the first two lines. The canvas() function of A3 will return an object we call the **canvas.** The plot() function of A4 will plot on the canvas, and then use the draw() function of A5 to actually draw it. After the graph is drawn, the canvas is still an object in memory. We need to use a special program to display it, that is, what to be done after clicking the button on the right, and the graph we see appears.

Computer drawing requires a plane rectangular area (because the screen and paper are all this shape), and the canvas simulates such an area. The plot() function is responsible for plotting on the canvas. The plot() function of SPL is a bit like a deferred cursor. It does not really draw the graph directly on the canvas, but just notes what to draw. Only when the draw() function is executed does the drawing really start, and a graphic object that can be used for display is returned (it is different from the canvas. You can click the cell to see the value).

The parameter of the draw() function is the number of pixels (readers familiar with mobile phones will not be unfamiliar with this concept), that is, it indicates how big the final graph to be drawn is. Only after knowing this information can SPL start real drawing. This parameter is not appropriate to be given when creating the canvas, because the graph produced by the same set of plot() statements can be presented in different sizes. For example, we can write another statement in A6

=A3.draw(400,300)

It will change the size of the graph and draw it again.

However, usually we don't need to change many sizes. Generally, there is only one draw(). Therefore, it can be simply understood that plot() is drawing, but it needs a draw() to specify the size before presenting. Let's focus on the plot() function in the future. All the plot collections in SPL are solved by this function.

Now let's change the first parameter of the plot() function in A4:

=A3.plot("GraphPie","categories":A2.(area),"values":A2.(amount))

The result is a pie chart:

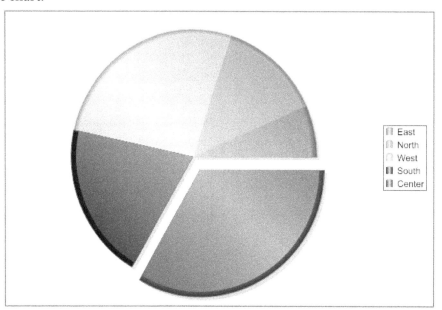

In the future, the screenshot only has the middle graphic part, not the window edge.
The outer frame is added during book typesetting, not the content of the graph itself. This will also happen later.

It seems that the plot() function can do many things. What are its parameters? What else can it draw?

Right click A4 and a menu will pop up, including an item "Graphics editor":

Select this menu item and a dialog box will pop up:

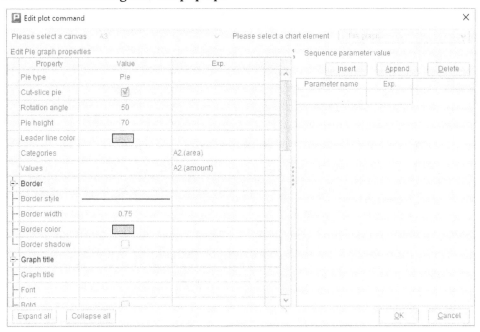

The first column on the left is the parameters of the plot() function! There are so many that it's easy to see when you have to expand and collapse. The right part is used to edit sequence type parameter settings, which will be used in the following section when we talk about legends.

There are too many parameters of the plot() function, and it is too difficult to fill in the code directly, so esProc has made an editing dialog to facilitate programmers to fill in the parameters.

You can try to modify these parameters to see the effect. Most of them are graphic appearance attributes, and there is no need to explain them here.

Now delete the code in cell A4, right-click to get the menu and select the graphics editor item. This dialog box will also pop up:

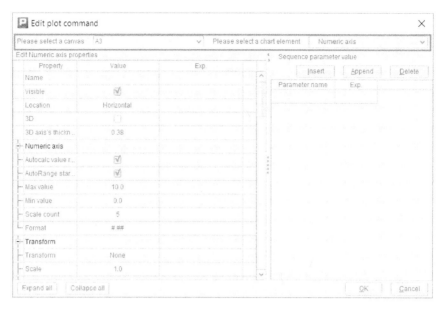

But unlike just now, the content on the top can be edited. The left is used to select the canvas. esProc knows which cells have the statement to create the canvas, and will list these cells for selection. The selection on the right is called an **element**. Open the drop-down box and the elements that can be selected will be listed here.

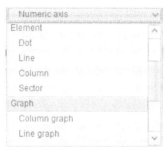

The graphics in SPL are composed of a batch of elements, and each kind of element has its own properties. After selecting an element, the below property list will change, and then fill in the properties of this element, the editing of this plot() function is finished. Each plot() will draw one or more elements of the same type on the canvas.

Some elements are very simple, such as a point, a line or a line of text. Some elements are very complex and are composed of other more basic elements. For example, the column graph and pie graph presented by us are called **finished graphs** in SPL. They are some statistical charts made in advance, which can also be understood as a complex element.

The finished graph is very convenient to use. You can draw the graph as long as you fill in the parameters, but it does not have much worth learning. We show the examples of finished graph just to let you feel how the program language draws and the editing method of plot() function. This book does not intend to introduce the parameters of these finished graphs. You can refer to the help documents when needed, and it is similar to the graphics of Excel.

We should learn more basic knowledge and understand how these finished graphs are drawn, and then we can make the desired graphics according to our own wishes without being limited to the fixed finished graphs.

12.2 Coordinate system

To draw a graph, we must first establish the concept of **coordinate system.** We all learned some knowledge of plane analytic geometry and rectangular coordinate system in middle school. We know that all dots on the plane can be represented by coordinates. The same is true of computer drawing, which usually uses **rectangular coordinate system** to determine the position.

Different from the coordinate system we are used to, the origin of the canvas coordinate system is in the upper left corner, its Y-axis direction is from top to bottom, and the whole canvas is in its first quadrant.

Let's try to draw a few dots with this coordinate system:

	A	B
1	[50,100,150,200,250]	
2	=canvas()	
3	=A2.plot("Dot","data1":300,"data2":50)	
4	=A2.plot("Dot","data1":A1,"data2":A1)	
5	=A2.draw(400,300)	=A2.draw(600,400)

The result is as follows:

Obviously, the dot on the upper right is drawn by A3, and the row of dots on the left that can form a slash is drawn by A4. Why are the dots in this row drawn in different colors? We'll explain later.

The plot() function can draw a single dot at a time or multiple dots at a time, as long as the coordinate value sequence is given. Data1 and Data2 correspond to the X-axis and Y-axis respectively. Note that if multiple dots are drawn, the two coordinate sequences should be of the same length.

You can try to use the plot() editing interface to change some appearance, such as the shape and color of dots.

The coordinate values are in pixels, so the results drawn in A5 and B5 are the same, both in the upper left part of the whole canvas, and the size is the same. However, we often want graphics to change with size (like the finished graph in the previous section), so it is not appropriate to use pixels as coordinate units.

SPL also provides relative coordinates. If the coordinate value is less than 1, it is considered as the proportion relative to the canvas, that is, the coordinate range of the whole canvas is within the [0,1] interval. Let's try.

	A	B
1	=10.((~-1)*0.1)	=A1.(~*~)
2	=canvas()	
3	=A2.plot("Line","data1":A1,"data2":B1)	
4	=A2.draw(400,300)	=A2.draw(600,400)

Now it can draw half a parabola, and B4 is larger than A4, realizing proportional scaling.

This time, line is used to draw. The dots in the figure are connected. You can change various appearance properties of the element by yourself. You can also choose not to draw dots.

In theory, with this coordinate system, we can draw any figure. Usually, the drawing mechanism that can be provided by a programming language that is not used for professional graphics can only provide the above content (of course, there will be some functions to complete complex composite actions). However, this is obviously inconvenient. Sometimes the drawing position is not exactly within the [0,1] range or the pixel range of the canvas, so you need to make some transformations yourself. Although SPL has strong computing power, it is not a problem to complete these things, but it is still a little troublesome.

Moreover, in the previous finished graphs, the parameters we passed to the element in the code are directly the region name and amount value, and it can draw very well. It will be much more convenient if we can draw like this.

When using pixel coordinates and relative coordinates to draw a graphic, we use a set of coordinate system that is inherent in the canvas, called **physical coordinates**. SPL allows programmers to draw with their own data as coordinate values, which requires the establishment of a **logical coordinate** system.

We know that a rectangular coordinate system always has two axes: the horizontal axis and the vertical axis. As long as the axes are determined, the coordinate system is determined. SPL uses this method to establish the logical coordinate system. Let's look at the list of elements on the upper right of the element editing box. The first part is the axis. There are three types:

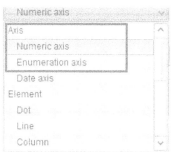

We select the first numeric axis and look at its properties, focusing on these:

Property	Value
Name	x
Visible	☑
Location	Horizontal
3D	☐
3D axis's thickn...	0.38
Numeric axis	
Autocalc value r...	☐
AutoRange star...	☐
Max value	3
Min value	-3

Property	Value
Horizontal axis	
X start	0.1
X end	0.9
Y position	0.5
Vertical axis	
Y start	0.8
Y end	0.1
X Position	0.1

The three properties on the left indicate that it is a horizontal axis and the value range is [-3,3] (the default value is not this, but this is a property that can be modified, including the above two checked items, which are checked by default). The actual position of the axis is defined on the right. Because there are only physical coordinates when defining the axis, its position can only be described by physical coordinates. These 0.1, 0.9 and 0.5 are the relative coordinates mentioned earlier (these are not the default values).

Use the element editing interface to add an element to the code, use the property values in the figure above, and use the default values for unlisted properties. Note that you should also name this axis (the first row of the property list), which is called x here.

Similarly, add a vertical axis named y, set the range as [-3,3], and uncheck the two items above the range. The position of the axis is filled as 0.9, 0.1 and 0.5. Note that the position of the vertical axis should be filled in the property of the vertical axis in the lower half of the right figure, and the start is 0.9 and the end is 0.1, from large to small. In this way, the y axis can be made from bottom to top, which is in line with our habit.

Add a draw() after the generated code:

	A	B
1	=canvas()	
2	=A1.plot("NumericAxis","name":"x","autoCalcValueRange":false,"autoRangeFromZero":false,"maxValue":3,"minValue":-3,"xEnd":0.9,"xPosition":0.5)	
3	=A1.plot("NumericAxis","name":"y","location":2,"autoCalcValueRange":false,"autoRangeFromZero":false,"maxValue":3,"minValue":-3,"yStart":0.9,"yEnd":0.1,"yPosition":0.5)	
4	=A1.draw(600,400)	

Execute it and take a look:

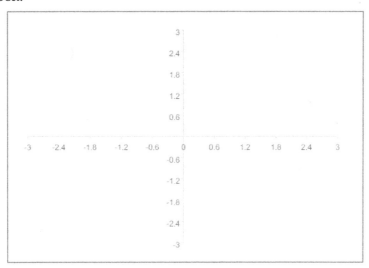

Sure enough, two axes are drawn. You can set various properties of the axis to control whether the scale and arrow are displayed.

Now let's draw with the coordinate system determined by these two axes, and continue to write code:

	A	B
1	=canvas()	=60.((~-1)*6*pi()/180)
...	...	
4	=B1.(2*cos(~)-cos(2*~))	=B1.(2*sin(~)-sin(2*~))
5	=A1.plot("Line","axis1":"x","data1":A4,"axis2":"y","data2":B4)	
6	=A1.draw(600,400)	

A5 uses these properties:

⊟ Data			
— Axis 1		x	
— Data 1/X			A4
— Axis 2		y	
— Data2/Y			B4

This indicates that the element drawn in A5 is positioned with two axes called x and y, and the coordinates of the dots to be drawn are in A4 and B4.

We succeeded in drawing this:

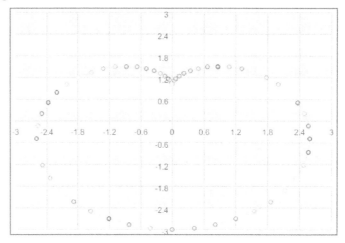

SPL graphics are mainly used to draw statistical charts for structured data. The default properties of these elements are not simple. For example, a dot will have different sizes to be seen clearly. Generally, the axis will have a scale, and there will be stripes by default when drawing the coordinate system. These can be adjusted by modifying properties, but after changing to non-default values, the parameters of the plot() function will be longer and inconvenient to be listed in the book, so we try to use the default properties, but it's a little strange to draw the function diagram. However, this does not affect the understanding of knowledge points.

These axes defined by ourselves are called **logical axes**, while the original two axes of the canvas are called **physical axes**. When drawing an element, the drawing of the two axes means that the logical coordinate system established by these two axes will be used, and then we can use our more convenient values as coordinate values. If no logical axis is selected, it means that physical coordinates will be used, such as the graph at the beginning of this section.

The essence of the logical axis is to map the familiar business values into the coordinate values of the physical axis. After the axis is defined, the business values are used in graphic drawing. The logical axis is responsible for finding the correct position. After modifying the mapping relationship between the logical axis and the physical axis, the graphic drawing code does not need to be changed, and the graphics will be drawn in another way.

For example, we can move the y axis up a little, change its start and stop position to 0.5 and 0.1, and then try to let SPL automatically find the range of coordinate axis at the same time:

	A	B
1	...	
2	=A1.plot("NumericAxis","name":"x","autoRangeFromZero":false,"xEnd":0.9,"xPosition":0.5)	
3	=A1.plot("NumericAxis","name":"y","location":2,"autoRangeFromZero":false,"yStart":0.5,"yPosition":0.5)	

To let SPL automatically calculate the coordinate axis range, check the first of the two items above the value range and leave the second unchecked. The value range can be left blank.

Now it's drawn like this. There is only graphic in the upper part of the canvas.

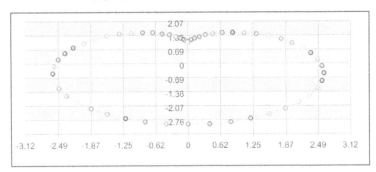

SPL provides three kinds of logical axes: numeric axis, enumeration axis and date axis. This is divided by the data type of business data. The numeric axis is used when the business data is numeric, the enumeration axis is used when it is a sequence, and the date axis is used when it is a date type.

In the previous finished graph, the enumeration axis is used, and the area values are in a sequence. At this time, we can ask SPL to draw a column at the position with the abscissa of East and the ordinate of 10. As for the specific position of East corresponding to the canvas, it is solved by the logical axis. When writing the drawing code, just care about its business significance.

Let's try to redraw the previous column chart using the logical axis.

	A	B
1	[10,20,40,30,50]	[East,North,West,South,Center]
2	=canvas()	
3	=A2.plot("EnumAxis","name":"area")	
4	=A2.plot("NumericAxis","name":"amount","location":2)	
5	=A2.plot("Column","axis1":"area","data1":B1,"axis2":"amount","data2":A1)	
6	=A2.draw(600,400)	

A3 creates the enumeration axis as the horizontal axis, named area, and other properties use the default values; A4 uses a conventional numeric axis as the vertical axis, named amount, and also uses the default properties. Then A5 draws a graph in the logical coordinate system established by the two axes with the data of A1 and B1.

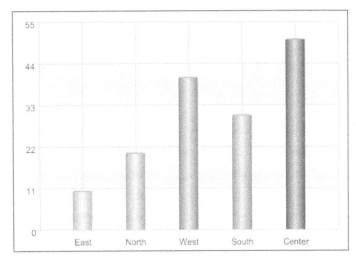

There is still a problem. Now that the order of these columns from left to right is the order of the data in B1. If we want to change the order, or if there are some regions that do not appear in the business data, but still want a position in the graph, do we have to modify the business data in B1?

No, how to find the physical position should be the task of the axis, which has nothing to do with the business data.

Change the code:

	A	B
1	[10,20,40,30]	[East,North,West,South]
2	=canvas()	[East,North,Center,West,South]
3	=A2.plot("EnumAxis","name":"area","categories":B2)	
...	...	

We deliberately fill in one less data of A1 and B1, but there is a complete region sequence in B2. When A3 establishes the enumeration axis, fill its "categories" property as B2, and draw it again:

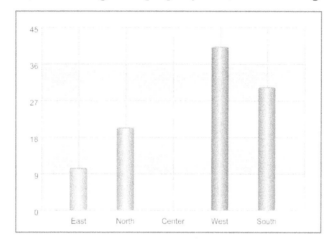

How to find the physical position is indeed the task of the axis, which has nothing to do with the data used for drawing. Only when the corresponding property of the axis is not filled in, SPL will automatically fill in one.

To sum up, SPL realizes the transformation from business data to physical position through the logical axis. If you understand this principle, the date axis is easy to understand (just converting the date into position). It is also easy to understand the properties of the logical axis element. For example, logarithmic and exponential transformation can also be done on the numeric axis. These contents no longer involve knowledge points, but specific syntax and editing schemes. Please refer to SPL documents when necessary.

12.3 More coordinate systems

We also saw a pie chart in the first section, but it seems too troublesome to describe the positions of these circles and sectors in the coordinate system. How was it drawn?

In addition to the rectangular coordinate system, SPL also provides the **polar coordinate system.**

The polar coordinate system also requires two axes (plane graphics always need two axes): polar axis and angular axis. In addition to selecting horizontal and vertical axes, polar and angular axes can also be selected for the location properties of axis element:

Property	Value		Property	Value
Name	area		Name	amount
Visible	☑		Visible	☑
Location	Polar ⌄		Location	Angle ⌄
3D	☐		3D	☐

Readers with polar coordinate system knowledge can easily understand the location properties of these two axis elements, which will not be repeated here.

Change the previous column graph to polar coordinate system:

	A	B
1	[10,20,40,30,50]	[East,North,West,South,Center]
2	=canvas()	
3	=A2.plot("EnumAxis","name":"area","location":3)	
4	=A2.plot("NumericAxis","name":"amount","location":4)	
5	=A2.plot("Column","axis1":"area","data1":B1,"axis2":"amount","data2":A1)	
6	=A2.draw(600,400)	

Only the definition of the axis is modified, and the element statement in A5 is not changed at all. But it is drawn like this:

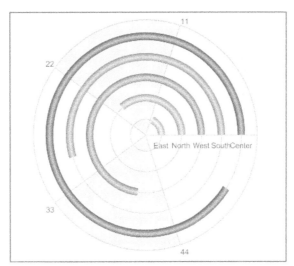

This is not what we want. But when you think about it carefully, SPL is right. It turns the horizontal axis and vertical axis into polar axis and angular axis. The position of the horizontal axis becomes the radius of the polar axis, while the value of the vertical axis becomes the angle of the angular axis. The column element has no problem in polar coordinate system.

We need to stack these "columns" in one position. We find that the element does have this property, but after using it, it draws five whole circles, which are not stacked in one position.

It turns out that the coordinate of the enumeration axis corresponds to a sequence composed of members of two sections. The former section is called category and the latter is called series. Stacking can only be between series. In fact, category and series are equivalent to two levels, but it is not easy to describe them with a two-layer sequence. It needs a table sequence with fields, which is troublesome, so SPL uses comma separated strings to describe this relationship. such as

["USA,NY","USA,CA","USA,TX",...,

"CHN,BJ","CHN,SH","CHN,TJ",...,

...]

It can describe a two-tier relationship. The same in the previous section is considered to be the same category. The series under different categories can be the same or different.

In our current situation, we should regard these areas as series under one category, and there is only one category.

Adjust the code:

	A	B
1	[10,20,40,30,50]	[East,North,West,South,Center]
2	=canvas()	=B1.("",+~)
...	...	
5	=A2.plot("Column","stackType":1,"axis1":"area","data1":B2,"axis2":"amount","data2":A1)	
6	=A2.draw(600,400)	

Percentage stacking shall be used in A5, which will ensure that the entire 360-degree angular axis is filled. At the same time, the data of the first axis should be changed to B2, preceded by a comma to turn the area list into a series (there is only one empty category).

Now it's drawn like this, and it's a little familiar. The rest is to adjust the width of the "column", and there is a lack of indication information. These can be realized step by step.

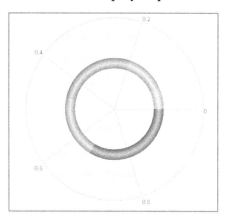

However, it is still too troublesome. SPL directly provides a sector element, which will automatically convert category into series and stack:

	A	B
...	...	
5	=A2.plot("Sector","axis1":"area","data1":B1,"axis2":"amount","data2":A1)	
6	=A2.draw(600,400)	

Use the default properties of the element to draw it, only the appearance is different from the previous graph. Just adjust the properties.

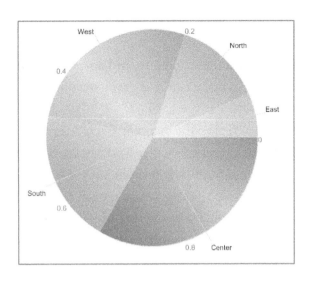

You may have found that we do not define a logical coordinate system, but set two axes for the element each time. So, if we have three axes x, y1 and y2, can x and y1 fit into a logical coordinate system and x and y2 fit into another logical coordinate system?

Yes. This is a biaxial graph.

	A	B	C
1	[10,20,40,30,50]	[4,2,3,4,9]	[East,North,West,South,Center]
2	=canvas()		
3	=A2.plot("EnumAxis","name":"area")		
4	=A2.plot("NumericAxis","name":"amount","location":2)		
5	=A2.plot("NumericAxis","name":"quantity","location":2,"yPosition":0.8)		
6	=A2.plot("Column","axis1":"area","data1":C1,"axis2":"amount","data2":A1)		
7	=A2.plot("Line","axis1":"area","data1":C1,"axis2":"quantity","data2":B1)		
8	=A2.draw(600,400)		

A4 and A5 define two vertical axes. A6 uses the coordinate system composed of A3 and A4, and A7 uses the coordinate system composed of A3 and A5. The drawn biaxial graph:

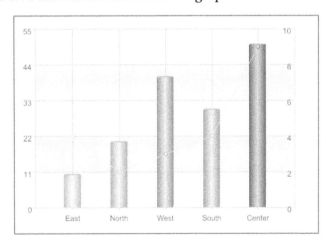

12.4 Legend

We never explained how the colors of these columns and dots came from. Moreover, there are legends in the finished graph, but it has not appeared when we draw a graph by ourselves. How should it be drawn?

The introduction of logical axis can realize the mapping from business data to physical position. We can draw a dot at the position of (East,40), and the logical axis will be responsible for finding the correct physical position.

Similarly, the legend is also a mapping, which is responsible for mapping the business data into colors. Since we can draw a dot at (East,40), we should also be able to use the East color to draw a column. Whether to use red or blue when drawing on the graph is determined by the legend. Later, to change the mapping mode in the legend, we can get different graphics without changing the plot() statement itself.

In this sense, the legend can also be regarded as some kind of axis, but it maps the business data to the color of the element, not the position. In fact, not only colors can be mapped, but colors are the most commonly used. If we want to obtain black-and-white graphics (such as for printing), it is easy to be confused to distinguish by color. At this time, we can use shape, linetype and other appearance properties to distinguish. The task of the legend is to map the business data to some appearance property of the element.

Let's try to control the color of the column by ourselves. First edit a legend, select the legend in the element list, give the legend a name (called manager here, which will be used later), and then find the arrow on the right of the following two properties in the property list and click:

Property	Value	Exp.	
Name	manager		
Legend data			⇒

⊟ Legend			
Legend type	Rectangle		⇒
Line type			⇒
Line weight	1.0		⇒
Line color			⇒
Fill color			⇒
Marker shape	○		⇒

A list will appear in the right half of the editing dialog, in which you can fill in the following lines (click the color column to pop up another dialog box to select the color):

Legend data ⇌	Exp.	Fill color ⊹
John		
Alice		
Mary		

You can see that the property list on the left has been filled in. Actually, it is OK to fill in directly on the left, but because the sequence members as properties should correspond one by one, it is easy to misplace if filling in directly, so use the list on the right to assist.

Because color is very complex information, the edited plot() statement is very complex and long.

Now let's use this legend:

	A	B	C
1	[10,20,40,30,50]	[East,North,West,South,Center]	[John,Alice,John,Mary,Alice]
2	=canvas()		
3	=A2.plot("Legend","name":"manager","legendText":["John","Alice","Mary"],"legendFillColor":[["ChartColor",0,false,-65536,-5252872,0],["ChartColor",0,false,-16776961,-5252872,0],["ChartColor",0,false,-16711936,-5252872,0]])		
4	=A2.plot("EnumAxis","name":"area")		
5	=A2.plot("NumericAxis","name":"amount","location":2)		
6	=A2.plot("Column","fillColor":C1:"manager","axis1":"area","data1":B1,"axis2":"amount","data2":A1)		
7	=A2.draw(600,400)		

A2 is the legend statement just edited.

A sequence is added to the data to represent the manager in charge of each region. There may be multiple regions that are in charge by the same manager. Seeing the names, we know that we are going to use different colors to represent different managers.

When editing the A6 plot column statement, fill in the appearance property like this, use the value in sequence C1 as the color, and the legend name is manager.

Property	Value	Exp.	Legend	
⊟ Appearance				
— Column width	0.9			⇒
— Column shape	Column			⇒
— Border style	————			⇒
— Border weight	0			⇒
— Border color	▬			⇒
— Fill color		C1	manager	⇒

SPL will successively use the members of C1 to get the actual colors from the legend manager to draw the picture.

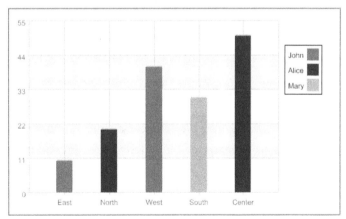

At the same time, the legend is also drawn to the edge. Modifying the properties of the legend element can change its position.

Let's go back to the question mentioned earlier. Why do a row of dots and columns automatically have different colors?

If no definite color is selected during drawing, SPL will automatically set a default legend for the element. If there is an enumeration axis in the drawing, the color will correspond to the coordinates of this enumeration axis. The default legend is called Legend. We can draw it:

	A	B
1	[10,20,40,30,50]	[East,North,West,South,Center]
2	=canvas()	=A2.plot("Legend")
3	=A2.plot("EnumAxis","name":"area")	
4	=A2.plot("NumericAxis","name":"amount","location":2)	
5	=A2.plot("Column","axis1":"area","data1":B1,"axis2":"amount","data2":A1)	
6	=A2.draw(600,400)	

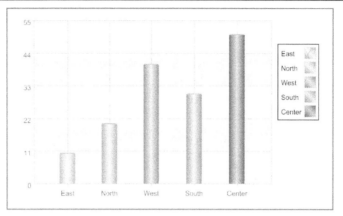

Let's try other appearance properties and draw this graph with dots of different shapes.

	A	B	C
1	[10,20,40,30,50]	[East,North,West,South,Center]	[John,Alice,John,Mary,Alice]
2	=canvas()		
3	=A2.plot("Legend","name":"manager","legendText":["John","Alice","Mary"],"legendType":2,"legendFillColor":["ChartColor",0,false,-16777216,-5252872,0],"legendMarkerShape":[1,2,3])		
4	=A2.plot("EnumAxis","name":"area")		
5	=A2.plot("NumericAxis","name":"amount","location":2)		
6	=A2.plot("Dot","markerStyle":C1:"manager","lineColor":-16777216,"markerColor":["ChartColor",0,false,-16777216,-5252872,0],"radius1":0.2,"radius2":1,"axis1":"area","data1":B1,"axis2":"amount","data2":A1)		
7	=A2.draw(600,400)		

When defining the legend in A3, use the dot type, select different shapes as the rendering properties of the legend, and select the fill color as black, otherwise SPL will draw the legend in color by default.

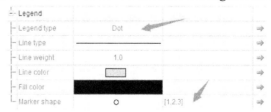

Use the dot element in A6 to correspond the shape to the legend, and increase the radius of the dot to see it more clearly (the unit of radius is determined by the logical axis of the horizontal axis and the vertical axis, and the distance between two adjacent members of the enumeration axis is 1), and the line color and fill color are set to black.

Marker			
Marker style	O	C1	manager
Line style	——		
Line weight	1.0		
Line color	▬		
Fill color	███		
Marker weight	0		
Radius 1	0.2		
Radius 2	1		

Draw a black-and-white graph without color:

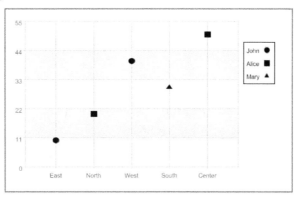

APPENDIX

More Resources

The following links and information will remain valid until at least December 31, 2026.

1. https://github.com/SPLWare/esProc

   The open source address of the esProc.

   However, it is difficult for non-professionals to use opensource code directly, you can use the below commercial edition.

2. https://www.scudata.com/download-Desktop

   The download address for the esProc desktop edition.

   The desktop edition is a commercial edition, but you can keep trying it for free to learn the contents of the book, please refer to the information on this page to obtain.

3. https://doc.scudata.com/esproc/func

   SPL function reference.

   This book focuses on the content related to the conceptual knowledge points, and does not introduce the use methods of various functions and options in detail. If you want to make the data processing at work more convenient, you need to practice more, especially be familiar with various common library functions.

4. https://c.scudata.com/article/1634722432114

   The web edition of this book (including some exercises), due to typographical limitations, is not as good as the reading experience of the paper book, but you can copy codes directly from these pages to practice.

5. https://c.scudata.com/article/1651916536524

   A set of Excel processing routines for non-professionals, including how to use SPL Excel plug-ins and a lot of samples.

6. https://c.scudata.com/article/1692757887444

   More Samples.

7. https://c.scudata.com/article/1662368734970

   SPL programming CookBook, slightly professional, can be used as an advanced reading.

What programming language should non professionals learn?

Programming was once considered a basic skill in modern society, just like driving, that none professionals should also master, and it is also taught in primary and secondary schools. But in reality, its popularity is far worse than driving, and there are very few people who master this skill. The knowledge learned in school is forgotten because it cannot be used in work.

Why is this happening?

To answer this question, we first need to answer: **Why do we need to learn programming?** What do you want to do after learning?

Except for a few individuals who are highly interested (who are likely to become professional programmers), the purpose of most none professionals learning programming should be to assist with daily work. There are indeed many things that can be easily solved by programming, while doing them manually can be very cumbersome. For example, merging 500 Excel spreadsheets, generating employee cards using a roster, and so on. There are many training classes on the street that advocate promoting work efficiency after learning XXX, which will also make many workplace people tempted.

This purpose requires learning two levels of content:

The first level is the basic logic of the program.

For example, variables, branches, loops, and so on. Without understanding these, almost no program can be written. However, this part of the content is not complicated or too much. Friends who have a basic understanding of using Excel formulas can master it with a little effort. Moreover, almost all programming languages have similar abilities in this area, and even use similar keywords and syntax rules. If you have mastered one language, it is easy to learn others, which can be extrapolated.

However, after learning this level of content, you can only solve some arithmetic problems of primary and secondary schools, such as solving chicken and rabbit problem, decomposing prime factors, etc. Practicing your brain is ok, and it is almost useless for assisting daily work.

Unfortunately, facing none professionals, many tutorial books and even training courses end here, or in other words, can only teach to this level, as will be explained later.

To apply what you have learned, you must also learn the second level of content, which is **structured data** and its operations.

The daily work that we hope to solve by programming, which is actually processing the data at hand, most of these are Excel spreadsheets or data that can be filled into Excel spreadsheets, such as:

This type of data has a name called **structured data.** Only by mastering the concepts of structured data and common operations such as tables, records, fields, grouping, joins, etc., can one truly cope with daily work. Structured data usually appears in batches (tables usually have many rows of data), so it is important to be familiar with the concepts related to sets, however high school mathematics knowledge is sufficient.

Unfortunately again, unlike countless courses on the first level of basic logic, tutorials for none professionals rarely involve knowledge of structured data. Perhaps only database courses will systematically explain these things, but they are the foundation of daily work and not so difficult for none professionals to master. For example, do you often use Excel for filtering, summarizing, and even doing joins (the word "join" may not be understood, but it is actually what VLOOKUP does)? But without systematic learning, one will become confused when encountering more complex situations.

After mastering both levels of knowledge, none professionals can truly handle daily work with ease, and their work efficiency is impressive.

Then, which programming language to learn?

For the first level of knowledge, there is theoretically a lot of room for choice, and even any language can be chosen, because this is a common content of all programming languages. Then just choose a programming language that is good at handling structured data, which is convenient for learning the second level of knowledge and can also be applied.

In principle, this is the case, but when facing friends with zero foundation, the environmental configurations cannot be too complicated, or they will faint. Zero foundation friends need to install and be ready to use, or even better without installation.

In the early days (over 30 years ago), machines had their own BASIC language, which was indeed usable without installation. But I can't figure out why it's all gone now, and I can't say if this is progress or regression.

There are two main languages that do not need to be installed now, one is JavaScript that comes with the browser, and the other is VBA that comes with Excel. Although these two things do not need installation, if you really want to use them, you need to understand many concepts inside browsers and Excel (called objects in professional terms), which are even more difficult than the program logic itself and are not suitable for beginners.

Sometimes I miss BASIC back then.

How about Python with training classes all over the street? It looks very beautiful.

If it is only used to learn the first level of knowledge, Python can be said to be no problem. It is not difficult to install only basic feature packages, and writing code to run in the development environment is not a problem.

But if you want to learn structured data, for most none professionals, we can confidently say: **you cannot master it!** Not to mention applying what has been learned. The detail reason can be referred the next article.

Not to mention Java, C/C++, and so on. Object orientation is originally an advanced thing that is not suitable for beginners to understand; Structured data processing ability is almost zero, and learning it is useless; The development environment is also very complex, after all, these things are for professionals to work on large software, and complexity has its own reason.

It is unimaginable for primary and secondary schools to teach Java as a computer enlightenment course.

What about SQL? Its structured data processing capabilities are sufficient for beginners, and it is truly something they can master. It is also a quirk that can skip to the second level without learning the first level (so we mentioned "almost" before, not absolutely), and can make quite complex queries without understanding the concepts of variables or loops.

However, there are still challenges. SQL needs to run in the database, but none professionals usually cannot handle the installation of the database and have no ability to dump Excel into the database (otherwise they cannot process it with SQL). As a result, even after learning, there is no place for practical application.

After all the talk, isn't there no suitable language to learn?

Yes, if you look at these mainstream programming languages, there really isn't. Either you cannot master it, or learning it won't be of much use.

Because of this, although programming concepts have been hyped up, none professionals have never been able to use them, constantly asking what to learn. No matter how many training classes there are, it's useless. The training classes don't have the ability to improve or invent programming languages. This is essentially a matter of not having eggs, not a matter of how to make an omelet.

Probably only esProc SPL is a programming language suitable for none professionals with zero foundation.

As a programming language, SPL has a complete set of basic program logic (first level knowledge); The full name of SPL is Structured Process Language, which was invented to deal with structured data. Its structured data processing ability is extremely strong, and it can be said that it has the most complete ability in this area among current programming languages, far exceeding Python and SQL, and we will not go to details here. One-click installation, easy to write and debug in a grid, carefully designed syntax and rich function library for easier mastery; It can directly read and write and calculate Excel files, and even execute SQL on files (so it can also be used to learn SQL).

However, SPL was not specifically invented for beginners, but to solve the problems of SQL being difficult to write and too slow. But when you actually use it, you will find that its system is simple and easy to use, which is very suitable for beginners to learn programming. The key is to truly apply what you have learned.

Actually, you will nevel be able to master Python

This article is a clickbait, there are thousands of Python programmers, of course, many people can master it. The term "you" here refers to none professionals in the workplace.

People in the workplace usually use Excel to process data, but there are also many helpless situations, such as complex calculations, duplicate calculations, automatic processing, etc. When encountering a crash without saving, it can often cause people to collapse. If you can master a programming language, these problems won't be a problem anymore. So, what should we learn?

Countless training institutions and online materials will tell us: Python!

The Python code looks very simple, it can solve many troublesome Excel problems in just a few lines, and it looks really good.

But is that really the case? As none professionals, can we really use Python to assist us in our work?

It just looks beautiful!

In fact, Python is not suitable for people in the workplace because it is too difficult. As a none professional in the workplace, you just cannot master it, and even **the difficulty of Python may be so great that you cannot understand why it is too difficult to learn.**

The data encountered in daily work is mostly in the form of Excel spreadsheets, known as structured data. To assist daily work, programming languages need to have strong structured data processing capabilities.

Python requires an open-source package called Pandas to handle structured data, which is not an inherent component of Python. You have to download and install it yourself, and the process is not very simple. It needs to be accompanied by a bunch of things that make beginners dizzy. Of course, third-party programs can also be used, but the installation of these third-party programs themselves is a problem, and there are a lot of engineering environment configurations when starting up that make people feel confused (they are designed for large applications). And also debugging, you can't write the code right all at once. The debugging function of the Python development environment is not very good, and Pandas is not native to Python, making debugging even more difficult.

These troubles are still off topic and can be overcome. The key issue is that Pandas is not designed for structured data, and there are many things that cannot be as desired and are very difficult to understand

Let's take a look at an example, such as this table:

EID	NAME	SURNAME	GENDER	STATE	BIRTHDAY	HIREDATE
1	Rebecca	Moore	F	California	1974/11/20	2005/3/11
2	Ashley	Wilson	F	New York	1980/7/19	2008/3/16
3	Rachel	Johnson	F	New Mexic	1970/12/17	2010/12/1
4	Emily	Smith	F	Texas	1985/3/7	2006/8/15
5	Ashley	Smith	F	Texas	1975/5/13	2004/7/30

Each row of data, except for the first row, is called a record, corresponding to an event, a person, an order... The first row is the title, indicating which attributes make up the record. These records all have the same attributes, and the entire table is a set of these records.

In Pandas, an object called DataFrame is mainly used to process this type of table data. After reading the table into DataFrame, it looks like this:

		EID	NAME	SURNAME	GENDER		STATE	BIRTHDAY	HIREDATE
	0	1	Rebecca	Moore	F		California	1974-11-20	2005-03-11
	1	2	Ashley	Wilson	F		New York	1980-07-19	2008-03-16
row index	2	3	Rachel	Johnson	F		New Mexico	1970-12-17	2010-12-01
	3	4	Emily	Smith	F	data	Texas	1985-03-07	2006-08-15
	4	5	Ashley	Smith	F		Texas	1975-05-13	2004-07-30

It looks similar to Excel, except the row numbers start from 0.

First, try summarizing the number of people in each department:

```
import pandas as pd

data = pd.read_csv('Employee.csv')

group = data.groupby("DEPT")

dept_num = group.count()

print(dept_num)
```

Grouping and then counting is a common approach, but the result is a bit awkward:

```
DEPT
Administration     4     4     4     4     4     4     4     4
Finance           24    24    24    24    24    24    24    24
HR                19    19    19    19    19    19    19    19
Marketing         99    99    99    99    99    99    99    99
Production        91    91    91    91    91    91    91    91
R&D               29    29    29    29    29    29    29    29
Sales            187   187   187   187   187   187   187   187
Technology        47    47    47    47    47    47    47    47
```

The number of department members, which is the number of members in each group, only needs one column. Why are there so many columns? It seems like it has done the same action for each column, which is strange.

This is because DataFrame is essentially a matrix, not a set of records, and Python does not have such a concept of record. When count is applied to a matrix, it counts each column, which is somewhat unexpected.

Simple filtering operations, such as extracting employees in the R&D department, may result in a subset of the personnel table, but in reality, it is the entire personnel table (matrix) and some selected row positions (called row indexes), which can be understood as submatrix. At this point, the output results may not show anything, but if you want to further operate, such as giving a 5% salary increase to R&D department employees, you will once again find it "unexpected".

When using DataFrame to process structured data, it is necessary to follow the matrix approach, which can be very challenging for beginners to understand.

How can we correctly output the number of department members? The size function needs to be used to view the number of members in each group.

```
import pandas as pd

data = pd.read_csv('Employee.csv')

group = data.groupby("DEPT")

dept_num = group.size()

print(dept_num)
```

This result is normal:

```
DEPT
Administration      4
Finance            24
HR                 19
Marketing          99
Production         91
R&D                29
Sales             187
Technology         47
dtype: int64
```

However, this result is no longer a two-dimensional DataFrame, but a one-dimensional Series, and it can no longer continue to apply the methods of DataFrame, which is another "unexpected".

Apparently the grouping and aggregation result is also a structured data table with rows and columns, is it not good to continue using DataFrame? Why do we need to create something else? It's puzzling.

Python does not stop at these two. For example, the essence of grouping operations is to partition a large set into small sets, and the result should be a set of sets. Then let's take a look at what DataFrame looks like after grouping? Print the grouping results in the above code to observe.

```
import pandas as pd
data = pd.read_csv('Employee.csv')
group = data.groupby("DEPT")
print(group)
```

It outputs:

```
"pandas.core.groupby.generic.DataFrameGroupBy object at 0x000001ADBC9CE0F0"
```

What is this thing? Is this a set of sets?

Search online, it turns out that this is called an iterable object. Each member of it is composed of DataFrame plus a group index, and there are also methods to split and observe. This object, known as " iterable object", is essentially a set of submatrixes of a large matrix, which can barely be considered a set of sets. However, it cannot directly use a sequence number to get a member like a regular set (such as group [0]).

I guess many people have already fainted at this point, and can't figure out what nonsense I'm talking about. Well, that's right, this is the normal state for people in the workplace.

Python has a lot "objects" to describe the same type of data, each with its own adaptation scenarios and operation rules. For example, DataFrame can be filtered using the query function, while Series cannot, and after grouping, this object becomes completely different. The transition between these things is also very "smooth", and if you're not careful, they become something else you don't know.

As a result, programming mostly relies on googling, and even if you run it right, you still can't understand why and can't remember it, and you'll have to google again next time.

Let's take a step further, to sort the employees of each department by hiredate from early to late.

This only needs to group and sort the grouped subsets by hiredate. The following is the code:

```
import pandas as pd
employee = pd.read_csv("Employee.csv")
employee['HIREDATE']=pd.to_datetime(employee['HIREDATE'])
dept_g = employee.groupby('DEPT',as_index=False)
dept_list = []
for index,group in dept_g:
```

```
        group = group.sort_values('HIREDATE')
        dept_list.append(group)
employee_new = pd.concat(dept_list,ignore_index=True)
print(employee_new)
```

It looks a bit verbose. You need to write a for loop to do it bit by bit, which doesn't seem to reflect the advantages of set-oriented data processing. After all, structured data is batch and set type, and writing it is so verbose, so the difference between it and VBA is not significant.

Well, actually Python also has a way of writing without a for loop:

```
import pandas as pd
employee = pd.read_csv("Employee.csv")
employee['HIREDATE']=pd.to_datetime(employee['HIREDATE'])
employee_new = employee.groupby('DEPT',as_index=False).apply(lambda x:x.sort_values('HIREDATE')).reset_index(drop=True)
print(employee_new)
```

But, can you understand the second to last statement, which is the most crucial one here, with the apply and lambda?

This is the concept of "functional language", and its writing complexity and understanding difficulty are beyond the capabilities of most none professionals. I will not go through the trouble to explain the specific meaning here, and you can search for it yourself to see if you can understand it.

To summarize briefly:

DataFrame is essentially a matrix, not a set of records. Programming requires thinking about it in a matrix like manner, which can often be a bit convoluted and result in "unexpected outcomes".

Even more troublesome is that Python has too many similar data types, such as Series, DataFrame, and the grouped objects can all represent a certain set, but each has its own rules, and the calculation method is even more elusive. To understand these principles and apply them correctly, the difficulty and complexity are not something that none professionals can and should do.

There are also things like apply+lambda, if you don't use them, the code for batch data processing is too verbose, but if you use them, they are difficult to understand.

In fact, Python is a highly ranked thing. For none professionals, the power and convenience of Python only exist in training classes. You rarely see people around you using Python to tinker with their Excel. The true users of Python are highly skilled professionals, mainly those who specialize in artificial intelligence.

For none professionals, esProc SPL is much simpler.

SPL has only one type of set, a structured data table is the set of records, and the grouping result is the set of sets. The same set of operations can be performed on these sets.

Looking at the previous example, grouping and aggregation and simple count can get normal result:

	A
1	=file("Employee.csv").import@tc()
2	=A1.groups(DEPT;count(~):cnt)

Index	♀ DEPT	cnt
1	Administration	4
2	Finance	24
3	HR	19
4	Marketing	99
5	Production	91
6	R&D	29
7	Sales	187
8	Technology	47

The result of grouping is the set of sets, which is easy to understand:

	A
1	=file("Employee.csv").import@tc()
2	=A1.group(DEPT)

Index	Member
1	[[18.Jonathan.Moore][20.Alexis.Allen,][26.Timothy.Miller]]
2	[[2.Ashley.Wilson][13.Daniel.Davis][23.Joseph.Turner]]
3	[[4.Emily.Smith][9.Victoria.Davis][64.Madison.Williams]]
4	[[8.Megan.Wilson][17.Hannah.Johnson][21.Jacob.Moore]]
5	[[16.Christopher.Hernandez][19.Samantha.Williams][28.Zachary.Wilson]]
6	[[1.Rebecca.Moore][5.Ashley.Smith][10.Ryan.Johnson]]
7	[[3.Rachel.Johnson][6.Matthew.Johnson][7.Alexis.Smith]]
8	[[55.Olivia.Anderson][56.Jacob.Smith][85.Hailey.Smith]]

Index	EID	NAME	SURNAME	GENDER	STATE	BIRTHDAY	HIREDATE	DEPT	SALARY
1	18	Jonathan	Moore	M	Florida	1971-03-07	2000-03-07	Administration	7000
2	20	Alexis	Allen	F	Florida	1977-08-07	2007-08-07	Administration	16000
3	26	Timothy	Miller	M	Florida	1977-12-24	2007-12-24	Administration	5000
4	42	Michael	Jones	M	Pennsylvania	1978-08-20	2008-08-20	Administration	12000

To sort grouped subsets does not require complex lambda, but remains concise. SPL has made functional languages unnoticeable.

	A
1	=file("Employee.csv").import@tc()
2	=A1.group(DEPT)
3	=A2.conj(~.sort(HIREDATE))

esProc SPL is the programming language that none professionals may truly master and use.